On Freud's "Neurosis and Psychosis" and "The Loss of Reality in Neurosis and Psychosis"

On Freud's "Neurosis and Psychosis" and "The Loss of Reality in Neurosis and Psychosis" explores these two key papers on the topics of psychosis and neurosis and their relationship to the unconscious and to reality.

The contributors to this book approach these texts from both a historical and a contemporary point of view, highlighting their fundamental contributions and comparing Freud's thoughts with modern psychoanalytic theory. The chapters demonstrate the ongoing richness of Freud's work and his legacy by highlighting new ideas and developments, and include both clinical vignettes and theoretical insight. The contributors also raise questions that deserve further study; about the understanding and treatment of psychosis in children, distinctions and similarities between autism and psychosis, and the way in which aspects of our rapidly changing world – social media, climate change, AI – influence the evolution of psychotic states.

On Freud's "Neurosis and Psychosis" and "The Loss of Reality in Neurosis and Psychosis" will be essential reading for psychoanalysts and psychoanalytically oriented clinicians in practice and in training. It will also be of interest to academics and scholars of psychoanalytic studies and to readers interested in how modern clinicians interpret Freud's work.

Gabriela Legorreta, PhD, is a member of the Montreal Psychoanalytic Society (French section of the Canadian Psychoanalytic Society), as well as a Training and Supervising Analyst at the Montreal Psychoanalytic Institute and President Elect of the Canadian Psychoanalytic Society. She is former Chair and present Consultant of the IPA Publications Committee.

Catalina Bronstein, MD, is a training and supervising analyst, and former president of the British Psychoanalytical Society. She is a child and adolescent and adult psychoanalyst working at the Brent Adolescent Centre in London and in private practice, and is Visiting Professor at the Psychoanalysis Unit, University College London.

The International Psychoanalytical Association Contemporary Freud Turning Points and Critical Issues Series

Series Editor: Silvia Flechner

IPA Publications Committee
Natacha Delgado, Nergis Güleç, Thomas Marcacci, Carlos Moguillansky, Rafael Mondrzak, Angela M. Vuotto, Gabriela Legoretta (consultant)

Titles in this series

On Freud's "Screen Memories"
Edited by Gail S. Reed and Howard B. Levine

On Freud's "Formulations on the Two Principles of Mental Functioning"
Edited by Gabriela Legorreta and Lawrence J. Brown

On Freud's "The Question of Lay Analysis"
Edited by Paulo Cesar Sandler and Gley Pacheco Costa

On Freud's "The Uncanny"
Edited by Catalina Bronstein and Christian Seulin

On Freud's "Moses and Monotheism"
Edited by Lawrence J. Brown

The Ego and the Id: 100 Years Later
Edited by Fred Busch and Natacha Delgado

On Freud's "Remembering, Repeating and Working-Through"
Edited by Udo Hock and Dominique Scarfone

On Freud's "Neurosis and Psychosis" and "The Loss of Reality in Neurosis and Psychosis": 100 Years Later
Edited by Gabriela Legorreta and Catalina Bronstein

On Freud's "Neurosis and Psychosis" and "The Loss of Reality in Neurosis and Psychosis"
100 Years Later

Edited by
Gabriela Legorreta and Catalina Bronstein

Routledge
Taylor & Francis Group
LONDON AND NEW YORK

Designed cover image: Freud by Julia Kotulova, Charcoal & digital, 2019

First published 2024
by Routledge
4 Park Square, Milton Park, Abingdon, Oxon OX14 4RN

and by Routledge
605 Third Avenue, New York, NY 10158

Routledge is an imprint of the Taylor & Francis Group, an informa business

© 2024 selection and editorial matter, Gabriela Legorreta and Catalina Bronstein; individual chapters, the contributors

The right of Gabriela Legorreta and Catalina Bronstein to be identified as the authors of the editorial material, and of the authors for their individual chapters, has been asserted in accordance with sections 77 and 78 of the Copyright, Designs and Patents Act 1988.

All rights reserved. No part of this book may be reprinted or reproduced or utilised in any form or by any electronic, mechanical, or other means, now known or hereafter invented, including photocopying and recording, or in any information storage or retrieval system, without permission in writing from the publishers.

Trademark notice: Product or corporate names may be trademarks or registered trademarks, and are used only for identification and explanation without intent to infringe.

British Library Cataloguing-in-Publication Data
A catalogue record for this book is available from the British Library

ISBN: 978-1-032-47000-9 (hbk)
ISBN: 978-1-032-46999-7 (pbk)
ISBN: 978-1-003-38412-0 (ebk)

DOI: 10.4324/9781003384120

Typeset in Palatino
by Taylor & Francis Books

Contents

Acknowledgements vii
Series Editor Foreword viii
The Standard Edition of the Complete Psychological Works of Sigmund Freud (1924). Standard Edition, (19):147–154 xi
The Standard Edition of the Complete Psychological Works of Sigmund Freud (1924). Standard Edition, (19):181–188 xv

1 Introduction to Freud's Papers "On Neurosis and Psychosis" and "The Loss of Reality in Neurosis and Psychosis" 1
CATALINA BRONSTEIN AND GABRIELA LEGORRETA

2 The Clinic of Psychosis. Challenges 15
ALTAMIRANDO MATOS DE ANDRADE JR.

3 Reality and Psycho(-Patho)logical Organisation of the Personality 34
ANTONIO PÉREZ-SÁNCHEZ

4 Some Observations on the Relation to Reality and the Function of Belief in Schizophrenia 52
DAVID BELL

5 The *Negative* in Psychosis 70
MARIE-FRANCE BRUNET

6 The Object of Psychosis 87
PAUL WILLIAMS

7 Psychosis and Neurosis: Which reality? 108
DOMINIQUE SCARFONE

8 Possessiveness and its Relation to Some Youthful Follies 118
CARLOS MOGUILLANSKY

9 The Regulation of Psychic Reality Through Sensory Perception 139
ELISABETH SKALE

Index 157

Acknowledgements

Gabriela Legorreta and Catalina Bronstein in our role as co-editors of this book wish to express our gratitude to all those people who have contributed to the publication of this volume.

We are grateful to our colleagues of the Publication Committee of the International Psychoanalytical Association and in particular, to the chair, Silvia Flechner, for their support and encouragement.

Special mention should also go to Rhoda Bawdekar the IPA Publications Manager IPA and to Susannah Frearson from Routledge.

We are also grateful to the British Psychoanalytical Society and the Standard Edition of the Complete Psychological Works of Sigmund Freud for permission to reprint Freud's two papers: (1924) Neurosis and Psychosis and (1924) The Loss of Reality in Neurosis and Psychosis.

Series Editor Foreword

Contemporary Freud Turning Points and Critical Issues Series

G. Legorreta and C. Bronstein: On Freud's Neurosis and Psychosis [1924] and The Loss of Reality in Neurosis and Psychosis [1924]

The Publications Committee of the International Psychoanalytical Association has the honor to include another publication to the series "Contemporary Freud Turning Points and Critical Issues."

This series was founded by Robert Wallerstein in 1991 and subsequently edited by Joseph Sandler, Ethel Spector Person, Peter Fonagy, Leticia Glocer Fiorini, Gennaro Saragnano, and most recently by Gabriela Legorreta. Its essential contribution has interested psychoanalysts of the IPA, a stimulating forum for exchanging ideas. This series has the main objective to approach Freud's work both from a historical perspective and a contemporary point of view, highlighting the central contributions of his work that constitute the core of the psychoanalytical theory and practice.

This publication in this series compiles the works of psychoanalysts from different geographical regions of the IPA; this fact results in observing different theoretical and clinical stances regarding these essential works of Freud.

Catalina Bronstein states in her Introduction:

> *These two papers of Freud need to be placed within the context of other works that he was engaged with at the same time, in particular the Ego and the Id (1923), a paper that marks the transition to the structural model of the mind. We however need to consider that many of the thoughts that appear in the Ego and the Id were themselves the continuation of other ground-breaking theoretical changes that he developed previously such as the role of Identification with the lost object in his paper on Mourning and Melancholia, his paper on*

Narcissism, the duality of the Life/Death drives (*Beyond the Pleasure Principle*), among other works.

In his 1924 paper "Neurosis and Psychosis", Freud proposed that whilst neurosis was the result of a conflict between the ego and the id, psychosis was the analogous outcome of a conflict between the ego and the external world (Freud, 1924). The rupture between the ego and reality leaves the ego under the power of the Id.

Gabriela Legorreta also states in her Introduction:

The reader will realize in exploring this volume that, in his two seminal papers "Neurosis and psychosis" and "The loss of reality in neurosis and psychosis", Freud continued to break new ground in his psychoanalytic investigations of the complex workings of the mind. Freud had been preoccupied with the question of psychosis for a long time, as could be seen in many papers such as "Formulations of the two principles of mental functioning", "President Schreber" "On Fetishism", "On Negation" and others. However, it is in these two papers that, using the new structural model he put forward in "The Ego and the Id", Freud proposes a new way of thinking about the differences between neurosis and psychosis regarding their relationship to reality. The richness and variety of the contributions in this book demonstrate that in these two papers, Freud left many questions open, providing a breeding ground for further development and evolution of psychoanalytic thinking on the subject.

Freudian clinical intuition is the author's understanding of the subject of psychosis. Beyond his theoretical formulations, he explored the plasticity of his concepts. Freud shows himself to be a great clinician, open to the subject's condition, no matter how enigmatic and irrational this subject may appear. In the case of psychosis, it is no different. We see, paradoxically, that which excludes it from the domain of the analyzable gives it a particular place in the construction of psychoanalytic theory.

Although Freud advanced in formulating the field of psychoses, associating paranoia as a regression to narcissism and schizophrenia to a regression to autoerotism, it cannot be affirmed that the psychotic patient would not be subject to the experience of analysis (Freud, 1923). These formulations are well known, but the place of psychosis in Freudian work is not limited to this point of impossibility; on the contrary, we can say that it represents an elementary piece in the framework of the field of knowledge of psychoanalysis, highlighting that clinical intuition surpasses the theory, and could be the compass that guides us.

The Publications Committee is pleased to publish "On Freud's Neurosis and Psychosis [1924] and The Loss of Reality in Neurosis and Psychosis [1924]." Gabriela Legorreta and Catalina Bronstein have expertly edited this new volume. They asked eight distinguished colleagues from different regions to discuss and locate Freud's ideas in the light of contemporary psychoanalytic thinking. This book is the conclusion of their work that will bring the continuity of this critical series.

Silvia Flechner
Series Editor
Chair, IPA Publications Committee

Neurosis and Psychosis

Sigmund Freud

In my recently published work, *The Ego and the Id* (1923b), I have proposed a differentiation of the mental apparatus, on the basis of which a number of relationships can be represented in a simple and perspicuous manner. As regards other points – for instance, in what concerns the origin and role of the super-ego – enough remains obscure and unelucidated. Now one may reasonably expect that a hypothesis of this kind should prove useful and helpful in other directions as well, if only to enable us to see what we already know from another angle, to group it differently and to describe it more convincingly. Such an application of the hypothesis might also bring with it a profitable return from grey theory to the perpetual green of experience.

In the work I have mentioned I described the numerous dependent relationships of the ego, its intermediate position between the external world and the id and its efforts to humour all its masters at once. In connection with a train of thought raised in other quarters, which was concerned with the origin and prevention of the psychoses, a simple formula has now occurred to me which deals with what is perhaps the most important genetic difference between a neurosis and a psychosis: *neurosis is the result of a conflict between the ego and its id, whereas psychosis is the analogous outcome of a similar disturbance in the relations between the ego and the external world.*

There are certainly good grounds for being suspicious of such simple solutions of a problem. Moreover, the most that we may expect is that this formula will turn out to be correct in the roughest outline. But even that would be something. One recalls at once, too, a whole number of discoveries and findings which seem to support our thesis. All our analyses go to show that the transference neuroses originate from the ego's refusing to accept a powerful instinctual impulse in the id or to help it to find a motor outlet, or from the ego's forbidding that impulse the object at which it is aiming. In such a case the ego defends itself against the instinctual impulse by the mechanism of repression. The repressed material struggles against this fate. It creates for itself, along paths over which the ego has no power, a substitutive representation (which forces itself upon the ego by way of a compromise) – the symptom. The ego finds its unity threatened and impaired by this intruder, and it continues to struggle against the symptom, just as it fended off the original instinctual impulse. All this produces the picture of a neurosis. It is no contradiction to this that, in undertaking the repression, the ego is at bottom following the commands of its super-ego – commands which, in their turn, originate from influences in the external world that have found representation in the super-ego. The fact remains that the ego *has* taken sides with those powers, that in it their demands have more strength than the instinctual demands of the id, and that the ego is the power which sets the repression in motion against the portion of the id concerned and which fortifies the repression by means of the anticathexis of resistance. The ego has come into conflict with the id in the service of the super-ego and of reality; and this is the state of affairs in every transference neurosis.

On the other side, it is equally easy, from the knowledge we have so far gained of the mechanism of the psychoses, to adduce examples which point to a disturbance in the relationship between the ego and the external world. In Meynert's amentia – an acute hallucinatory confusion which is perhaps the most extreme and striking form of psychosis – either the external world is not perceived at all, or the perception of it has no effect whatever. Normally, the external world governs the ego in two ways: firstly, by current, present perceptions which are always renewable, and secondly, by the store of memories of earlier perceptions which, in the shape of an "internal world", form a possession of the ego and a constituent part of it. In amentia, not only is the acceptance of new perceptions refused, but the internal world, too, which, as a copy of the external world, has up till now represented it, loses its significance (its cathexis). The ego creates, autocratically, a new external and internal world; and there can be no doubt of two facts – that this new world is constructed in accordance with the id's wishful impulses, and that the motive of this dissociation from the external world is some very serious frustration by reality of a wish – a frustration which seems intolerable. The close affinity of this psychosis to normal dreams is unmistakable. A precondition of dreaming, moreover, is a state of sleep, and one of the features of sleep is a complete turning away from perception and the external world.

We know that other forms of psychosis, the schizophrenias, are inclined to end in affective hebetude – that is, in a loss of all participation in the external world. In regard to the genesis of delusions, a fair number of analyses have taught us that the delusion is found applied like a patch over the place where originally a rent had appeared in the ego's relation to the external world. If this precondition of a conflict with the external world is not much more noticeable to us than it now is, that is because, in the clinical picture of the psychosis, the manifestations of the pathogenic process are often overlaid by manifestations of an attempt at a cure or a reconstruction.

The aetiology common to the onset of a psychoneurosis and of a psychosis always remains the same. It consists in a frustration, a non-fulfilment, of one of those childhood wishes which are for ever undefeated and which are so deeply rooted in our phylogenetically determined organization. This frustration is in the last resort always an external one; but in the individual case it may proceed from the internal agency (in the super-ego) which has taken over the representation of the demands of reality. The pathogenic effect depends on whether, in a conflictual tension of this kind, the ego remains true to its dependence on the external world and attempts to silence the id, or whether it lets itself be overcome by the id and thus torn away from reality. A complication is introduced into this apparently simple situation, however, by the existence of the super-ego, which, through a link that is not yet clear to us, unites in itself influences coming from the id as well as from the external world, and is to some extent an ideal model of what the whole endeavour of the ego is aiming at – a reconciliation between its various dependent relationships. The attitude of the super-ego should be taken into account – which has not hitherto been done – in every form of psychical illness. We may provisionally assume that there must also be illnesses which are based on a conflict between the ego and the super-ego. Analysis gives us a right to suppose that melancholia is a typical example of this group; and we would set aside the name of 'narcissistic psycho-neuroses' for disorders of that kind. Nor will it clash with our impressions if we find reasons for separating states like melancholia from the other psychoses.

We now see that we have been able to make our simple genetic formula more complete, without dropping it. Transference neuroses correspond to a conflict between the ego and the id; narcissistic neuroses, to a conflict between the ego and the super-ego; and psychoses, to one between the ego and the external world. It is true that we cannot tell at once whether we have really gained any new knowledge by this, or have only enriched our store of formulas; but I think that this possible application of the proposed differentiation of the mental apparatus into an ego, a super-ego and an id cannot fail to give us courage to keep that hypothesis steadily in view.

The thesis that neuroses and psychoses originate in the ego's conflicts with its various ruling agencies – that is, therefore, that they reflect a failure in the functioning of the ego, which is at pains to reconcile all the various demands made on it – this thesis needs to be supplemented in one further point. One would like to know in what circumstances and by what means the ego can succeed in emerging from such conflicts, which are certainly always present, without falling ill. This is a new field of research, in which no doubt the most varied factors will come up for examination. Two of them, however, can be stressed at once. In the first place, the outcome of all such situations will undoubtedly depend on economic considerations – on the relative magnitudes of the trends which are struggling with one another. In the second place, it will be possible for the ego to avoid a rupture in any direction by deforming itself, by submitting to encroachments on its own unity and even perhaps perversions, through the acceptance of which they spare themselves repressions.

In conclusion, there remains to be considered the question of what the mechanism, analogous to repression, can be by means of which the ego detaches itself from the external world. This cannot, I think, be answered without fresh investigations; but such a mechanism, it would seem, must, like repression, comprise a withdrawal of the cathexis sent out by the ego.

The Loss of Reality in Neurosis and Psychosis

Sigmund Freud

I have recently indicated as one of the features which differentiate a neurosis from a psychosis the fact that in a neurosis the ego, in its dependence on reality, suppresses a piece of the id (of instinctual life), whereas in a psychosis, this same ego, in the service of the id, withdraws from a piece of reality. Thus for a neurosis the decisive factor would be the predominance of the influence of reality, whereas for a psychosis it would be the predominance of the id. In a psychosis, a loss of reality would necessarily be present, whereas in a neurosis, it would seem, this loss would be avoided.

But this does not at all agree with the observation which all of us can make that every neurosis disturbs the patient's relation to reality in some way, that it serves him as a means of withdrawing from reality, and that, in its severe forms, it actually signifies a flight from real life. This contradiction seems a serious one; but it is easily resolved, and the explanation of it will in fact help us to understand neuroses.

For the contradiction exists only as long as we keep our eyes fixed on the situation at the *beginning* of the neurosis, in which the ego, in the service of reality, sets about the repression of an instinctual impulse. This, however, is not yet the neurosis itself. The neurosis consists rather in the processes which provide a compensation for the portion of the id that has been damaged – that is to say, in the reaction against the repression and in the failure of the repression. The loosening of the relation to reality is a consequence of this second step in the formation of a neurosis, and it ought not to surprise us if a detailed examination shows that the loss of reality affects precisely that piece of reality as a result of whose demands the instinctual repression ensued.

There is nothing new in our characterization of neurosis as the result of a repression that has failed. We have said this all along, and it is only because of the new context in which we are viewing the subject that it has been necessary to repeat it.

Incidentally, the same objection arises in a specially marked manner when we are dealing with a neurosis in which the exciting cause (the "traumatic scene") is known, and in which one can see how the person concerned turns away from the experience and consigns it to amnesia. Let me go back by way of example to a case analysed a great many years ago, in which the patient, a young woman, was in love with her brother-in-law. Standing beside her sister's death-bed, she was horrified at having the thought: 'Now he is free and can marry me.' This scene was instantly forgotten, and thus the process of regression, which led to her hysterical pains, was set in motion. It is instructive precisely in this case, moreover, to learn along what path the neurosis attempted to solve the conflict. It took away from the value of the change that had occurred in reality, by repressing the instinctual demand which had emerged – that is, her love for her brother-in-law. The *psychotic* reaction would have been a disavowal of the fact of her sister's death.

We might expect that when a psychosis comes into being, something analogous to the process in a neurosis occurs, though, of course, between different agencies of the mind; thus we might expect that in a psychosis, too, two steps could be discerned, of which the first would drag the ego away, this time from reality, while the second would try to make good the damage done and re-establish the subject's relations to reality at the expense of the id. And, in fact, some analogy of the sort can be observed in a psychosis. Here, too, there are two steps, the second of which has the character of a reparation. But beyond that the analogy gives way to a far more extensive similarity between the two processes. The second step of the psychosis is indeed intended to make good the loss of reality, not, however, at the expense of a restriction of the id – as happens in neurosis at the expense of the relation to reality – but in another, more autocratic manner, by the creation of a new reality which no longer raises the same objections as the old one that has been given up. The second step, therefore, both in neurosis and psychosis, is supported by the same trends. In both cases it serves the desire for power of the id, which will not allow itself to be dictated to by reality. Both neurosis and psychosis are thus the expression of a rebellion on the part of the id against the external world, of its unwillingness – or, if one prefers, its incapacity – to adapt itself to the exigencies of reality, to Ανάγκη [Necessity]. Neurosis and psychosis differ from each other far more in their first, introductory, reaction than in the attempt at reparation which follows it.

Accordingly, the initial difference is expressed thus in the final outcome: in neurosis a piece of reality is avoided by a sort of flight, whereas in psychosis it is remodelled. Or we might say: in psychosis, the initial flight is succeeded by an active phase of remodelling; in neurosis, the initial obedience is succeeded by a deferred attempt at flight. Or again, expressed in yet another way: neurosis does not disavow the reality, it only ignores it; psychosis disavows it and tries to replace it. We call behaviour "normal" or "healthy", if it combines certain features of both reactions – if it disavows the reality as little as does a neurosis, but if it then exerts itself, as does a psychosis, to effect an alteration of that reality. Of course, this expedient, normal, behaviour leads to work being carried out on the external world; it does not stop, as in psychosis, at effecting internal changes. It is no longer *autoplastic* but *alloplastic*.

In a psychosis, the transforming of reality is carried out upon the psychical precipitates of former relations to it – that is, upon the memory-traces, ideas and judgements which have been previously derived from reality and by which reality was represented in the mind. But this relation was never a closed one; it was continually being enriched and altered by fresh perceptions.

Thus the psychosis is also faced with the task of procuring for itself perceptions of a kind which shall correspond to the new reality; and this is most radically effected by means of hallucination. The fact that, in so many forms and cases of psychosis, the paramnesias, the delusions and the hallucinations that occur are of a most distressing character and are bound up with a generation of anxiety – this fact is without doubt a sign that the whole process of remodelling is carried through against forces which oppose it violently. We may construct the process on the model of a neurosis, with which we are more familiar. There we see that a reaction of anxiety sets in whenever the repressed instinct makes a thrust forward, and that the outcome of the conflict is only a compromise and does not provide complete satisfaction. Probably in a psychosis the rejected piece of reality constantly forces itself upon the mind, just as the repressed instinct does in a neurosis, and that is why in both cases the consequences too are the same. The elucidation of the various mechanisms which are designed, in the psychoses, to turn the subject away from reality and to reconstruct reality – this is a task for specialized psychiatric study which has not yet been taken in hand.

There is, therefore, a further analogy between a neurosis and a psychosis, in that in both of them the task which is undertaken in the second step is partly unsuccessful. For the repressed instinct is unable to procure a full substitute (in neurosis); and the representation of reality cannot be remoulded into satisfying forms (not, at least, in every species of mental illness). But the emphasis is different in the two cases. In a psychosis it falls entirely on the first step, which is pathological in itself and cannot but lead to illness. In a neurosis, on the other hand, it falls on the second step, on the failure of the repression, whereas the first step may succeed, and does succeed in innumerable instances without overstepping the bounds of health – even though it does so at a certain price and not without leaving behind traces of the psychical expenditure it has called for. These distinctions, and perhaps many others as well, are a result of the topographical difference in the initial situation of the pathogenic conflict – namely whether in it the ego yielded to its allegiance to the real world or to its dependence on the id.

A neurosis usually contents itself with avoiding the piece of reality in question and protecting itself against coming into contact with it. The sharp distinction between neurosis and psychosis, however, is weakened by the circumstance that in neurosis, too, there is no lack of attempts to replace a disagreeable reality by one which is more in keeping with the subject's wishes. This is made possible by the existence of a *world of phantasy*, of a domain which became separated from the real external world at the time of the introduction of the reality principle. This domain has since been kept free from the demands of the exigencies of life, like a kind of 'reservation' it is not inaccessible to the ego, but is only loosely attached to it. It is from this world of phantasy that the neurosis draws the material for its new wishful constructions, and it usually finds that material along the path of regression to a more satisfying real past.

It can hardly be doubted that the world of phantasy plays the same part in psychosis and that there, too, it is the store-house from which the materials or the pattern for building the new reality are derived. But whereas the new, imaginary external world of a psychosis attempts to put itself in the place of external reality, that of a neurosis, on the contrary, is apt, like the play of children, to attach itself to a piece of reality – a different piece from the one against which it has to defend itself – and to lend that piece a special importance and a secret meaning which we (not always quite appropriately) call a *symbolic* one. Thus we see that both in neurosis and psychosis there comes into consideration the question not only of a *loss of reality* but also of a *substitute for reality*.

1 Introduction to Freud's Papers "On Neurosis and Psychosis" and "The Loss of Reality in Neurosis and Psychosis"

Catalina Bronstein and Gabriela Legorreta

Introduction I

Catalina Bronstein

A simple formula…

"Neurosis and Psychosis" was written during late autumn 1923 and published in 1924. This paper, together with the one that followed shortly, "The Loss of Reality in Neurosis and Psychosis" (1924b) sit among a number of highly relevant papers that Freud wrote after the ground breaking development of the structural theory, when he explored the role of the Ego in its connection to the Superego and to the Id. A door had been opened to new discoveries that expanded the understanding of psychoanalysis in both its theoretical and clinical perspectives.

In his Introduction to Freud's paper "Neurosis and Psychosis", Strachey points out (Strachey, in Freud, 1924 a, p. 148, SE Vol XIX) that the roots of this paper could be found much earlier, in Freud's paper on the Neuro-Psychoses of Defence (1894) where for the first time he mentions concepts such as "defence", "conversion" and "flight into psychosis" (Strachey, in Freud, 1924 a, p. 148, SE Vol XIX). These initial psychoanalytical explorations led Freud to link the development of neurosis to the role played by trauma which he initially connected to external events such as to experiences of early sexual seduction. Control and discharge of excitation and mental energy were considered in relation to *quantity* that could be accumulated or discharged. Freud initially distinguished between the *psychoneuroses* and the *actual neuroses (neurasthenia and anxiety neuroses)*. The *actual* neuroses (standing for "something current') were regarded as manifestations of current physical factors (such as coitus interruptus, that prevented proper discharge of excitation and of satisfaction) and underpinned Freud's first theory of anxiety. The emphasis was here on the accumulation of undischarged

DOI: 10.4324/9781003384120-1

somatic tensions which were transformed into anxiety. This notion can be contrasted with what he denominated "psychoneurosis" (such as *hysteria* and *obsessional neurosis)* and which Freud linked to incompatible ideas that were transformed into something somatic via what he called, *conversion*. Even though this first phase in his explorations were very much connected to what Sandler described as "the affect-trauma frame of reference" and to identifying the cause of trauma as one that was always connected to external reality, I think that Freud was also already implicitly holding some notion of psychic conflict (Sandler J and others, 1997, p. 41).

Three years later, following his letter 69 to Fliess he expressed his disappointment with his own investigations, and in contrast with centring his research mainly on the impact of external events, he stated:

> … I will confide in you at once the great secret that has been slowly dawning on me in the last few months. I no longer believe in my *neurotica* [theory of the neuroses].
> (Freud, 1897, p. 259)

Freud shifted his interest to what we could think of as "psychic reality". This move heralded the development of further explorations and ideas on the role of the drives and on the Unconscious. They formed part of what Freud called "a topography of the mind" (Freud, 1915, p174)) with an emphasis placed on the psychological qualitative interactions and relationships between different strata of the psychic apparatus which he distinguished as composing three systems, Conscious, Preconscious and Unconscious. The notion of a "topography" was explored by Freud in several papers that advanced ideas on childhood sexuality, the nature of the drives, and the centrality of psychic conflict where the understanding of pathological formations was based on instinctual wishes, defences, and compromise formations. He stressed that he was not indicating any psychical locality in any anatomical fashion and that he was remaining "upon psychological ground" (Freud, 1900, p. 536). In Freud's words conflict was aroused by the drives, specifically by the self-preservative drives or ego-instincts:

> …opposition between ideas is only an expression of struggles between the different instincts…
> (Freud, 1910a, p. 213)

However, the interaction between the drives and the relation to external reality continued to occupy an important place in Freud's thinking about the development of pathological processes. In Formulations on the Two Principles of Mental Functioning (1911)

Freud worked on the distinction between two regulating principles: the pleasure principle and the reality principle. He described how

> every neurosis has as its result, and therefore as its purpose, a forcing of the patient out of real life, an alienating him from reality... . Neurotics turn away from reality because they find it unbearable – either the whole or parts of it.
> (Freud, 1911a, p. 218)

He continues by mentioning that

> The most extreme type of this turning away from reality is shown in certain cases of hallucinatory psychosis...
> (Freud, 1911a, p. 218)

The term "psychosis" has been defined by psychiatry and this has influenced the way it is being used in psychoanalysis. It involves a large group of mental disorders that could be seen to have as a common factor a serious difficulty to remain in contact with reality, with the production of delusional thinking, hallucinatory experiences, distortion of perception and thought disorder. In psychoanalytic theory too, the relationship to external reality lies at the centre of the psychotic process. (Bronstein, 2020; Freeman, 1969; Hartmann, 1953). However, psychoanalytic thinking on psychosis is very much centred on addressing internal, psychic reality.

Freud's interest in understanding paranoia (psychosis) started very early on and was already mentioned in his correspondence to Fliess, but according to Strachey, Schreber's *Memoirs* (published in 1903) did not attract his attention till the summer of 1910. His early writings on psychosis were further developed with his thoughts on the memoirs of Schreber, where he looked at the catastrophic internal state that gives rise to the creation of delusions, the relationship between delusion and reparation, and the role of narcissism and sexuality in psychotic disorders (Freud, 1894, 1896, 1911b).

Freud's work on Schreber was published in 1911 (Freud, 1911b), so it is likely that his work on the two principles of mental functioning bear the influence of thoughts he had in relation to his ideas on Schreber. In Formulations on the Two Principles of Mental Functioning Freud proposed that the demands brought by internal needs and by the pleasure principle need to meet "a new principle of mental functioning": the setting up of the *reality principle* proved to be a momentous step" (Freud, 1911a, p. 219) (italics in original). Freud follows this assertion with ideas on how notation, memory, *phantasying*, day-dreaming and thinking develop.

The paper on the two principles was highly influential to many authors, among them Wilfred Bion, for whom the distinction between the pleasure principle and the reality principle was central for the understanding of psychosis (Bronstein, 2017).

Freud's exploration of the connection to reality-testing and to reality continued in many papers, among them, A Metapsychological Supplement to the Theory of Dreams (1917). It shows his interest in trying to explain the workings of the mind in relation to reality and to the principles involved in it, as well as to the mental agency responsible for it. We can see a movement between the topographical model of the mind towards the structural model. In this paper the role of the ego acquires specific relevance. Freud's attempt to work out differences between early mental processes and psychotic manifestations will be continued in the two papers that we are revisiting in this volume.

In 1917 Freud wrote,

> … we gave up hallucinatory satisfaction of our wishes at a very early period and set up a kind of "reality-testing. The question now arises in what this reality-testing consisted, and how the hallucinatory wishful psychosis of dreams and amentia and similar conditions succeeds in abolishing it and in re-establishing the old mode of satisfaction…
>
> (Freud, 1917, p. 232)

> On the other hand, we can already learn from pathology the way in which reality-testing may be done away with or put out of action. We shall see this more clearly in the wishful psychosis of amentia than in that of dreams. Amentia is the reaction to a loss which reality affirms, but which the ego has to deny, since it finds it insupportable. Thereupon the ego breaks off its relation to reality; it withdraws the cathexis from the system of perceptions, *Cs.* – or rather, perhaps, it withdraws *a* cathexis, the special nature of which may be the subject of further enquiry. With this turning away from reality, reality-testing is got rid of.
>
> (Freud, 1917, p. 233)

The relation to reality continues to exert a dominant place in the papers we are revisiting here and in many of the contributions to this volume.

These two papers of Freud need to be placed within the context of other works that he was engaged with at the same time, in particular the Ego and the Id (1923), a paper that marks the transition to the structural model of the mind. We however need to consider that many of the thoughts that appear in the Ego and the Id were themselves the continuation of other ground-breaking theoretical changes that he developed previously such as the role of Identification with the lost object in his paper on Mourning and Melancholia, his paper on Narcissism and the duality of the Life/Death drives (Beyond the Pleasure Principle), among other works.

In his 1924 paper "Neurosis and Psychosis", Freud proposed that whilst neurosis was the result of a conflict between the ego and the id, psychosis was the analogous outcome of a conflict between the ego and the external world (Freud, 1924a). The rupture between the ego and reality leaves the ego under the power of the Id. The ego then reconstructs a new reality in accordance with the desires of the Id. He states:

> ... a simple formula has now occurred to me which deals with what is perhaps the most important genetic difference between a neurosis and a psychosis: *neurosis is the result of a conflict between the ego and the id, where psychosis is the analogous outcome of a similar disturbance between the ego and the external world* (italics in original).
>
> (1924a p. 149)

We are here presented with some very interesting ideas such as the ego's conflict with the Id in the service of the super-ego and of reality and the potential threat to the ego's unity (initially by the instinctual impulse but later by the defences from it, by the symptom). It seems that the main danger is the possibility of a "rupture" of the ego which needs to be defended from in many possible ways, including by disavowal of reality.

Freud goes back to describe in psychosis, the process of dissociation from the external world as the consequence of a serious frustration of a wish, by reality. In the conflict between the three agencies (ego, super-ego and id in relation to reality), "the pathogenic effect depends whether "... the ego remains true to its dependence on the external world and attempts to silence the id, or whether it lets itself be overcome by the id and thus torn away from reality" (Freud, 1924a, p151). The question that he seems to be trying to work out is where is the conflict centred?: between the ego and the id (as in transference neuroses), between the ego and the super-ego (narcissistic neuroses) or between the ego and the external world (as in psychoses). The role of the super-ego seems also crucial for the understanding of psychotic functioning. As Fenichel stressed, delusions "attempt to supplant the lost parts of reality, they often contain elements of the repudiated reality, which return nevertheless, and portions of warded-off-drives as well as projected demands of the superego" (1946, p. 427). Many of the works on psychosis by Kleinian and contemporary Kleinian analysts focus on the centrality of the conflict between the ego and the superego.

The points Freud makes in the second paper we are revisiting, "The Loss of Reality in Neurosis and Psychosis" expand his earlier assumptions and open the door to a further discussion on the mechanisms involved in a psychosis. Freud points out that whilst in neurosis there is also a disturbance in relation to reality (he is talking here of external reality, "a "flight from real life" (Freud, 1924b p. 363)), this is the result of the failure of the defensive mechanisms, particularly of repression. The psychotic reaction, instead, would be have been a disavowal of reality and the creation of a "new reality'. It seems to me that a very important contribution that Freud makes is that

> In a psychosis, the transforming of reality is carried out upon the psychical precipitates of former relations to it – that is, upon the memory-traces, ideas and judgements which have been previously derived from reality and by which reality was represented in the mind. But this relation was never a closed one; it was continually being enriched and altered by fresh perceptions.
> (Freud, 1924b, p. 185)

and

> In psychosis "…the rejected piece of reality constantly forces itself upon the mind, …"
> (Freud, 1924b, p. 186)

Freud continued to explore these issues in his papers on Negation (1925) "Fetishism" (1927) and in "Splitting of the Ego in the Process of Defence". (1940[1938])

Following his 1920 paper on the death drive, Beyond the Pleasure Principle (1920), Freud retakes the study on psychosis that he described in his two 1924 papers and makes a link to the fusion of "two primal forces (Eros and destructiveness) in varying proportions", also signalling the risks to the psyche of a de-fusion of instincts (Freud, 1938, p. 197). He expanded on some of these thoughts in "An Outline Of Psycho-Analysis" (1938) where he describes the task of the ego fighting to defend its existence against an external world that threatens it with annihilation as well as against the demands of the internal world. He concludes that

> *the precipitating cause of the outbreak of a psychosis is either that reality has become intolerable painful or that the instincts have become extraordinarily intensified… .*
> (Freud, 1938, p. 201)

He adds that it would be extremely rare that the ego's detachment from reality could be carried through completely. Freud described the co-existence of two psychical attitudes, one which took account of reality and another which under the influence of the instincts detaches the ego from reality, stating that when the abnormal one gained the upper hand then the situation was ripe for the onset of psychosis.

In the history of the psychoanalytic movement, we can find many important contributions to the understanding of the psychological mechanisms and unconscious conflicts underlying the development of both neurotic and psychotic pathologies. Among them, the understanding of the role of projective identification and of the disturbances in symbol formation, Segal and Rosenfeld), played an important role in advancing our knowledge on psychotic processes (Segal, 1950, 1957, 1972, Rosenfeld, 1947, 1954).

For reasons of space I will just mention here some of the developments brought by Bion as his understanding of psychosis had an important influence on how we think nowadays.

Expanding on Freud's 1911 paper Formulations on the "Two Principles of Mental Functioning", Bion stressed the relevance of Freud's description of the mental apparatus being called into activity by the demands of the reality principle and *"in particular of that part of it which is concerned with the consciousness attached to the sense-organs"* (Bion, 1957). He also mentions the relevance to the understanding of psychosis of Klein's description of the phantasized sadistic attacks that the infant makes on the breast in the P-S position and the discovery of projective identification.

Bion was particularly interested in the patient's attitude towards reality and the distinction between measures to evade and to modify reality. He followed Freud's proposal in his 1924 papers that in psychosis the main conflict lies between the Id and reality, that is, that in *psychosis the ego, in the service of the id, withdraws itself from a part of reality"* (Freud, 1924a, p183). For Bion, the notion of reality included both external as well as internal reality as sometimes the denial of external reality is a correlate to the inability to tolerate internal reality (Bion, 1965)

> ... *consciousness of an external reality depends on the person's ability to tolerate being reminded of an internal reality.*
> (Bion, transformations p. 86)

He proposed that in the development of a psychosis (he mentions specifically schizophrenia) we should consider a preponderance of destructive impulses, *a hatred of reality internal and external which is extended to all that makes for awareness of it; a dread of imminent annihilation and, finally, a premature and precipitate formation of object relations, foremost amongst which is the transference, whose thinness is in marked contrast with the tenacity with which they are maintained* (Bion, 1957, p. 44). There is an oscillation between these states of mind where the subject tries to broaden contact with reality and his need to restrict it. The accent is placed by him on the fragmentation of the personality, particularly of the apparatus of awareness of reality.

Bion proposed that contact with reality is masked by the dominance of an *"omnipotent phantasy that is intended to destroy either reality or the awareness of it, and thus achieve a state that is neither life or death"* (Bion, 1957 p. 46). Some of the central issues that he explores are the role played by the Oedipal conflict and the hatred of the reality of the primal scene which are connected to the subject's attack on his own mental functioning and on the capacity to make links (Bion, 1959; Bronstein and O'Shaughnessy, 2017).[1]

Bion developed these ideas further by characterizing the two coexisting psychical attitudes as the psychotic and non-psychotic parts of the personality. (Bion, 1957; Lucas, 2009). There seems to be an agreement among psychoanalysts that there are healthy elements in the psychotic patient but is far less clear how this relates to the illness itself. Rather than using the term "psychotic and neurotic parts of the personality" I prefer to see it in a more dynamic way, as states of mind that fluctuate according to a constellation of anxieties and unconscious phantasies that determine the type of defence mechanisms that are put in place. There are times when these different states of mind might not be able to be distinctly identified and when neurotic and psychotic processes might be operating simultaneously, where the subject tries to broaden contact with reality but needs to restrict it.

In this volume these two inspiring papers of Freud are being revisited by eminent psychoanalysts whose original contributions enrich and deepen our understanding of unconscious mental processes.

Introduction II

Gabriela Legorreta

> The world of fantasy, the pool from which neurosis and psychosis draw the material to create a more satisfying real past....

The reader will realize in exploring this volume that, in his two seminal papers "Neurosis and Psychosis" and "The Loss of Reality in Neurosis and Psychosis", Freud continued to break new ground in his psychoanalytic investigations of the complex workings of the mind. Freud had been preoccupied with the question of psychosis for a long time, as could be seen in many papers such as

"Formulations of the two principles of mental functioning", "President Schreber" "On Fetichism", "On Negation" and others. However, it is in these two papers that, using the new structural model he put forward in "The Ego and the Id", Freud proposes a new way of thinking about the differences between neurosis and psychosis regarding their relationship to reality. The richness and variety of the contributions in this book demonstrate that in these two papers, Freud left many questions open, providing a breeding ground for further development and evolution of psychoanalytic thinking on the subject. The major themes that preoccupied and interested the contributors, who come from the four regions of the IPA, are:

The evolution of the theory and practice of understanding psychosis. Post-Freudian contributions

Several authors of this book delve into the evolution of the theory and practice of treating psychosis after Freud's seminal papers. Brunet gives a comprehensive account of important post-Freudian authors such as Searles, Bion, Aulagnier and Green who proposed new ways of understanding psychosis. Brunet's paper examines the first step described by Freud in the development of psychosis, that is, the withdrawal of the ego from contact with reality. She underlines the importance of negative aspects in psychotic states which Green developed in depth in his "Work of the Negative". These aspects are characterized by the absence of the usual psychotic symptoms. The author elaborates on this based on Bion's notion of -K and on Green's and Jean Luc Donnet's concept of "white psychosis".

De Matos, who also focused on post Freudian's contributions, develops in depth the importance of Kleinian theory, in particular, the concepts of projective identification, the paranoid/schizoid position and the depressive position. Bell, in his paper, describes in detail the way in which Bion, deeply influenced by Melanie Klein, developed his own way of working with psychotic patients, shedding light on the distinction between psychic reality in psychotic and non-psychotic manifestations.

Contemporary theoretical and clinical perspectives in the treatment of psychosis

In his chapter, Sanchez constructs the argument that, in these two seminal papers, one can find the roots of a conception of psychosis that is accessible to psychoanalysis, although paradoxically, Freud considered it untreatable. A careful reading of Freud's two papers allows the author to develop the idea that treatment is possible if one takes a perspective where psychosis is considered closer to neurosis than it seems, taking into account that psychotic features are also present in neurotic cases. Sanchez highlights that Freud not only develops what makes neurosis and psychosis different but that, in various arguments throughout the two papers, he also brings to light what is similar amongst the two, adding that neurotic and psychotic features are also present in "normal" personalities. Sanchez's contribution convincingly illustrates how approaching Freud's texts meticulously can uncover unidentified richness in the text.

Also interested in the question of the treatment of psychosis, Williams proposes that, when treating psychotic conditions, the analyst should be mindful of the possible need for hospitalization. He underlines that it is crucial to identify the limits of psychotic functioning as well as its continuity or lack of continuity with normal psychic functioning. For Williams, it is essential to establish clinical links between psychotic and non-psychotic mental states in the transference-countertransference relationship.

In another chapter regarding the relationship between psychotic and non-psychotic states, De Matos underlines the fundamental importance of taking into consideration the mechanisms of projective identification and the paranoid-schizoid position in clinical work with psychotic patients. The author develops the original idea that an essential aspect of the work with these patients involves building a mutual psychic apparatus capable of thinking, feeling, and relating, which makes possible a psychoanalytic dialogue.

We are fortunate in this volume to have all eight authors provide clinical material to clarify and illustrate the ideas put forward in their chapters. Brunet's case is an example of psychosis without restitutive symptoms ("white psychosis"). Scarfone, basing himself on the notion of psychic reality, reference to which, he rightly underlines, is surprisingly absent in Freud's papers, proposes a different understanding of the role of reality in psychopathology. His clinical case serves as an illustration. Skale's case illustrates the way in which a patient used sensory perception in the service of neurotic and psychotic defenses (distorted sense of smell and sometimes changes in visual perception). The patient's hallucinatory experience expressed in a distortion of his sense of smell and taste was useful in regulating or at times interrupting contact in relationships and with reality. Sanchez's case is used to illustrate the importance, in the treatment with these patients, of considering psychosis as a disorder closer to neurosis, considering that psychotic features are also identified in neurotic cases. Bell's description of the treatment of a schizophrenic patient illustrates the existence of a devastated internal world where the capacity to believe is extremely fragile as the patient lacked the capacity to believe in the existence of anything with any conviction. This case helps to highlight that, according to Bell, internal and external reality are experienced as being under omnipotent control and are treated interchangeably. In the patient's experience, internal and external reality do not exist as separate entities that can be brought to mind in order to help make distinctions. This serious impairment also interferes with the capacity to think.

Most of the authors highlight the intense and challenging countertransference experiences the analysts lives through when working with these patients. These experiences range from a feeling of deadness (Bell) and confusion (Skale) to the pressure that patients exert in a hidden and unconscious way on the analyst's mind, reactivating infantile aspects of the analyst's psychic functioning (Altamirando).

The question of reality

The notion of reality stimulated much discussion amongst the authors and their contributions enlarged and enriched the psychoanalytic perspective of this notion. Scarfone, focusing on the notion of psychic reality which, he points out, is absent in both papers, proposes a different way of understanding the role of reality in psychopathology. Inspired by the work of Laplanche, Scarfone states that it is not the material aspect of the relation that poses a problem for the patient, but the psychical reality which is a result of the patient's confrontation with the "enigmatic messages" that the individual receives from his significant others, an idea that Laplanche elaborated in depth within his conceptualization of the Fundamental Anthropological Situation. In addition, Scarfone, referring to Aulagnier's contributions on psychosis, proposes that the psychic reality that the psychotic creates, no matter how distorted, should be considered a genuine effort at constructing a meaningful conception of the world in order to respond to the impact which results from a violent, crazy making intrusion exerted in the mind of the patient by significant others. Following this conceptualization, psychosis and neurosis will be different depending on the individual's capacity to elaborating the enigmatic messages at the center of the encounter with the other.

In his paper, while allowing us to share in the depth of his understanding of Freud, Melanie Klein and Bion, Bell underlines that "the fact that we live in two worlds or realities, at the same time, namely the subjective/internal world and the shared or objective external world, is part of what we mean by what it is to be human, have subjectivity and self-consciousness". Based on his experience with schizophrenics, Bell states that these patients' psychic and external realities are not separate categories of experience. The capacity to maintain a difference and establish a complex relationship between internal and external reality is impaired. A consequence of this is that both internal and external realities are changeable, in that external reality can be handled as if it were an internal imaginative fantasy, and under the subject's control. Bell puts forward a most interesting idea regarding the capacity for "belief". Based on his clinical experience with schizophrenics he argues that what distinguishes their psychosis from other forms of psychotic states is the deep impairment in the capacity to believe. Bell's argument is supported by Freud's paper on "Negation" and in particular the function of judgement which is what allows the psyche to decide (and to believe) whether something is real and whether or not it exists.

On the question of reality, Moguillansky's uses his rich theoretical and clinical experience with adolescents to propose that, in some cases their contact with reality is compromised. He refers to cases where the adolescent creates a rather delusional world that often acquires a possessive qualities, that are manifested by a strong need to possess and control the other In his clinical case, Mogouillanky describes the way in which these experiences of possessiveness are not based in reality, they have a psychotic quality that can sometimes be accompanied by hallucinations or delusional phenomena, (what the author calls "explicit insanity'). However, in other cases the lack of contact with reality is not accompanied by psychotic symptoms ("a mute insanity"). Mogouillansky's contribution is particularly important in that it helps keep in mind the presence of psychotic phenomena in adolescence that may in some situations be dismissed. Elaborating on this idea, the author argues that the construction of a delusional world with possessive qualities is a defensive move, it creates an illusion of protection against uncertainties and the unknown, which because of the challenges of adolescence, are particularly intense experiences.

In conclusion, the authors of this book have succeeded in taking Freud's contributions further and in opening up a vast horizon in our understanding and treatment of psychosis. They have also raised questions that deserve further study. Some of these new directions are the understanding and treatment of psychosis in children, the distinctions and similarities between autism and psychosis and the way in which our present world's rapid changes, in particular those associated with the rise of social media, with climate change, AI, amongst many others, influence the evolution of psychotic states.

Note

1 Bion's notions of alpha function and contact barrier are particularly relevant to understanding psychotic manifestations with respect to modifying frustration and/or evading it (Bion, 1957, 1962, 1967)

References

Bion, W.R. (1957) Differentiation of the Psychotic from the Non-Psychotic Personalities. IJP Vol 38, Parts 3–4. In *Second Thoughts*, ed. Jason Aronson, NY 1967, 43–63.
Bion, W.R. (1959) Attacks on Linking. *Int. J. Psycho-Anal.*, 40: 308–315.
Bion, W.R. (1965) *Transformations: Change from Learning to Growth*, 5: 1–172.
Bronstein, C. (2017) Introduction. In Bronstein, C. and E. O'Shaughnessy, eds. 2017. *Attacks on Linking Revisited*. London: Karnac, xxxiii–xxxvii.
Bronstein, C. (2020) Psychosis and Psychotic Functioning in Adolescence. *International Journal of Psychoanalysis*, 101: 136–151.
Fenichel, O. (1946) *The Psychoanalytic Theory of Neurosis*. London: Routledge.
Freeman. (1969) *Psychopathology of the Psychosis*. New York: International University Press.
Freud, S. (1894) The Neuro-Psychoses of Defence. *The Standard Edition of the Complete Psychological Works of Sigmund Freud* 3:41–61.
Freud, S. (1896) Further Remarks on the Neuro-Psychoses of Defence. In *The Standard Edition of the Complete Psychological Works of Sigmund Freud, Volume III (1893–1899)*: Early Psycho-Analytic Publications, 157–185.
Freud, S. (1897) Letter 69: Extracts from the Fliess Papers. *The Standard Edition of the Complete Psychological Works of Sigmund Freud* 1:259–260.
Freud, S. (1900) The Interpretation of Dreams. *The Standard Edition of the Complete Psychological Works of Sigmund Freud* 4:ix–627.
Freud, S. (1910) The Psycho-Analytical View of Psychogenic Disturbance of Vision. *The Standard Edition of the Complete Psychological Works of Sigmund Freud* 12:213–226.
Freud, S. (1911a) Formulations on the Two Principles of Mental Functioning. *The Standard Edition of the Complete Psychological Works of Sigmund Freud* 12:213–226.
Freud, S. (1911b) Psychoanalytic notes on an autobiographical account of a case of paranoia (Dementia paranoides). *SE* 12:3–79.
Freud, S. (1915) The Unconscious. *The Standard Edition of the Complete Psychological Works of Sigmund Freud* 14:159–215.
Freud, S. (1917) A Metapsychological Supplement to the Theory of Dreams. *The Standard Edition of the Complete Psychological Works of Sigmund Freud* 14:217–235.
Freud, S. (1920) Beyond the Pleasure Principle. *The Standard Edition of the Complete Psychological Works of Sigmund Freud* 18:1–64.
Freud, S. (1923) The Ego and the Id. *The Standard Edition of the Complete Psychological Works of Sigmund Freud* 19:1–66.
Freud, S. (1924a) Neurosis and Psychosis. *The Standard Edition of the Complete Psychological Works of Sigmund Freud* 19:147–154.
Freud, S. (1924b) The Loss of Reality in Neurosis and Psychosis. *The Standard Edition of the Complete Psychological Works of Sigmund Freud* 19:181–188.
Freud, S. (1925) Negation. *The Standard Edition of the Complete Psychological Works of Sigmund Freud* 19:233–240.
Freud, S. (1927) Fetishism. *The Standard Edition of the Complete Psychological Works of Sigmund Freud* 21:147–158.

Freud, S. (1938) An Outline of Psycho-Analysis. *The Standard Edition of the Complete Psychological Works of Sigmund Freud* 23:139–208.
Freud, S. ([1940]1938) Splitting of the Ego in the Process of Defence. *The Standard Edition of the Complete Psychological Works of Sigmund Freud* 23:271–278.
Hartmann, H. (1953) Contribution to the Metapsychology of Schizophrenia. *Psychoanal. St. Child*, 8: 177–198.
Rosenfeld, H. (1947) Analysis of a Schizophrenic State with Depersonalization. *International Journal of Psychoanalysis*, 28: 130–139.
Rosenfeld, H. (1954) Considerations Regarding the Psycho-Analytic Approach to Acute and Chronic Schizophrenia. *International Journal of Psychoanalysis*, 35: 135–140.
Sandler J., Holder A., Dare C., Dreher A. U. (1997) *Freud's Models of the Mind*. London: Karnac.
Segal, H. (1950) Some Aspects of the Analysis of a Schizophrenic. *International Journal of Psychoanalysis*, 31: 268–278.
Segal, H. (1957) Notes on Symbol Formation. *International Journal of Psychoanalysis*, 38: 391–397.
Segal, H. (1972) A Delusional System as a Defence Against the Re-Emergence of a Catastrophic Situation. *International Journal of Psychoanalysis*, 53: 393–401.

2 The Clinic of Psychosis. Challenges

Altamirando Matos de Andrade Jr.

Since the beginning of psychoanalysis, treatment of serious cases such as psychoses, have been a constant challenge because of the difficulties to access the patients' mind and the work of transference that was considered not possible for the psychotics. Freud introduced several clinical examples of critical patients, and throughout his vast work, he discussed the psychoanalytic treatment of *psychoses*, often considering that treatment was not possible due to the fact that these patients were not able to develop transference. Freud postulated that these patients abandoned their object cathexes, and that the object libido was transformed into the cathexis onto the ego, preventing this transference to develop.

In one of his *Introductory Letters* (1917) as Freud was discussing psychotics, he stated: "They do not show transference, and for this reason, they are inaccessible to our efforts, they cannot be cured by us." He considered that analysis was essentially the resolution of a transference neurosis, and therefore, the narcissism in a schizophrenic was a factor that prevented analysis.

In pioneering papers such as *The Project* (1895), *Letters to Fliess* (1892–1899), *The Neuropsychosis of Defense*, and later, in the *Schereber Case* (1911), several descriptions were made by Freud regarding psychotic phenomenon. In 1924, in his seminal works "Neurosis and Psychosis" and "The Loss of Reality in Neurosis and Psychosis", the topic was taken up in a more focused manner and important additions were considered. In these works, there is an effort to understand the psychotic functioning. However, despite subsequent contributions, Freud maintained the idea that these patients were not suitable to undergo psychoanalytic treatment. These last two works were influential on the development of the work of several authors who were interested in the psychoanalytic treatment of psychoses. Even though Freud disagreed that a psychoanalytical approach was possible, his understanding of these states of mind allowed him to advance in his studies, theory, and in the techniques with these patients.

DOI: 10.4324/9781003384120-2

Freud seems to have become even more pessimistic in relation to the psychoanalytic treatment of psychoses when he put forward his understanding of the destructive burden of the death instinct, that is, the excessive constitutional burden of death instincts. But he also did not fail to observe that somewhere hidden in the patient's mind there were also healthy aspects which were necessary to establish a useful and beneficial alliance, as described in the *Outline of Psychoanalysis* (1938). Several times, he suggested that future research would allow psychotic phenomena to be better understood, and the analyst would therefore find ways to embark in psychoanalytic treatment with psychotic patients. In the paper *The Future Prospects of Psychoanalytic Therapy* (1911/1970), considering the innovations of the technique in relation to the analyst himself, Freud argued that: "We become aware of the countertransference which, in him, arises as a result of the patient's influence on his unconscious feelings and we are almost inclined to insist that he will recognize the countertransference, in himself, and overcome it." Further on: "… we note that no psychoanalyst advances beyond what their own internal complexes and resistance allow …" In a clear demonstration of the evolution of his understandings, Freud gave us an optimistic sign towards the analysis of psychotic patients, recognizing the importance of the analyst's thinking about himself and even analyzing himself to overcome resistances that could prevent the understanding of the patient's material. Although he did not develop these issues in the analysis of psychotics, Freud opened the possibility for others to do so; as we will see throughout this text.

Freud oscillated between a pessimism about the possibility of treating psychoanalytically psychotics and an understanding of psychotic functioning, where the splitting of the ego between a normal and a psychotic part proved to be quite important for the understanding of the psychotic mind. Later, following these ideas about the splitting of the ego, other authors developed a greater understanding of these aspects and postulated a theory that made this treatment possible.

Melanie Klein was perhaps the most important author in contributing knowledge about the development and functioning of the baby's mind since its beginnings. By describing the schizoparanoid and depressive positions and the defense mechanisms such as projective identification and splitting of the ego and of the object in the text *Notes on Some Schizoid Mechanisms* (1946), she opened the door to the psychoanalytic treatment of psychoses. In the introduction to this text (page 1), she stated: "In early infancy, anxieties characteristic of psychosis arise which drive the ego to develop specific defense mechanisms. In this period the fixation points for all psychotic disorders are to be found."

Klein listed some defense mechanisms, such as splitting of the ego, splitting of the object, denial of internal and external reality, and she also stated that these mechanisms, present in the first months of life, are found later in psychotic states, mainly schizophrenia. She also considered that problems related to the precocious ego, such as its cohesion or lack of it, were due to constitutional factors, and that they were important factors in the origin of psychoses, determining if the ego is able to establish integration, or not. She also suggested: "... that the primary anxiety of being annihilated by a destructive force within, with the ego's specific response of falling to pieces or splitting itself, may be extremely important in all schizophrenic processes."

The understanding of projective identification and its effects, described by Klein, led many psychoanalysts to think about the development of transference in psychotics patients, making it possible to understand not only the projective aspect, but also the communication contained in this mechanism, allowing to explore what goes through the psychotic mind and how it relates to the object.

Her followers, such as Rosenfeld (*Psychotics States* 1965), postulate that confusional states arise when the ability to differentiate between good and bad objects is lost, between libidinal and aggressive impulses, causing the splitting mechanisms to be reinforced. Klein's understandings carried out by Rosenfeld, highlighted the relationships of schizoid objects, and made it possible to understand psychotic transferences.

For Freud, the psychoanalytical approach to psychoses has been a great challenge from the very start of his career, because he did not consider the possibility of transference in psychotics. The recommendations from those as Klein, Segal, Bion and Rosenfeld were to maintain the classical technique recommended for neurotics. A significant leap was made when, from the understanding of the psychotic mind, the interaction between the analyst and the patient started to be considered, creating an understanding of the analyst's mind as an important factor in this therapeutic context.

Rosenfeld (1987) explains: "He [Money Kyrle] also described the unconscious interplay between the patient's and the analyst's mental processes and the analyst's need to be able to be conscious of what is going on in the patient and in himself, in order to disentangle and interpret to the patient the aspects belonging to the patient" (12).

In chapter 2, "Some Therapeutic and Anti-Therapeutic Factors in the Functioning of the Analyst" of his book *Impasse and Interpretation* (1987), Rosenfeld described the importance of the analyst's analysis and the skill required to deal with the analyses of psychotic patients, as, for instance: "The analyst's state of mind, his capacity to function well is an essential therapeutic factor in analytic therapy."

I believe that the biggest challenge was, and continues to be, the understanding of the pressure that patients exert, in a hidden and unconscious way, on the analyst's mind and the analyst's infantile aspects that are reactivated by this pressure. Money Kyrle's statement above serves as a guide for us to understand and think about these aspects while dealing with the analyses of these patients.

An interesting postulation is June Felton's understanding of psychoses, cited by Rosenfeld (1987), in which massive projections on the foetus and later on the baby are exerted by the mother, which would be reactivated in the transference bond, leading the analyst to suffer pressure of the primitive transference that once was suffered by the baby/patient which, as described by Felton, makes it difficult to understand the ongoing process.

Wilfred R. Bion, an early follower of Klein, investigating both the schizophrenics' language and their thought disorder, also understood the pressure exerted by the psychotic mind on the analyst, as described in several works gathered in *Second Thoughts* (1967). Later (1976–1979), he also understood that aspects he called embryological remains, which have not yet gained symbolic expression, "make pressure" to gain representation, and thus to be understood. In some supervisions (1973, 2013, 2018), and in his book *Taming Wild Thoughts* (1997), these aspects were discussed in more detail. These embryological remains are not necessarily psychotic aspects, although they may seem to be. In my view, they function with a certain proximity to psychoses, and depending on their evolution, they may even turn into a psychosis. Bion said that certain people are often considered insane, but that, in fact, they could be trying to express something, a state of mind, for example, which has remained undeveloped, and which they have not gained conditions to represent or the ability to think about them.

This dynamic of understanding transference/countertransference is only possible because psychotic patients transfer their primitive emotional experiences on to the analyst, although in a different way from that carried out by neurotics or by the neurotic parts of patients in general, as demonstrated by several post-Freudian analysts.

In the paper *Notes on the Theory of Schizophrenia*, published in *Second Thoughts* (1967), Bion told us: "Language is employed by the schizophrenic in three ways; as a mode of action, as a method of communication and as a mode of thought." In this text, as in many others, Bion developed his ideas about psychotic thinking and his psychoanalytical approach, although with some divergences in relation to Freud, mainly with regard to the early relations of the ego with objects, transference in psychoses, and the role of libidinal and object cathexes. If for Bion, following Klein, the precocious ego already establishes relations with the object, albeit partial, this means that the object libido has not turned to the ego to a point that does not allow a relation with the object therefore liable to being transferred. The important Freudian texts already mentioned in 1924, contain bases for the development of Bion's ideas regarding reality, reality testing, hallucination and delirium as containing something in terms of healing or of the reconstruction of contact with reality. The same can be said for Rosenfeld and his works, both the pioneer *Psychotic States* (1965) and the later *Impasse and Interpretation* (1987).

It is important to remember Freud's (1924) seminal papers on psychoses where he states that delusion and hallucination were attempts to cure or reconstruct contact with the lost reality. Freud had a very important theoretical and clinical insight on the psychotic mind of the patients that contribute to giving meaning to hallucinations and delusions. This insight opened the possibility to interpret the origin of hallucination and delusions, and link the hallucination to a possible recovery of object relation. Later Klein and her followers made important contributions to these issues.

An important view of Bion on psychotic transference can be found in Andrade Jr. (2015), who quoted Bion (1962):

> Bion called alpha function the transformation of rudimentary emotions into alpha elements. That is the function that the object has of containing rudimentary emotions and experiences that are projected by the subject so that they can be slowly digested psychically and thought by the object. In his model container/contained, Bion (1962) calls our attention to the object that receives the projections of the baby, metabolizes them, and returns them to the baby giving a different meaning to the projected. In this model, the baby introjects an object that receives and understands its anxieties. These experiences, common to humans, form a pattern of object relations that develops throughout the individual's life. This pattern of relationship is what arises in the transferential context of an analysis.

Segal, another important follower of Klein, contributed greatly to the advancement of work with psychotics. Her work *Notes on Symbol Formation* (1957) can be considered, in my view, of fundamental importance to understand and approach the way patients work, communicate or act. The concept of symbolic equation, showing the relationship between the original object and the symbol in the internal and external world, has brought an understanding of the basis of the schizophrenics' concrete thinking. Segal stated:

The formation of symbols governs the ability to communicate, since all communication is done through symbols. When schizoid disturbances occur in object relations, the ability to communicate is similarly disturbed, firstly because the differentiation between subject and object falls apart, and secondly because the means of communication are absent, since the symbols are felt in a concrete way and, therefore, are not available for communication purposes.

Segal was clear with respect to schizophrenic thinking being directly linked to the difficulty in forming or using symbols. In the 1979 postscript to the mentioned work, Segal affirmed, based on Bion's concept on the relationship between contained and container, that it is not the projective identification itself that leads to a concrete thought, but that it is necessary to take into account the relationship between the projected part and the object on which it is projected, that is, the contained and the container. This leads us to the understanding that, in the external world, there may be real objects that the projection can adapt to. The analyst may become this real object that receives what is projected and sometimes can function as an inadequate container meaning not able to think about the elements projected on him, allowing what is projected to adapt to the real object/analyst, finding reinforcement in the external reality. If the analyst is able to contain and think about the projected, he can offer an interpretation to the patient in order to clarify what is going on in that moment of the session.

De Masi (2006), in his book *Vulnerabilitá alla Psicosi* (Vulnerability to Psychosis), described two unconscious systems: the dynamic system on the one hand, which would be characteristic of neurosis, and the emotional system of psychosis on the other. For the apprehension of the emotional unconscious of the psychotic patient, it becomes of great importance to understand the concept of projective identification as a form of communication, since this unconscious model being primitive, it manifests itself through bodily sensations, though certain qualities of the analyst's dreams, and countertransference feelings. De Masi differentiated the dynamic unconscious, stating that it manifests itself through content that have been repressed. Therefore, to understand the manifest content, it would be necessary to unveil the latent content. The emotional system, on the other hand, made of sensations that have never been represented or repressed and that manifest themselves by preverbal language. Elaborating further on the notion of the emotional unconscious, the author states that it is a source of affective nourishment from the affective life and the first experiences of childhood relationships. The emotional unconscious continuously builds the sense of personal identity, determines the way of relating to the world, and generates the ability to perceive and treat emotions. Elsewhere in the book, the author states that Freud described another way in which the unconscious functions, he brought the understanding that everything that is repressed is unconscious, De Masi states that not everything that is unconscious is repressed. This leads the author to consider that Freud foresaw what he, De Masi, postulated as being the emotional unconscious.

Considering that the emotional unconscious would be that of any individual's psychosis and psychotic experiences, while the dynamic unconscious would correspond to that of neuroses, De Masi affirmed that different techniques are necessary to approach one and the other. He also stated that interpretation has an effect on neurotic patients, as they are able to symbolize and understand interpretations. With psychotics, due to the symbolic deficit, it becomes necessary to help the patient build a psychic apparatus that would be able to symbolize, communicate and understand the interpretations given by the analyst. De Masi considered that transferential interpretations were experienced by psychotic patients as aggressions since they were not understood, which explains why it is necessary to first help these patients build a psychic device capable of thinking and understanding. He also stated that transferential interpretations to psychotic patients can lead to increased confusion because of their not being able to understand them.

I think that treating psychotics patients we need to be tuned to the different moments of the session to understand if neurotic or psychotics aspects prevail once they are separated only in order to describe them, but both are present in the emotional system and in the dynamic system. Here the skill of the analyst is necessary to give a proper interpretation to the patient. I understand De Masi concepts of emotional system and dynamic system as a way to better capture the communication of the patient during the session.

In his book, De Masi provided us with a commented review of the work on psychoses and also on several authors and their approaches to the psychoanalytic treatment of psychoses. It is interesting to see that all the authors discussed are anchored in Freud's seminal concepts regarding the knowledge and functioning of psychotics. Several of the developments of the authors discussed, such as those of Klein, Bion, Segal, Rosenfeld and some Americans such as Giovacchini and Schaeffer relate to the two important texts of 1924. The above developments were in terms of the understanding of the mental apparatus of the psychotics and the way work with them is done. The understanding of projective identification was very important in analysing psychotics, to which Rosenfeld and Bion made huge contributions.

Winnicott also described psychoses, starting from a different model from Klein and her followers. For Winnicott, psychosis was due to an environmental deprivation in the early days of a baby's life. He also considered in some of his work in 1963), that psychosis would be a defensive organization that protects the true self; therefore, the regression proper to the course of a psychotic episode can be valued as a necessary measure to restart the development of personal identity.

My experience with the psychoanalytic treatment of psychotic patients, whether they were in crisis or not, has shown me the importance of building a psychic apparatus together with the patient (Andrade Jr., 2015), capable of thinking, feeling, and relating, which enables understanding of interpretations, as well as communication with a more evolved part of the patient, where transferential interpretation is understood, and the possibility of a psychoanalytic dialogue is viable. Being aware of these two aspects of the patients' experiences, and being in tune with the patients' state of mind, are both particularly important for the development of work, confidence and any collaboration that may arise.

I will present below some fragments of sessions of the treatment of a psychotic patient. I intend to illustrate the transference work and the evolution of the treatment.

About twenty years ago I was approached by a very anxious lady who asked me to see her daughter. It was a Saturday morning, and this mother told me that her daughter was undergoing psychiatric treatment and had a diagnosis of schizophrenia. She informed me that her sister, who was a doctor, had recommended me to her, and added that she was very distressed and could not wait until Monday to call me.

I proposed that the lady took the patient to my office but given the fact that the patient was desperate and frightened to leave her house, I went to her home. She received me in a huge room with two large dogs lying at her feet. We started talking and the patient informed me that she was hearing voices and was very scared. The atmosphere was tense, she was terrified and was crying a lot.

Suddenly the dogs came towards me and got close to my face. I was panic-stricken, I was terrified that they would attack me. I looked at the patient and suddenly the patient's mother entered the room and took the dogs out. I noticed that the patient had rung a bell calling someone and the mother appeared.

The patient looked at me and said:

P: You were scared!

I replied with an embarrassed smile, kind of agreeing.

P: I am also very scared.

I said, at one point, that she had noticed my fear and that it made her imagine that I could feel and understand what she felt.

After the visit at her house, the patient started treatment in my office, which lasted for about a year, and was then interrupted, and I had no more news from her.

About ten years ago and about ten years after the initial consultation, the patient called me and asked to see me again. With a smiling voice, she asked if I remembered her. I confirmed I did and recalled the fear I felt of the dogs.

In the office, the first thing she told me was that she remembered how terrified I was of the dogs. I smiled, and she said that I mentioned to her a few times that she expelled her fear outside of her in an attempt to get rid of it. She also said that she never forgot that. I understood this situation as the patient saying to me that I was able to contain her projections and give meaning to her. I think that doing this both of us can create a collaborative work able to differentiate her projections from my feelings. In fact I experienced some feelings of fear when the dogs approached me but the possibility to contain it and think about it led me to give an interpretation trying to clarify the projective process. The patient as she mentioned several times took this interpretation as something that touched her and made sense to her feelings of fear and despair.

I then said that this had made sense to her. She confirmed it and added that that was why she had come to me. She said that she hoped I could do something about her fear, since I was familiar with that kind of feeling and that it also seemed to her that I could suppress her fear.

She told me that the fact that she saw that I was afraid and did not despair, gave her confidence that her fear could be lessened and even dealt with, and that was why she had come to me again.

Since then, we have continued work in analysis typical of serious cases of psychosis that develops during the treatment that usually started in childhood. Several times, I found myself in situations where the atmosphere of the session was one of extreme tension and anguish. I had enormous difficulty to understand what was going on and even how to formulate an interpretation.

It was necessary to be tolerant with her and with myself, to let the tension subside to a reasonable level that would allow me to think. I believe that the analyst's confidence in being able to try to understand the psychotic patient's material can function as a model which, if introjected by the patient, allows him to also have confidence in the analytical work, however difficult it may be.

Here is a session that took place during this period of analysis:

The patient entered the room, lay on the floor, and started looking at my books on the bookshelf. She then looked at me and said:

P: Have you read this one? (it was a book about schizophrenic disorders).
P: I know that I am not schizophrenic, you may think that I am. This book, why is it here? You are provoking me with all these books. You'll want to convince me that I'm crazy, you're going to put me in a hospital.

I said that I understood that she was scared and frightened about not knowing what I thought of her, and whether I would be able to understand all those thoughts that were unbearable.

She walked around the room shaking her head and swinging her legs and arms.

A: Perhaps through these movements, you are letting out something that is disturbing you.
P: The voices, the fears…
A: The fears of feeling schizophrenic and what these fears may mean to you.

Suddenly she pulled up her shirt and showed me a tattoo where a bird was wrapped in leaves. She explained to me that one day, she heard a voice about freedom and death, and decided to get this tattoo done. I told her that I thought the tattoo meant something to her. She told me that the voices were telling her to try to fly and be free, and that she was afraid of dying.

She got near the window, opened the curtains, and said she could do stunts between buildings. I said that she seemed to be scared of the idea of death and killing herself, so she said she didn't know if she had dreamed of it or if she was awake, but that she saw me entering her room and sitting in the same chair where I sat when I attended her at her house around 10 years ago.

I told her that the fact that I entered her room disturbed her, but that she also felt she wanted me close to her so as not to leave her alone with the voices and thoughts that disturbed her.

Soon afterwards, she told me that her thoughts were terrifying, there was a lot of death, sex, and forbidden things.

The patient was visibly disturbed at that moment, very agitated, swaying her entire body while making disconnected sounds. So, I said that something very disturbing was happening to her at that moment, and she said that what was going on in her mind was just sex, which could kill.

A: Fear that because of your sexual thoughts we were going to have sex, and thereby kill your treatment.
P: Sex can kill, end life.
A: It can put an end to this analysis, or to the life of one of us.
P: Of both of us. Kill.
A: You may be very afraid that, thinking about something, means this something is happening. Thinking about sex is having sex here with me, thinking about my death is like killing me.
P: … having sex can kill…

(The patient started crying and looked at me with an expression of anguish).

A: You fear that the only way to stay connected to me is through sex, and that this could lead to the death of everything here. And you are afraid that if I do not understand this, I will not be able to help you go home and not feel dead. You are also afraid to feel that if I am not with you, I may be dead.
P: Why does sex kill? Confusion?
A: Because there is some confusion in you about sex. If, on the one hand, it generates life, feelings of connection with me and others, on the other hand, it is felt as something that kills, that will happen because of what you thought. This seems to explain the confusion a little.

She was silent until the end of the session, which was about to happen.

I realized that there was a real threat of death, because the patient was delusional about doing acrobatics, jumping between the buildings on the street where my office is located. The impact of the possibility of suicide made me afraid for a while in the analysis of this patient, which may have prevented me from understanding her better during that period. I gradually worked on those issues, and the fear lessened to the point where we openly talked about it, and the patient confirmed that she was afraid of killing herself. We even explored possible command voices ordering her to kill herself. This was an example of how my feelings sometimes disturbed me in the sense that the patient's suicidal ideas made it difficult for me to think and I had to calm myself so I could think about me, and about the relationship with the patient, and understand that the terror inside the patient was threatening me. It is important to take in consideration that the analysis of the analyst and his capacity to self-analyse, as well as the containment of the terror are very important in facing situations such as the one I am describing here.

Gradually and throughout the treatment, the patient talked about her childhood and the confusion arisen in her family relating to the secrets of her parents' love relationships with other people, but everything was said in an obscure way, as if not said, but lingering in the air. The father was the lover of a sister-in-law and the mother had an affair with a family dentist. Those issues were hinted at during family dinners, and she was told it was not quite what she was understanding, and that she was confused about hearing things. Her parents were cold and distant and had a truncated communication with each other and with the patient. At least, that was what I was able to understand from her associations and information given by her during the analysis.

She reported that, as a child, she kept quiet beside her parents, listening to the conversations which, although friendly at first, always ended up with accusations and aggressions. A few months before the visit I made to her house, her father had suddenly died, and her mother was very sad, which left the patient confused because if her parents were so aggressive towards each other, why was her mother so sad about the loss of her husband!? This was one question among many that the patient described as having no words to explain. She further affirmed that she never understood what was going on with her family and their feelings. Regarding herself, she said that since she was a child, she had beliefs and imaginations, which I gradually understood as being hallucinations and delusions. She explained that she saw and heard conversations between people, even though she was alone in her room, or in the bathroom. She noticed that her dogs talked to her, and when she was still a child, her dolls fought with her and complained about her being very curious.

The patient's report on the confused atmosphere at her home was a way for her to express the confusion in which she lived, and the tensions she experienced due to hallucinations. I was under the impression that in those moments we were talking about very precocious feelings and experiences in her life, and which gained an attempt to be understood through delusions and hallucinations, as well as through the tense and confused atmosphere in the sessions. Freud (1924) described that "delirium is applied as a patch on the place where a crack had originally appeared in the ego's relationship with the external world" (189). He added that delusion and hallucination were attempts to cure or reconstruct contact with the lost reality.

The understanding that delusions and hallucinations are an attempt to cure or reconstruct contact with reality has followed a model since the times of "Project for a Scientific Psychology" (1895), and later on in Chapter VII of *Dreams Interpretations* (1900), in which

Freud described that it is the real object which gives the character of communication to what the individual expresses. In this understanding, I see an immense wealth for the development of the psychoanalysis of psychoses. In a way, the role of countertransference developed later by Racker (1948, 1953) and Heimann (1950, 1960), is present.

Freud (1900) says that the mother gives the character of communication when the baby cries, he says that the mother can say if it is hungry, thirsty or needs to be hold. In this way when facing psychotic experiences with patients we can help them give meanings to their communications. Many times do we construct with the patients meanings about what is going on in the session and in the mind of the patients. Some patients do not have the capacity to symbolize so they have great difficulty to understand our interpretation, and in this case we need to construct meanings. Instead of a direct interpretation of some content we can interpret what the feelings present in a moment of the session are, and moreover, we can patiently show to the patient his difficulty to understand and give meanings to his feelings. It is this work together with the patient that I see as an important tool to face psychotics states.

I disagree with De Masi when he says that it is not useful to interpret a psychotic transference because the patient is not able to understand the meaning of the interpretation and that can lead to paranoid feelings. What I think is that we can help the patient to have capacity to symbolize, to think and feel feelings that create the possibility to understand the interpretations. The patient I am presenting here, for instance, has many times received my interpretations using her listening in the wrong track. Instead of listening to me, she was listening to what she thought and projected her thoughts in my words giving a different meaning to what was interpreted and developing the paranoid feelings that I was accusing her. Carefully, I described to her the way she was listening to me and comparing this with other situations in our transference relationship and also with experiences she had with other people. It is a work done step by step until the patient is able to understand what is going on. The wrong track of the listening is something that, when understood by the patients, creates a relief and opens the possibility to accept transference interpretations. So I think that it is possible to interpret psychotic transference even if the patient is not able to receive them at first; but we can patiently help them to develop this capacity.

These concepts were particularly useful to me when working with the patient I am reporting on. Understanding and working on what was described in the clinical material above, was a job that required patience. Understanding was made difficult by the patient's quite precarious symbolic resources. Furthermore, I myself needed to set myself apart from the confusion, and gain understanding, so as to communicate to the patient what I perceived. That was not always easy and it did not happen frequently. My understanding often arose only after a long period of confusion and tension in the sessions. I think that we count on our self-analysis to cope with such experiences of fear, terror, and confusion, and it is often difficult to understand what is going on. We have to allow patience it's their job!

Here is a session that took place about four years into the treatment:

> She entered the office, talking on her cell phone, then hung up and explained to me that when she left home, she did not leave a message to her mother to feed the dogs she had just bought. She said that if the dogs were not fed, they could die.

P: This morning I saw an object on top of my bookcase. It looked like one of these statuettes you have here.
P: I saw a person on television who looked like you. I know he wasn't you, but I was confused if he was or not. When I walk down the street, I always see things that I don't know if they are real or not. Sometimes I say that they are true, so as to get rid of the doubt. There are also voices that drive me crazy. I don't know where they are coming from. I had a tattoo made on my shoulder, so as to get rid of the idea of death.

> She spent a few minutes in silence and then said:

P: Are you sure I can get well? I want to go back to school. Everything is so confusing. I am afraid of dying, going crazy, being hospitalized, and receiving shock treatment.
A: I see that you can express what you're feeling in words and tell me about the fear and anguish that you're experiencing from hearing voices.
P: I feel less agitated, but the voices and things I see are scary. Sex also makes me afraid, I'm afraid of going crazy for thinking about sexual things.
A: Your agitation has lessened, which allows you to think more about what is going on with you, and even to understand the voices.
P: The other day, I think it was today, I thought you wanted to have sex with me. No! I think it was the other way around, I wanted to have sex with you.

A: It seems that thinking about these things makes them come true, as if they were going to happen or were already happening. And you don't know if it's me or you who are having these thoughts.
P: I don't know if I'm thinking or if I'm experiencing something.
A: This confusion makes you feel crazy, afraid of what you think, unable to separate what you are thinking from what is happening.

She got up from her chair, crying. She walked towards me, and said: "You have to help me, can you?"

I told her she was afraid that I would be confused by her and could not help her. That I would not be able to discriminate between thoughts and facts, that is, what was a thought and what was a fact.

She went back to her chair, and said that she always got confused, not sure if she did things right.

I told her that when she thinks about something sexual in relation to me, she feels like the same thing is happening to me, and that then we are going to do what she is thinking of.

She said she was going to lie on the couch, and the rest of the session was spent in silence. Towards the end of the session, I told her that she must have understood what I explained to her, as lying on the couch was a sign of confidence. She smiled, and the session ended.

The night after the session, she called me, and left a message on the office's answering machine, saying she was thinking about going to sleep without taking her medication. She wanted to try it, but before talking to her psychiatrist, she wanted to talk to me. I understood that phone call as a way of communicating a greater deal of trust in me and in the analysis, a fact that we were able to better explore in other later sessions. Since that phone call, the patient has started to oscillate less between a high level of tension and despair in the sessions, to a more collaborative relationship with me in relation to the analytical work. Clearly, a greater deal of trust was achieved when the patient understood the difference between thinking and acting, which led to a decrease in the confusion and fear of what could happen between us. We were also able to discuss and examine her experiences in relation to her father's death, where she thought she could have caused his death through her thoughts.

The work described above led the patient to seek to question childhood memories, trying to understand if they were real facts, or emotional experiences experienced as real. The conversation with the dolls, the voices that accused her, the noises she heard, and the visions she had come to a more palatable dimension to be understood, and less embedded in a delusional or hallucinatory truth. Realizing a few years ahead that her delusional and hallucinatory productions were feelings and realities produced by her and not coming from outside, albeit a great cause for suffering, brought her the hope of "repair", a word she started using to refer to what was possible to do.

At the beginning of the treatment I experienced some fears as for example the dogs and later the patient suicidal ideas. I believe that when it was possible for me to think and contain these terror states I could relieve and be able to help the patient. It is necessary to count on our self-analysis in order to understand what is happening as, for example, with my fears. Recovering the capacity to think gives us more conditions to work and we can separate the analyst's fears and the patient's fears, and at the same time connect them once what is projected by the patient reactivates the mind of the analyst.

In this report, I sought to expose what I think to be the current and eternal challenges in the treatment of psychotic patients, that is, the capacity of the analyst's mind to develop the ability to think in and cope with a confused, tense atmosphere; the capacity that is necessary for the patient to gain conditions to think.

Freud's seminal papers on psychoses opened the possibility to study and understand the psychotic mind and the treatment of psychoses by psychoanalysis. Contributions by Klein and her followers built on Freud's first ideas on the subject and thus opened important and decisive ways to work with such patients. We can see in Klein and her followers many aspects that are in Freud's papers on psychoses, such as the idea that the interpretation of the hallucinations might be a way to know aspects of reality, the healing process and so on.

In "Neurosis and Psychosis" (1924), Freud explained that transferential neuroses correspond to a conflict between the ego and the id, narcissistic neuroses to a conflict between the ego and the superego, and psychoses, to a conflict between the ego and the external world (p. 192). This understanding led Freud to postulate how "the ego can avoid a rupture by deforming itself, subjecting itself to usurpations in its own unity, and even by performing a cleavage or division in itself."

Later in other texts, such as *Fetichism* (1927) and *Splitting of the Ego in the Defensive Process* (1938), Freud advanced in the understanding of mechanisms used by the ego, such as refusal, disapproval, rejection, and denial, which led to the understanding of important psychotic phenomena, such as attempts to substitute reality for the remodeling of reality through hallucinations and delusions – a topic that had already been developed in the texts of 1924.

These understandings were seminal for the further development of the treatment of psychoses, with the work of Rosenfeld published in *Psychotic States* (1965) and *Impasse and Interpretation* (1987), as well as in several other pieces of work. The advancement in the psychoanalytic treatment of psychoses took place all over the world with European, American, and South American authors publishing their findings and their experiences. Among the pioneers, we can mention the work of Abraham (1924/1927), Stern (1938) and Federn (1943). In different approaches, work by Winnicott (1963, 1978), and more recently, by De Masi (2006), Kernberg (1984), Searles (1959, 1965), and Bryce Boyer (1961) in the United States, while the work of Almeida Prado (1979, 1983) in Latin America.

In conclusion, I would like to say that it has been a long journey since Freud's seminal work on psychoses with many other significant contributions. I want to add that the capacity to survive the confusion and terror experienced while treating psychotics patients gives us analysts a stimulus to cope with the difficulties. We need to show to the patient that although it is extremely difficult both to bear and to make sense of, patients' suffering is a human experience and as such it is possible to understand. I tried to show this in the clinical material presented.

References

Abraham, K. (1927). *Selected Papers of Karl Abraham*. London: Hogarth (reprinted London: Karnac, 1988).
Abraham, K. (1955). *Clinical Papers and Essays on Psychoanalysis*. London: Hogarth (reprinted London: Karnac, 1988).
Almeida Prado, M.P. (1979). *Identificação Projetiva no Processo Analítico*. (*Projective Identification in Analytic Process*). Rio de Janeiro: Author Edition.
Almeida Prado, M.P. (1983). *Psicanálise de Psicóticos*. (*Psychoanalysis of Psychotics*). Rio de Janeiro: Plurarte Ed.
AndradeJr, A.M. (1990). *Una Defesa Contra o Sentimento de Morte*. (*A Defense Against Death Feelings*). Scientific Bulletin SBPRJ. N° 11. Rio de Janeiro.
AndradeJr, A.M. (2012). *Clinical Material presented to the 29th Latin America Congress*. São Paulo.
AndradeJr, A.M. (2015). Recovering Psychic Apparatus. Published as a Keynotes Paper to 49th IPAC. Boston in the *Int. Journal of Psychoanalysis*, 96, n° 3, 521–533.
Bion, W.R. (1962^a). *Learning from Experience*. London: Heinemann, New York: Basic Books.

Bion, W.R. (1967). *Second Thoughts*. Selected Papers on Psychoanalysis. London: Heinemann. (reprinted by Karnac1984).

Bion, W.R. (1973/1974). *W.R. Bion. Conferências Brasileiras*. Rio de Janeiro: Imago Editora. (Bion's Brazilian Lectures 1).

Bion, W.R. (1997). *Taming Wild Thoughts*. London: Karnac.

Bion, W.R. (2013). *Wilfred Bion Los Angeles Seminars and Supervision*. Edited by Joseph Aguayo and Barnet Malin. London: Karnac.

Bion, W.R. (2018). *Bion in Buenos Aires Seminars, case Presentation and Supervision*. Edited by Joseph Aguayo, Lia Pistiner de Cortinas and Agnes Regeczkey. London: Karnac.

Boyer, L.B. (1961). Provisional Evaluation of Psychoanalysis with Few Parameters in the Treatment of Schizophrenia. *Int. Journal of Psychoanalysis*, 42: 389–403.

Boyer, L.B. (1990). Introduction: Psychoanalytic Intervention in Treating the regressed patient. In *Mater Clinicians on Treating Regressed Patient*. Edited by L.B. Boyer and P.L. Giovacchini. 1–32. Northvale, NJ: Jason Aranson.

De Masi, F. (2006). *Vulnerabilità alla Psicosi. Raffaello Cortina Editore*. (*Vulnerability to Psychosis*).

De Masi, F. (2000). The Unconscious and Psychosis. Some Considerations on the Psychoanalytic Theory of Psychosis. *Int. J. Psychoan.*, 81: 1–20.

Federn, P. (1943/1952). *Ego Psychology and the Psychosis*. New York: Basic Books.

Freud, S. (1892–1899/1969). *Extratos dos Documentos Dirigidos a Fliess*. (*The Origins of Psychoanalysis*). Standard Edition Brasileira (SEB). Vol. 1. Rio de Janeiro: Imago Ed.

Freud, S. (1895/1969). *Projeto Para uma Psicologia Científica* (*Project for a Scientific Psychology*). SEB. Rio de Janeiro: Imago Ed.

Freud, S. (1894/1969). *As Neuropsicoses de Defesa*. (*The Defense Neuro-Psychoses*). SEB. Vol. 3. Rio de Janeiro: Imago Ed.

Freud, S. (1900/1972). *A Interpretação dos Sonhos*. (*Dreams Interpretation*). SEB. Vol 5. Rio de Janeiro: Imago Ed.

Freud, S. (1911/1970). *As perspectivas Futuras da Terapêutica Psicanalítica*. (*The Future Prospects of Psychoanalytic Therapy*). SEB. Vol. 11. Rio de Janeiro: Imago Ed.

Freud, S. (1911/1969). *Notas Psicanalíticas sobre um Relato Autobiográfico de um Caso de Paranoia*. (*Psychoanalytic Notes upon an Autobiographical Account of a Case of Paranoia*). SEB. Vol. 12. Rio de Janeiro: Imago Ed.

Freud, S. (1917/1976). *Conferências Introdutórias Sobre Psicanálise. A Transferência. – XXVII*. (*Introductory Letters on Psychoanalysis*). SEB. Vol. 16. Rio de Janeiro: Imago Ed.

Freud, S. (1924/1976). *Neurose e Psicose*. (*Neurosis and Psychosis*). SEB. Vol. 19. Rio de Janeiro: Imago Ed.

Freud, S. (1924/1976). *A Perda da Realidade na Neurose e na Psicose*. (*Loss of Reality in Neuroses and Psychosis*). SEB. Vol. 19. Rio de Janeiro: Imago Ed.

Freud, S. (1927/1974). *Fetichismo*. (*Fetishism*). SEB. Vol. 21. Rio de Janeiro: Imago Ed.

Freud, S. (1940/1975). *Esboço de Psicanálise*. (*An Outline of Psychoanalysis*). SEB. Vol. 23. Rio de Janeiro: Imago Ed.

Freud, S. (1940/1975). *A Divisão do Ego no Processo de Defesa*. (*Splitting of the Ego in the Defensive Process*). SEB. Vol. 23. Rio de Janeiro: Imago Ed.
Heimann, P. (1950). On Counter-transference. *International Journal of Psychoanalysis*, 31: 81–84.
Heimann, P. (1960). Counter-transference. *British Journal of Medical Psychology*, 33: 9–15.
Kernberg, O. (1984). *Severe Personality Disorders*. New Haven, CT: Yale University Press.
Klein, M. (1946/1975). Notes on Some Schizoid Mechanisms. In *The Writings of Melanie Klein Vol. 3*: 1–24. London: The Hogarth Press.
Money-Kyrle, R.E. (1956). Normal Counter-transference and some of its Deviations. *Int. J. Psychoan*, 37: 360–366.
Racker, H. (1948). Aportacion al problema de la contratransferência. *Revista de Psicanálise*, 12: 481–499.
Racker, H. (1953). A Contribution to the Problem of Counter-transference. *International Journal of Psychoanalysis*, 34: 313–324.
Rosenfeld, H. (1965). *Psychotic States*. London: Maresfield Reprints.
Rosenfeld, H. (1983). On the Psychology and treatment of Psychotic Patients (Historical and Comparative Reflections). In: *Do I dare Disturb the Universe? A memorial to Wilfred R. Bion*. Edited by James S. Grotstein. London: Maresfield Reprints.
Rosenfeld, H. (1987). *Impasse and Interpretation*. London: Tavistock Publications.
Searles, H.F. (1959[a]). The effort to drive the analyst crazy – An element in the Aetiology and Psychotherapy of Schizophrenia. *British Journal of Medical Psychology*, 32: 1–18.
Searles, H.F. (1965). *Collected Papers on Schizophrenia and Related Subjects*. London: Hogarth Press.
Segal, H. (1957). Notes on Symbol Formation. *Int. J. of Psychoanal.*, 38: 391–397.
Stern, A. (1938). Psychoanalytic Investigation of and Therapy in the Borderline Group of Neuross. *Psychoanalytic Quarterly*, 7: 467–489.
Winnicott, D.W. (1963) Fear of Breakdown. In Winnicott, D.W. *(1989) – Psycho-Analytic Explorations*. Cambridge, Massachusetts: Harvard University Press.
Winnicott, D.W. (1978). *Textos Selecionados: Da Pediatria a Psicanálise*. (*Collected Papers: Through Paediatrics to Psychoanalysis*). Rio de Janeiro: Francisco Alves Ed.

3 Reality and Psycho(-Patho)logical Organisation of the Personality

Antonio Pérez-Sánchez

1 Introduction

The central theme of Freud's publications we are discussing lies in establishing a differentiation between neurosis and psychosis with reality as a point of reference. But alongside this intention, almost a hundred years after it was written, and in the light of subsequent psychoanalytical developments, it is possible to grasp another and no less important purpose. In contrasting neurosis and psychosis, Freud not only marks out what separates them but also describes what makes them similar. Moreover, the narrative technique used, apart from showing Freud's literary ability, is a convincing discursive procedure in itself for the reader. Indeed, throughout both articles, the arguments that separate neurotic and psychotic functioning alternate with others that argue that what we find in the psychotic is also found in the neurotic. And then he again disabuses the reader by reminding them that, despite these similarities, the neurotic and the psychotic contain differences. Freud then shows these only to explain precisely that which unites them. So, through this movement from distance to proximity to distance between neurosis and psychosis, we end up convinced that psychosis, although different from neurosis, is not as different as we sometimes think, and especially at the time when this work was written. But Freud goes further still, for he dares to suggest that even in "normal" behaviour we might find some of the characteristics that are present in both neurosis and psychosis.

Therefore, the first consideration to be drawn from reading these two papers is the current validity of an assertion implicit in them: that it is not possible to establish a clear dividing line between neurosis and psychosis. Moreover, every personality organisation, even the non-pathological, participates in both functions. I will try to show what the seeds of these ideas are in Freud's two papers and then connect them with some of the later developments. Clinical material from a schizophrenic patient will help me illustrate these connections.

DOI: 10.4324/9781003384120-3

The two papers we are discussing here are part of a line in Freud's research that shows his interest in psychosis (and its relation to the non-psychotic), which can be traced throughout his work. As a complementary theoretical element, I would also add *The Two Principles of Psychic Functioning* (1911) because of the importance given to phantasy and the relationship with reality in delimiting psychosis and neurosis. Although I will only mention those that seem to me to be the most outstanding.

Thus, thirty years before the 1924 publications, Freud showed interest in psychosis in *The neuro-psychoses of defence* (1894a). In this work, he considers psychosis as a "defence" which he places alongside other defensive mechanisms, such as hysteria and phobia. He furthermore speaks of a "flight into psychosis", which he would later generalise as a "flight into illness", or as a defence against a painful reality. Freud makes two further points: one is that while psychosis has a conflict with reality, and consequently reacts by withdrawing from it, it does not, however, do so completely. Thus, in explaining hallucinatory states, he considers that there are elements of reality preserved, from which the hallucination is constructed. He puts it like this:

> the ego has fended off the incompatible idea through a *flight into psychosis* [...] The ego breaks away from the incompatible idea; but the latter *is inseparably connected with a piece of reality*, so that, insofar as the ego achieves this result, it, too, has detached itself wholly or in part from reality. In my opinion this latter event is the condition under which the subject's ideas receive the vividness of hallucinations.
> (Freud, 1984, 50–51) (Author's italics)

The other issue already mentioned in this early work is the complex composition of all psychopathology:

> The three methods of defence here described and, along with them, the three forms of illness [hysteria, phobia and hallucinatory confusion] to which those methods lead, *may be combined in the same person*.
> (1984a: 60) [Author's italics]

In other words, even psychopathological mental life is susceptible to a malleability that goes beyond rigid diagnostic schemes.

2 Works of 1924

In *Neurosis and Psychosis,* Freud begins by establishing the "genetic" difference between the two: *Neurosis* is the result of a conflict between the ego and the id, whereas psychosis depends on the relationship between the ego and the external world. In neurosis, the part of the ego that seeks satisfaction is repressed. But the repressed part rebels and finds ways to give substitute satisfaction to the tendencies of the id by means of the symptom; the ego fights against the symptom, as it did before against the instinctual tendency, giving rise to the picture of neurosis. Thus, the ego obeys the commands of the superego, which is the result of the influences of the external world that have been represented in it, meaning that the ego has come into conflict with the id, siding with the superego and with reality.

Freud says:

> Normally, the external world governs the ego in two ways: firstly, by current, present perceptions which are always renewable, and secondly, by the store of memories of earlier perceptions which, in the shape of an 'internal world', form a possession of the ego and a constituent part of it.
>
> (1924b: 150)

In psychosis (amentia: an acute hallucinatory confusion), on the other hand, not only are the new perceptions rejected, but the inner world, which hitherto has been a copy of the external world and has represented it, loses its meaning, as it is no longer invested (catechised). The ego then imposes the creation of an outer and an inner world, due to two undoubted facts: that this new world is constructed following the tendencies of the id, and that the cause of the detachment from external reality is due to an intolerable frustration with reality.

In other words, psychosis is the result of the ego's extreme intolerance of psychic pain due to contact with reality. An incapacity that is difficult to resolve, since it dominates the dynamic of denying the perception of reality, and consequently not registering it, which prevents it from forming part of the ego; thus, each new reality is treated as if it were something completely alien that has to be rejected. This dynamic obstructs learning from experience, as there is no interaction, through introjection (of what is perceived) and projection (of what is internal), between external and internal reality, thus perpetuating the withdrawal from reality. As we have just seen, Freud also states that the internal world is generated as a copy of the perceptions of the external world, except when there is a psychotic conflict that excludes external reality. As we shall see later, we now know that the relationship between external and internal reality is rather one of mutual influence, of interaction, as a result of which an internal world is established.

Freud then forgets that he is talking about the differences between neurosis and psychosis, and, as if in passing, establishes a similarity of psychosis, not to neurosis, but to a normal psychic process: *dreams*. Indeed, dreaming requires a state, sleep, which implies a withdrawal from reality. Therefore, both psychosis and sleep share the withdrawal from the real world and from all perception, although the purpose is different: in sleep it is to achieve rest, in psychosis, to detach from a painful reality. This subtly leads us to think that psychosis is not alien even to normal psychic processes, even if only in a superficial way.

He then speaks of schizophrenia, in which he distinguishes two features: an "affective hebetude" which hinders perception and separates the individual from reality, and delusion. About the latter he says that it is a creation of a sort of "patch" that arises at those points in the relationship between the ego and reality in which a hole has been made. He adds that sometimes this conflict with the outside world is not so obvious, the reason for this is that the conflict is covered up by the attempt at "healing or reconstruction", through delusion. Freud thus offers a psychodynamic explanation of delusions, insofar as they make up or compensate for that part of reality in which a discontinuity has been generated. In other words, the delusion is thus created in order to maintain contact with reality, even it is only apparent. It can therefore be deduced that in schizophrenic psychoses (not in extreme psychoses such as amentias) only a part of external reality is disavowed, and it is there that delusion acts. This observation will not be taken up by Freud in the following work, *The Loss of Reality in Neurosis and Psychosis*, because, in differentiating between neurosis and psychosis, he considers that in the former only a 'piece' of reality is dissociated, whereas in psychosis the external "imaginary world" is put in the place of external reality.

Freud then points out that neurosis and psychosis have a common aetiology: the experience of frustration stemming from the non-fulfilment of infantile desires, deeply rooted in our organisation. The origin of frustration is external, although sometimes it arises from within, from the superego, as the representation of external demands. He then adds:

> The pathogenic effect depends on whether, [...], the ego remains true to its dependence on the external world and attempts to silence the id, or whether it lets itself be overcome by the id and thus torn away from reality.
>
> (1924a:151)

And he outlines the differences between the various pathologies, now including the superego: in *transference neurosis*, the conflict arises between the ego and the id; in *narcissistic neurosis* (melancholia), between the ego and the superego; and in *psychosis*, between the ego and the external world.

Freud then indicates that, in order to overcome the conflict with the different psychic instances, the ego depends on two factors: first, the economic factor, i.e. the magnitude of the conflicting forces, and, secondly, through the deformation of the ego, tolerating damage to its unity and even through splitting or division of itself. He will discuss this in later works (1927e, 1940e) were he will delve deeper into the concept of the splitting of the ego. Freud ends his paper on *Neurosis and Psychosis* by questioning whether the mechanism by which the ego separates itself from the external world in psychosis is *analogous* to repression.

In the following work, *The Loss of Reality in Neurosis and Psychosis* (1924e), Freud summarises the differences between neurosis and psychosis established in the previous paper by saying that the loss of reality would be a characteristic phenomenon of psychosis and alien to neurosis. But he immediately questions this distinction, noting that clinical observation indicates that in every neurosis there is some disturbance in the patient's relationship with reality: he flees from real life and creates a refuge. This seems like a contradiction if we only consider the first moment of the emergence of neurosis: when the ego represses the tendencies of the id, obeying reality. But the emergence of neurosis does not end there, it is completed by a second step, the reaction of the ego to repression, the consequence of this repression is a certain loss of reality that takes place in order to compensate for the damaged part of the id. In psychosis, similarly, the pathological process consists of two steps. However, contrasted with neurosis, the ego is torn away from reality in the very first step, while in the second step, it tends to compensate for the loss of reality in a different way than in neurosis: by creating a new reality through delusion. He immediately points out again that what they have in common is that both respond to the same tendency to be at the service of the aspirations of the id, that is to say, of the id's incapacity to adapt to the demands of reality. In other words, neurosis and psychosis differ more in the first stage than in the second, where there is an attempt at repairing.

Freud then highlights a different aspect. In neurosis, says Freud:

> the initial difference is expressed thus in the final outcome: *in neurosis a piece of reality is avoided by a sort of flight, whereas in psychosis it is remodelled*. Or we might say: in psychosis, the initial flight is succeeded by an active phase of remodelling; in neurosis, the initial obedience is succeeded by a deferred

attempt at flight. Or again, expressed in yet another way: *neurosis does not disavow the reality, it only ignores it; psychosis disavows it and tries to replace it.*

[SE: 185. (Author's italics)]

The description is eloquent, because not only does he find different ways of expressing the differences, but it alternates where the comparison begins. I think that this sort of dance between neurosis and psychosis leads us to a consideration of the latter as close to and with many points of contact with the former, and vice versa.

He then subtly introduces a change of subject, and slips – as he did in the previous work when introducing the subject of dreams – from the similarity between neurosis and psychosis to *'normal'* behaviour, which combines both neurotic and psychotic functioning:

> We call behaviour 'normal' or 'healthy', if it combines certain features of both reactions – if it disavows the reality as little as does a neurosis, but if it then exerts itself, as does a psychosis, to effect an alteration of that reality.
>
> (Freud, 1924b): 185)

However, it must be pointed out that normal behaviour leads to working on the external world and does not stop, as in psychosis, at making internal (perceptual) changes.

Freud then explains that in psychosis there is a transformation of the mentally represented reality through psychic precipitations from the relationships maintained until then with external reality. But in order for this internal reality to correspond to the external reality, renewed perceptions must be produced, which are adapted to the new reality, the ultimate expression of which would be a hallucination.

And without pausing, in the same paragraph, so that it may go unnoticed that he is talking about something new, he introduces the idea that in many forms of psychosis the defensive mechanisms (false memories, delusions, and hallucinations) against intolerable reality are generators of anxiety, which leads him to the conclusion:

> If it [normal behaviour] is without doubt a sign that the whole process of remodelling is carried through against *forces which oppose it* violently.
>
> (186) [author's italics]

And to explain this he resorts to the model of neurosis, "with which we are more familiar", in which anxiety arises every time the repressed instinct tries to reach consciousness, generating a conflict that is resolved by a transaction, which does not provide complete satisfaction. In psychosis, on the other hand,

> the rejected piece of reality constantly forces itself upon the mind, just as the repressed instinct does in a neurosis, and that is why *in both cases the consequences too are the same.*
> (186) [author's italics]

Consequently, we find ourselves with a new analogy, says Freud, in that both neurosis and psychosis partially fail at the second stage of the pathological process, as he says in the next paragraph:

> For the repressed instinct is unable to procure a full substitute (in neurosis); and the representation of reality cannot be remoulded into satisfying forms (not, at least, in every species of mental illness).

In psychosis, however, the emphasis is on the first step of the process, whereas in neurosis it is on the second.

Two points are worth noting here. One, which has already been mentioned, and which is present in both papers, is that Freud has no qualms about explaining – although partially – psychosis on the model of the dynamics of neurosis, with which he is more familiar. The other issue is the observation of the existence of forces that oppose the predominance of pathological defences, which would indicate a foretaste of what we know today as those aspects of the individual – including the psychotic – that always remain in contact with reality.

Next, the Freudian text brings us a new similarity. While neurosis tries to avoid the painful part of reality, there is no lack of attempts to replace the undesired reality with one that is more in tune with the subject's desires. This is made possible by the existence of the *world of fantasy*, a field that was separated from the external world with the irruption of the principle of reality and remained "like a kind of 'reservation'" (1924b:187). It is from this that neurosis draws its material "for its new wishful constructions". And Freud has "no doubt" that this world of fantasy is the same source that feeds psychosis in order to construct new realities. Although they differ in that in psychosis *"imaginary external world of a psychosis attempts to put itself in the place of external reality,"* whereas in neurosis, it relies on a different piece of reality from the one it had to defend itself against. However, and so ends the second paper:

Thus we see that both in neurosis and psychosis there comes into consideration the question not only of a *loss of reality* but also of a *substitute for reality*.

(1924b: 187)

That is to say, there is not so much difference between neurosis and psychosis, except in the question of the extent of the two phenomena. In both, there is a loss of reality, being lesser in the former than in the latter; and there is also a substitution of reality, being greater in psychosis than in neurosis.

In retrospect, both articles, as I said above, are woven compositions, where similarities and differences alternate in an exercise of exposition. This is not only a stylistic device as it raises an underlying question that Freud could perhaps not conceptualise sufficiently at the time. That is, that both the neurotic and the psychotic are present in every personality organisation, be it psychotic, neurotic, or "normal". This was a starting point for later developments which I will discuss below.

But I would first like to bring up another subject dealt with by Freud in later works, which I consider important for what we are examining. This is the ratification of the existence of the splitting of the ego in all psychoses. A mechanism that he was able to explore in depth when studying fetishism (1927e). Later, however, he was able to conclude that this mechanism is not something exclusive to this perversion, but a universal mechanism of all neurotics, and already present in childhood: "the disavowal [of reality] is always supplemented by an acknowledgment: two contrary and independent attitudes always arise and result in the situation of there being a splitting of the ego" (1940a: 204).

3 Current developments on the relationship between neurosis, psychosis, and organization of the personality

For all that has been said, it is reasonable to think that Freud left open some questions that later psychoanalytic thought has tried to answer over the years since the works we are commenting on were written. I think that Freud's interest in differentiating neurosis from psychosis, and at the same time emphasising what they have in common, is nothing more than putting the two pathological entities together, as coexisting, even though they are separate. This is precisely the description he gives of the universal mechanism, the splitting of the ego, to explain its psychopathology. It is well known that, despite his interest in psychosis, Freud dismissed the psychotic patient from psychoanalytic treatment as incapable of establishing "a transference" (1914c), so Freud was unable to study these patients in his clinical experience. He therefore needed to borrow observations from other psychosis scholars, or from patients' own testimonies (such as his essay on the Shreber case: Freud, 1911 *c*), and try to understand it from what he was most familiar with: the neuroses.

Therefore, in order for further contributions to be possible, it was necessary to include the treatment of psychotic patients into the psychoanalytic practice. A Kleinian group in Europe and a group of American analysts made this possible, and allowed Freud's original ideas to be developed by later psychoanalysts: the idea that psychosis is accessible through psychoanalysis, and that psychotic elements exist in every individual, even if they do not predominate. Taking Kleinian thought as a theoretical frame of reference, I will devote special attention to Bion's contributions.

One of the most prominent contributions to the analysis of psychotic patients has been that of Bion (1957), who described "the psychotic personality" as one that consists of a certain psychic functioning not only present in the psychotic patient, where it predominates, but in every individual – albeit to a lesser extent. This idea has led to distinguishing the existence in every person of "a psychotic part" and "a non-psychotic part" of his personality. Based on clinical work with difficult, psychotic, and borderline patients, future analysts have developed the defensive forms involved in the articulation between the psychotic and the non-psychotic. Defensive strategies that include both parts of the split mind. These developments have been given different names: "highly organised defensive system" (Riviére, 1936), "pathological narcissism" (Rosenfeld, 1964, 1971; Meltzer, 1968), and "defensive organisation" (Segal, 1972; O'Shaughnessy, 1981). J. Steiner took up and developed these contributions and coined the term "pathological organisations". (Steiner, 1983), which has become widely accepted. This chapter continues that line of thought, with special emphasis on the concern of how the coexistence of the neurotic and the psychotic parts of the personality are articulated. Elsewhere, I propose a distinction between different types of pathological personality organisation depending on the nature of the articulation between the psychotic and the non-psychotic part of the personality (Pérez-Sánchez, 2018). This in turn depends on the tolerance to mental pain involved in facing reality.

We could consider psychopathology as a function of how an individual's personality is organised when faced with the pain of recognising reality; depending on whether there is a predominance of the tendency to *avoid* it or to *modify* it, according to Bion's parameters (Bion, 1962). To a certain extent, both tendencies are present in all individuals, as it is not always possible to transform reality completely, as we should be omnipotent, and neither is it possible to totally elude it, for that would mean death. The degree of psychopathology in the organization of the personality will be larger the more the psychic activity leans towards the second option: the avoidance of reality. In most serious cases, psychopathology involves setting in motion a whole series of strategies and defence mechanisms which, even though they may succeed in the avoidance of direct contact with reality, generate another type of pain which, in turn, will need new strategies and defence mechanisms, in an endless spiral, with an end to not only suffering less and less from pain but even to feeling it less, which leads to an ever-greater emptying, distortion, and fragmentation of psychic life (affective and cognitive). This is the mental deterioration we find in long-term psychotic and schizophrenic patients.

In the neurotic organisation there is an acceptable tolerance of pain concomitant with contact with reality, so that in the inevitable interaction between the non-psychotic and psychotic parts there is a predominance of the former. In contrast, in the psychotic organisation the non-psychotic part has been losing strength in its defence of being in contact with reality and has been subjected to the dynamics of the psychotic part, with a consequent detachment from reality.

Another way of considering the dynamics of the relationship of the psychotic and non-psychotic parts with reality – which is the central theme of Freud's papers – is to attend to the existence of an adequate perception of reality, based on the different perceptive organs, and whether or not they harmonise with each other; that is to say, of "common sense". Therefore, the degree of distortion of "common sense" is another of the substantial elements of all personality organisations, from the psychotic to the neurotic. Britton, in discussing my proposal (Pérez-Sánchez, 2018) of the core of the conflict between the psychotic and the non-psychotic part of the personality, says:

> it is perhaps best to describe the competition as between the psychotic pathological organisation and the common sense view of reality. Taking common sense as Bion does in its two references: common to our different senses of the external and internal perceptions and also as reality as perceived in common with others.
>
> (Britton, 2018, p: XV)

According to Bion, the basis of contact with reality lies in the adequate conjunction of different sensory routes of access. Each route contributes a dimension that is not sufficient by itself and needs the assistance of others; that is, the pooling of all the senses that participate in perceiving an aspect of a certain reality (object) in order to define the characteristics of that reality. The ordinary expression "common sense" implies this "collective" of the senses. And so Bion defines an individual's common sense as "an adequate description covering an experience felt to be supported by all the senses without disharmony" (Bion, 1992, p. 10). But it also means something shared by other individuals, leaving hardly any room for doubt. The first conception of "common sense" would be the private, individual one, while the second takes on a social dimension: the most frequent use of the expression.

In another work, Bion insists that the purpose of communication is to achieve a correlation between the different elements of reality. And if this communication is private, thoughts and their verbalization need to facilitate the conjunction of one series of sensory information with another. If there is harmony in this conjunction of data, one experiences the sense that it is true. On the other hand, the failure of this conjunction of sensory data, and therefore of common sense, induces in the patient a mental state of weakness, as if the lack of truth were to the psyche what lack of food is to the body. This function of the senses concerning physical objects (situated in space and time) correlates to the function that emotions have in the psyche. So we could say that since there is an individual common sense, its psychic counterpart would be a common emotional point of view. Bion illustrates this with his example of the vision of a hated object that is put in conjunction with the vision of the same loved object, and if the result is that the object experienced in both emotions is the same object, one has a more complete feeling; that is, it better reflects the "truth" of the reality being experienced (Bion, 1967, p. 119).

According to Freud (1940a), at the onset of normal development of the individual, it is necessary to resort to splitting mechanisms in order to tolerate painful reality. But Kleinian thought delved deeper into the nature and diversity of the forms of splitting, and distinguished between splitting into a good and a bad object, and a good and a bad self, on the one hand, and splitting that tends to fragmentation of reality, on the other. The first splitting, which we call binary, would correspond to what Freud considers proper to the development of the individual. The fragmentary split, on the other hand, would be the one that takes place in pathological organisations.

Translated into Bionian terms, binary splitting would be nondestructive, while fragmentary splitting would be splitting with destructive intentionality. For the psychotic patient, his insufficient capacity for tolerating the experience of the necessary correlation of different vies of perception, because of the inevitable psychic pain involved in this emotional perception, leads to this kind of splitting;

to be effective, the splitting must be multiple, with the consequence of a fragmentation of reality.

We could say that these ideas about the Bionian "common sense" are an extension of his concept of "binocular vision", a metaphor often used by Bion to describe the "visualisation" of psychic reality. This deals with the conjunction of two "views" while "common sense" deals with the correlation established between the different sensory and emotional components that may constitute a relationship with the object.

Regarding the other meaning of "common sense", that of participating in a certain reality that others share, with the exception of folie a deux and collective delusions, the individual delusional experience is not usually shared by others. However, the analyst himself is not exempt from this risk with his patient; this may occur, at least to a certain degree, when the analyst colludes with the psychotic part of the patient or, perhaps more commonly, addresses the non-psychotic part, overlooking the psychotic part in order to avoid confronting it, thereby implicitly accepting it. I will give an example. A neurotic patient who lost her father at the age of three looked for partners to fill the gap of the father's absence, as a way of "resurrecting" the father (a delusional unconscious fantasy). In the transference, there was also this expectation until I realised that I unconsciously held the idea that I would fill her void, meaning that I colluded with her delusion of becoming her "resurrected" father. By becoming aware of my countertransference, I was able to verbalise it.

Finally, I am interested in reviewing the importance of the *"world of fantasy"* in its influence on psychic life, as understood by Freud, in the light of later developments. Freud regards phantasy in isolation from the rest of psychic life and the external world, as a kind of "natural reservoir", to which the ego has little access, and which emerges when the reality principle is established (Freud, 1911). Today we know two things from Melanie Klein and her followers along with other analysts. Firstly, that phantasy is not a stronghold apart from external reality; although its origin is linked to basic somatic drives and movements, it acquires form, i.e. representation, in its encounter with external objects. Thus, unconscious phantasy pervades the whole of psychic life, it accompanies it; alongside the manifest level, there is always the level of unconscious phantasy. M. Klein (1921) was able to observe how children's actual behaviour is accompanied by unconscious phantasy; S. Issacs (1948) conceptualised unconscious phantasy as the psychic representation of drives, and, according to her, they are therefore the primary content of unconscious mental processes. In other words, the primary nuclear activity that expresses both drives and defences (Segal, 1991). The other issue is that unconscious phantasy is the result of the interaction between the perceived external world and basic somatic vicissitudes. Thus, internal objects are not an exact reflection of external objects, but the result of the interaction between the latter and the unconscious phantasies activated by them. Unconscious fantasy thus reflects defences against reality, which is many times difficult. But, as Segal points out, unconscious fantasy is also a way of making hypotheses about reality in advance: What would happen to me if such and such happened. In the psychotic, unconscious fantasy is reality itself. (Segal,1994).

4 Clinical material. Working with the sane part against the psychotic part of personality

This material corresponds to the analysis of a schizophrenic patient in her fifth year of analysis of five weekly sessions during the first four years. It's a Thursday, the last session of a week in which we were able to do the four sessions, after several weeks in which it was not possible to complete all the sessions of the week.

She arrives around five minutes late. (After searching for her cigarettes and lighter and putting the ashtray on the couch, she lies down)

P: I must be stupid, masochistic or I don't know what... It turns out that the builder came to do another set of plans for the flat refurbishment. I guess I was the protagonist, because it is for me. Well I was hell bent on feeling down, until I managed it and ended up crying my eyes out, thinking about how I wanted to get cancer... [*The patient makes an effort, lies down on the couch, not always easy, begins to talk about the frustration she has experienced, and her intolerance towards the pain of that reality, with the consequent flight to desire a physical illness, in order to place her pain in her body.*]

A: Or rather, you realize that the project of having your own flat is something that could satisfy you, as is the project of you having your own mental space, with the work we do here, but insofar as this involves an effort, it seems to you as though you will not be able to bear it, and this could be avoided with the thought of having cancer.

P: Yes, it was difficult for me to come here. I went to catch the bus and not only that, it didn't come. And then I thought that if it takes another quarter of an hour, I won't go to Dr PS. And I was almost hoping it would not arrive. When I got on, I had the thought that I hope the bus crashes, I want to die (crying). But then I realized that there were innocent people on that bus... And I thought about the bus driver, doing the same route every day...

A: But you were finally able to come to the session. In spite of a part of you that is against it. You didn't want to take the bus, and once inside you wanted it to crash. But you immediately thought of the innocent aspects of yourself, in need of help, and of the "poor" analyst, who every day takes this route, driving this analysis to take you a little further. And that made you feel bad, but it allowed you to come.

P: God is unfair, because he does not send me cancer... [*Somewhat calmer. Although my interpretation has awakened in her a strong sense of guilt, she has not taken refuge in delusion as she did a year ago, when she was convinced, she had cancer. However, she has limited herself to missing it and wishing for it.*] Because yes, obviously, I am making efforts. But what is the use? What good are they? if only to survive... This week I've had some busy days and I have done things, but then?... I don't feel capable of doing anything (weeping).

A: I think that this week's sessions have been busy, we have been able to do them all, which was not possible last weeks; and for that reason now the week is over it becomes more difficult to bear the discomfort of stopping here and waiting until Monday...

P: Yes... I was thinking: "Dr. PS give me a cancer ..." Why shouldn't I have the chronic diarrhoea I had last winter? If I had any major disease ...! [*Again, in the face of almost unbearable psychological pain, she wishes for a somatic disease, which she asks me for. But she does not attack reality, as was her first impulse of not coming to the session, or distorting it to reconstruct it in a delusional way*].

A: You are asking me to give you an illness, not life, not to help you in your life. Perhaps you are asking me to tolerate it when you say that what I give you is of little use, and also to tolerate your particular discomfort.

P: But I am the one who cannot tolerate all of this, because it is such a struggle... [*she pauses. And, eventually, after my interpretation of her projective identification she can tolerate the pain, and go on with the session*]. Yesterday, after the session I went to see P. (a friend). I felt better (than how she felt in the session) but he had work to do. We talked a little but he didn't want to come to the cinema. I didn't want to go alone. I felt rejected, and I feel ugly and old (she cries, in fact she spends almost the entire session crying); I felt as though life was not worth living. So I went home and started to write. I wanted to write a long story... [*She often writes, and while in analysis she has been able to publish a few texts*] I thought of something autobiographical. About a girl who could not leave her neighbourhood. She met a boy she liked. But he was a citizen of the world, while she could not leave the neighbourhood… Now I think that I do actually leave my neighbourhood when I come here… (pause). I called M (a female friend). And she spoke to me about the translation she was doing and I talked through the story I was writing. She told me that she wasn't doing badly, just not great… Afterwards I couldn't write more than the four pages I had done… [*Her weeping intensifies again. Turning her head every so often*] I'm sorry but it's just that today I am that childish with such basic things…

A: You are realizing that it is possible to have come here for us to make a session journey, even if that journey is not quite as long as you would like, and that having to stop now until Monday requires a significant effort.

P: You don't know how hard it is for me… (She pauses) I wish I could be prescribed cyanide; I wish I could go to a motel and kill myself. I don't like the idea of pills because it's very slow (melancholy tone of desperation, while at the same time conveying that this is not something she is about to do). [*Again, the contact with a painful reality, the analytic separation, gives rise to another extreme defence: the death wish. Years ago, before starting psychoanalysis, she had made several suicide attempts*].

A: That is to say, I talk to you about the week coming to an end after having been productive and you tell me that you would like to commit suicide, that you are leaving with this idea, so I am left with the worry of how hard it is for you to endure this wait, just so I keep it in mind.

P: It's just so hard… (weeping). [*Once again, after interpreting her projective identification into me, she is able to accept her pain, although complaining about how hard it is. I think it also helped that I held back my concern about her threat of suicide*]

I tell her that it is time. [*I did not respond with reassuring interventions or by modifying the setting. In other words, I trusted her, simply by pointing out the reality of the end of the session*]

P: (She stands up, collects her things, slowly and miserably, exhaustedly, as if with great exertion. I withstand Ms B's pressure not to make some banal reassuring comment. Now on her feet she says:) How I wish it were last winter with the dreams of then.

A: ¿? (With an interrogative expression on my face)

P: Yes, when you and I were here. (She means the state of delusional fusion between her and me.)

At the weekend she did not call me urgently, as she used to do in the past because she could not bear the separation, and returned to the Monday session.

Comments on the session. This is one of the many moments in her analysis of this last period, in which the patient begins to emerge from the psychotic world in order to connect with reality. It is evident how hard and painful it is for her, the dramatic struggle between her psychotic and non-psychotic parts.

She has been able to tolerate the continuity of the four sessions, but today, the last of the week, is an almost impossible reality to tolerate. The session indicates the tremendous effort she is making to rebuild her mental (not just physical) space. It has been hard for her to come to the session and she would have preferred the bus not to arrive (psychotic part). But reality does not fulfil her wish. In spite of her frustration, she does catch the bus (non-psychotic part). And immediately, the psychotic part of her attacks reality (she wants the bus to crash), but the non-psychotic part reacts by thinking of the infantile innocent aspects of herself that want the treatment to go ahead. She (non-psychotic part) is also able to recognise the hard task of the driver-analyst, at the wheel of the analysis, every day. But her mental pain of guilt is so intense, as she cannot resort to psychotic functioning to avoid it because she now recognises its destructive consequences (crashing the bus-analysis), that she asks for the analyst's complicity. She asks me to give her a cancer. That is to say, to transform her psychological pain into physical pain. But she does so without conviction, because she knows that I am not omnipotent nor do I claim to be, and that I have also given her proof that I am in favour of the life tendencies, not destructive ones.

Afterwards, she talks of the meeting with her friend, and how she felt rejected. But instead of sinking into despair, she (non-psychotic part) begins to write. And the "autobiographic" story is about someone who did not leave her neighbourhood, like her… Although she soon realises that she is not imprisoned as it might seem, because her analytical sessions allow her to leave the "neighbourhood", or rather, her psychotic organisation, every day.

Indeed, all of this is requiring a great deal of effort from her, and it is still a precarious situation, as the end of the session shows: first, wishing to kill herself, and at the last moment, longing for the "dreams" of last winter, referring to the delusional state of the relationship between her and I. But it stays as a longing, since she has now managed to leave her "psychotic neighbourhood-organisation" and finds herself in a different realm, that of the differentiated relationship with the analyst. That is to say, the resources used some time ago to deal with the unbearable painful reality are no longer useful, and are limited to verbalising them in the form of desires, hoping that the analyst will contain them.

In other words, common sense in the Bionian double sense prevails. In the recognition of the 'real' object who is both the source of the liberating vital thrust, and at the same time the one who places her in a situation of increased effort, and of living the painful experience of separation. And also the common sense shared with the analyst, as the non-psychotic part prevails, of not accepting the delusional reality as a solution to her difficulties; and neither the physical illness, nor the suicide attempt. It is also evident the recognition of her psychotic aspects in their clearly destructive dimension, for her and for me, as well as her concern (from the non-psychotic part) for their consequences: destroying the needy and depending infantile aspects, as well as the driver-analyst analytic function. This brings her into contact with the unbearable guilt that she has to soften by her longing to return to the delusional world, although this remains an unfulfilled wish, which makes the situation more painful but contained with the help of the analyst's containment. In any case, we are faced with another of the many moments of emergence from the delusional world, which will appear again and again for quite some time, until a greater strength of self and confidence in reality can be established.

Concluding remarks

This chapter has attempted to show that Freud's discussed articles constitute the origin of a conception of psychosis that makes psychosis accessible to psychoanalysis, despite the fact that, paradoxically, Freud had considered it untreatable. And that this is possible is the result of Freud's approach to consider psychosis to be an ailment closer to neurosis than it might seem, in so far as we can see features of psychosis in neurosis.

In the description of psychosis in this chapter, two aspects have been highlighted: extreme intolerance to the experience of psychic pain and defensive reactions to it. In relation to the latter, I emphasized pathological splitting whilst placing less emphasis on omnipotent projective identification. This is due to the fact that, having taken Freud's ideas as a starting point, I have followed more his emphasis on the internal processes of the patient, and less on the involvement of the object in them. However, as I show in my clinical example, I do consider that projective identification too plays a very important role in psychosis.

References

Bion W. R. (1957) Differentiation of the Psychotic from the Non-psychotic Personality. In: *Second Thought*. London: Karnac. 1993.

Bion W. R. (1962) *Learning from Experience*. London: Karnac. 1991.
Bion W. R. (1967) *Second Thought*. London: Karnac. 1984.
Bion, W. R. (1992) *Cogitation*. London: Karnac.
Britton, R. (2018) Foreword. In: Pérez-Sánchez, A.: *Psychotic Organization of the Personality*. London: Routledge.
Freud, S. (1894a) Neuro-psychosis of Defence. In: *S.E.*, 3: 43–61. London: Hogarth.
Freud, S. (1911b) Formulations on the Two Principles of Mental Functioning. In: *S.E.*, 12: 213–217. London: Hogarth.
Freud, S. (1914c) On Narcissism: An introduction. In: *S.E.*, 14: 73–102. London: Hogarth.
Freud, S (1924b) Neurosis and Psychosis. In: *S.E.*, 19: 149–153. London: Hogarth.
Freud, S. (1924e) The loss of reality in neurosis and psychosis. In: *S.E.*, 19. London: Hogarth, 183–187.
Freud, S. (1927e) Fetishism. In: *S.E.*, 21: 149–157. London: Hogarth.
Freud, S. (1940a [1938]) An Outline of Psychoanalysis. In: *S.E.*, 23. London: Hogarth.
Freud, S. (1940e [1938]) Splitting of the Ego in the Process of Defence. In: *S.E.*, 23. 271–278. London: Hogarth.
Isaacs, S. (1948) The Nature and Function of Phantasy, *Int. J. Psycho-Anal.* 29: 73–97.
Klein, M. (1921) The development of a child. In: *The Writings of Melanie Klein*. Vol. I. London: Hogarth Press, pp. 1–53.
Meltzer, D. (1968) Terror, Persecution and Dread, *Int. J. Psycho-Anal.* 49: 396–400.
O'Shaughnessy, E (1981) A Clinical Study of Defensive Organization, *Int. J. Psycho-Anal.* 62: 359–369.
Pérez-Sánchez, A. (2018) *Psychotic Organization of the Personality*. London: Routledge.
Rivière, J. (1936) A Contribution to the Analysis of the Negative Therapeutic Reaction. *Int. J. Psycho-Anal.* 17: 304–320. And also in Joan Riviere, *The Inner World and Joan Riviere*. London: Karnac Books, 1991, pp. 134–153.
Rosenfeld, H. (1964) *On the Psychopathology of Narcissism: A Clinical Approach*.
Rosenfeld, H. (1971) A Clinical Approach to the Psychoanalytic Theory of life and Death Instincts: An Investigation into the Aggressive Aspects of Narcissism. *Int. J. Psycho-Anal.* 45: 332–337.
Segal, H. (1972) A Delusional System as Defence Against the Re-Emergence of a Catastrophic Situation, *Int. J. Psycho-Anal.* 53: 393–401.
Segal, H. (1991): *Phantasy, in Dream, Phantasy and Art*. London: Routledge, pp. 16–30.
Segal, H. (1994) Phantasy and reality. *Int. J. Psycho-Anal.* 75: 395–401.
Steiner, J. (1993) *Psychic Retreats*. London and New York: Routledge.

4 Some Observations on the Relation to Reality and the Function of Belief in Schizophrenia

David Bell

In this paper, I wish to focus on two aspects of the schizophrenic's experience that, as I will show, are related in important ways. These are 1) The schizophrenic's relation to the distinction between internal (psychic) reality and external reality and, 2) the phenomenological status of "belief" in the schizophrenic situation. This paper develops ideas presented to the panel on "Psychic reality in psychosis" at the San Francisco Congress. My focus, there, was not on psychic reality as a thing in itself, but more on the way the psychotic patient deals with psychic reality and objective reality and the relationship between them. In this chapter I will elaborate further on the development of Freud's attempts to differentiate neurosis from psychosis, which will lead to a consideration of Bion's return to this problematic. I will then present clinical material from the treatment of a schizophrenic patient to illustrate the way the patient deals with reality and also the intimate connection between the schizophrenic catastrophe and the capacity to maintain belief.

Psychic reality and external reality

The fact that we live in two worlds or realities, at the same time, namely the subjective/internal world and the shared or objective external world, is part of what we mean by what it is to be human, have subjectivity and self-consciousness. It is also clear that normal mental functioning hinges on being able to make the distinction between internal and external, a function that paradoxically derives from the capacity to know internal reality as real, yet different from the reality of the external world. The link between mental health and acceptance of reality is quite clear in Freud but was substantially enriched by Klein's (1952) conception of the nature of the constant interplay between internal and external worlds, particularly through the mechanisms of projection and introjection.

A normal relation to reality, then, is partly based on the ability to hold in the mind a view of both internal and external situations,

DOI: 10.4324/9781003384120-4

sustain the inevitable tension that arises from the awareness of non-identity between them, and thus become able to make a judgement as to what is real. This reality testing is, much of the time, largely an unconscious process. It is this "judging activity" which forms the centre of Freud's paper "Negation" Freud (1925), which I will have cause to consider further below.

Our understanding of subjectivity has been substantially enriched by Freud's conception of "psychic reality" a term which has come to have a number of different references. Caper (1988) has usefully located the distinction between psychic reality and material reality as that between the world of immaterial facts and material facts. However, immaterial facts also have their place in external reality and these would include: other minds, human knowledge, history and abstract qualities such as space and time.

Psychic reality is layered and includes aspects of conscious experience and imagination but for the purposes of this paper I wish mainly to refer to that aspect of psychic reality which is beyond any ordinary awareness, namely unconscious phantasy. It is at this level of psychic reality that we find representations of the mind's conceptions of its own activity.[1]

Main thesis

I will suggest firstly, that for the schizophrenic patient psychic reality and external reality are not separate categories of experience which have a complex relation to one another. This way of categorising experience into different phenomenal worlds is itself disturbed. Rather than these realities being available for comparison, they are treated interchangeably so that external reality can be handled as if it were internal imaginative fantasy, and under control of the subject, whilst aspects of internal reality (i.e. unconscious phantasies including those which underlie psychic function) can be held to be external or objective facts of the world. Thus, the schizophrenic patient "sees" his psychic reality in the functioning of the world around him.

Secondly, I will maintain that one of the things which distinguishes the schizophrenic patient from the other psychoses and borderline states is not just the nature of what is believed but the profound disruption in the very capacity to believe. The capacity to believe something to be or not be the case is a vital psychic function closely linked to Freud's concept of "judging" (see below, in discussion of Freud's " Negation"). Disturbance in the capacity to believe both reflect and cause important disturbances in thought and in the relation to reality, inner and outer. This was the focus of Britton's paper to the 1995 San Francisco conference (Britton, 1995).

Though not referring to schizophrenia, Britton makes the point that the annihilation of the capacity to believe results in a world of meaninglessness. This, I will contend, is central to the catastrophe at the core of schizophrenia.

Freud's differentiation of neurosis from psychosis on the basis of the relation to reality

Freud was much preoccupied by the issue of distinguishing neurosis/ normality from psychosis throughout his work but this problematic is at its most overt at three distinct periods. Firstly, it is an important part of the theoretical considerations from his earliest writings, namely The Project for a Scientific Psychology (Freud, 1895), reworked in Chapter 7 of *The Interpretation of Dreams* (Freud, 1901); secondly in the period 1910–1912 during which he wrote "Formulations on the two principles of mental functioning" (Freud, 1911b), which draws substantially on the Project and was written almost contemporaneously with his account of Schreber (Freud, 1911a).

Lastly, there are the three papers that cluster around 1924–1925, that is the two papers on Neurosis and Psychosis (Freud, 1924a,b) and the paper "On Negation" (Freud, 1925).

In "Formulations on the two principles of mental functioning", Freud compares that state of mind where: "What was thought of (or wished for) was simply presented in an hallucinatory manner" with that "momentous step" that is made when (on the abandonment of satisfaction by means of hallucination) "a new principle was introduced; what was presented in the mind was no longer what was agreeable, but what was real even if it happened to be disagreeable" (Freud, 1911 p219)

So, here Freud draws the distinction between two fundamentally different ways of dealing with reality: either the replacement of external reality by hallucination, under the aegis of the pleasure principle, or the recognition of the external world in accordance with the reality principle.[2] From this perspective, hallucination is instantaneous, evades all frustration, and does not involve any psychic work. The pleasure principle distorts reality in such a way as to disburden the mind of its disagreeable qualities, whereas the reality principle brings a world where a distinction can be made between internal and external and thus a judgement be made as to what is real. The dominance of the reality principle can only be achieved at the cost of frustration, though I think the implication here is that this frustration results from the lack of satisfaction of instinctual drives. However, slightly later, Freud makes the interesting comment that "the dissatisfaction which results from the replacement of the pleasure principle by the reality principle *is itself a part of reality"* (Freud, 1911 p224 my italics). I quote this because the dissatisfaction referred to here is quite distinct from instinctual frustration. Reality itself is painful as it inevitably brings awareness that one's wishes (internal reality) are not realised in external reality. The psychotic situation is precipitated by the minds inability to tolerate this sort of dissatisfaction; it is as if the messenger (awareness of reality) is murdered to evade the message (the reality of frustration, the gap between that which is wished for and that which is real).

Freud elaborates further on this theme in the papers on Neurosis and Psychosis (Freud, 1924a,b). In the first of these two papers he draws the distinction by asserting that in neurosis there is suppression of a piece of instinctual life, for example sexual or murderous wishes, whereas in psychosis there is a withdrawal from reality. In his second paper written as an addendum to the first, he expresses his dissatisfaction with this formulation of the distinction for, as he put it, "[we know that] every neurosis disturbs the patient's relation to reality in some way, that it serves him as a means of withdrawing from reality, and that, in its severe forms, it actually signifies a flight from real life" (Freud, 1924b p183). He points out that whereas the neurotic patient effects changes in reality by acting on the world, in the psychotic patient changes in reality are effected merely through changes in the representation of reality.

It is, however, in the paper "Negation" (Freud, 1925) that a substantial step forward is made. In this paper Freud describes and formulates the preconditions for that process he calls "judging" and brings greater clarity to the distinction between neurosis and psychosis. As the judgement referred to arises from the capacity to discriminate what is real from what isn't, and as it is this capacity which is so compromised in psychosis, the link between these two theoretical issues is immediately apparent.

Freud describes two quite distinct categories of negation. In the first place, there is the familiar type of negation which is "a way of taking cognisance of what is repressed… .already the lifting of repression" (p235–236) i.e. the emergence into consciousness of an unwelcome idea which makes its first appearance through denying it reality, such as occurs when the central character in Dennis Potter's "Singing Detective" pursues the identity of the murderer of a woman (symbolically his mother) and announces "Well one thing is for sure, it wasn't me".

Secondly, Freud describes something that is qualitatively quite distinct, the "general wish to negate, the negativism which is displayed by some psychotics" (p239).

So, whereas the neurotic negates aspects of reality, aspects that have a special significance, in the case of psychosis it is the whole relation to reality itself which is compromised. It is my view that it is this type of negation that underlies the schizophrenic catastrophe of "no belief". Freud goes on in this paper to consider what factors might contribute to this more massive negation and cites firstly a precondition for reality testing "namely that objects shall have been lost which once brought real satisfaction" (p238) and secondly a constitutional factor which he links to the instinct of destruction.

Bion's work

Bion, in what I have described elsewhere as "a return to Freud" (Bell, 1992), confronts the same problematic which preoccupied Freud in the papers on Neurosis and Psychosis and "Negation". He brings a clarification that is at once both logical and has important clinical implications. His focus as with Freud is on "thinking" (which bears a close relation to, though is distinct from what Freud termed "judging") and the nature of the differentiation of neurosis from psychosis. Throughout the whole corpus of his works he quotes extensively from "Formulations on the two principles of mental functioning", and from Freud's papers on neurosis and psychosis. Now armed with Klein's understanding of primitive mental states, the distinction between the paranoid schizoid and the depressive positions and his own refinement of technique gained from treating psychotic patients, he brings great clarity to the distinction between psychic reality in psychotic and non-psychotic situations.

Freud emphasised that a requirement for the development of the capacity for thinking was the loss of an object that had once brought real satisfaction. However, he appears here to be referring only to external reality. Bion's (1962a) unpacking and clarification of this issue is central to his theory. Given that it is internal experience that is the basis of psycho-analytic theory, it cannot be the actual loss of the object (i.e. an external fact) that is essential but **the awareness of the loss,** namely the object's continued existence in the mind as an object that had once brought satisfaction when the object is no longer present in external reality.

Following Klein's description of the binding of psychotic anxiety (Klein, 1952) he described a mental apparatus (or function) which binds raw experience which can be contained in the mind, transformed, and thus become a "thought". Without the availability of this function there can be no dreaming, ordinary fantasying or myth making, all of which require the ability to separate internal and external reality, and so bring them into relation with one another. Freud tended at times to equate psychosis with dreaming. For Bion, dreaming is an achievement of the non-psychotic personality.

Bion, described, here closely following Freud, how the apparatus that performs this function, the binding of raw experience, is called into operation by the awareness of the absent object. The capacity to think about an object that isn't there is a fundamental step forward. The absent object can become one of two things: not a good object absent but only a bad object present, fit only for expulsion. On the other hand, if it remains in the mind as a good object absent (namely there is the capacity to bear the frustration inherent in that situation), it becomes a thought. "The choice that matters to the psycho-analyst is one that lies between procedures designed to evade frustration and those designed to modify it. That is the critical decision." (Bion, 1962 p29)

Bion (1962b) described a process, "-K", which functions to strip experience of meaning, and I would add thus strip the individual of the capacity to believe anything to be true or untrue in any ordinary sense. It is this process which, I am suggesting, underlies the more malignant type of negation, linked to the death instinct, referred to in Freud's paper.

Some clinical features of schizophrenia

Following on from the above, negation by the psychotic personality is NOT a first step towards making judgement but an attack on the apparatus that makes judgements.

Such a process precipitates a psychic catastrophe where what remains is a destroyed world in which there can be no belief and anything is true, seen at its most extreme form in hebephrenic schizophrenia. It is a world of disconnected events which lack significance and appear to be uncaused and unmotivated. In such a meaningless world, which I think never occurs in totality, there can be no belief. Delusion formation, as Freud pointed out in the Schreber case, is not the illness per se, but an attempt at recovery, to recreate a world of meaning and, therefore, of belief, with the limited resources available. The clinical state that we encounter in schizophrenia thus has a number of different constituents. There are the phenomena that represent the effects of the psychic catastrophe, the devastated inner world where nothing can be believed. Secondly there are those phenomena that result from attempts to recreate a world of meaning, that is through the construction of delusions.[3] Lastly there are the effects of the omnipotent manipulation of reality, internal and external, and of the relationship between them.

A clinical example of delusion formation to evade a psychic catastrophe

Before illustrating these themes as they arose in the analysis of a patient, I would like to bring a vignette which illustrates how a breakdown in the belief in the omnipotent control of reality, resulted in the formation of a delusional experience, which protected the patient from a far worse psychic catastrophe.

Mr. A., a schizoid young man, was apparently unaffected by breaks in his psychotherapeutic treatment. He continued conversations in his mind between sessions, but treated these conversations as realities. He thus regarded his actual sessions as continuations of these conversations and negated those aspects of the session which might have challenged this view. Although he was not formally hallucinated, these experiences clearly derive their origin from that phase of life where "what was thought of (wished for) was simply presented in an hallucinatory manner" (Freud, 1911).

His psychotherapist felt pressured to be either silent or to collude with the patient's view that the conversations in his imagination occupied the same ontological world as the conversations with his real therapist. When his psychotherapist pointed out to him that he made no differentiation between the therapist in his head, under his own control, and the therapist in the room who came and went, and thus never experienced any separation, the patient felt momentarily disturbed. Following this session he went to the waiting area of the psychiatric clinic, where he was being seen, purchased a drink from a vending machine and, on starting to drink it, complained that the drink had been poisoned.

So, Mr. A's internal conversations were not ways of preserving inside himself the good experiences of his now absent object but instead served to replace the absence of his external object with the presence of an object under his own omnipotent control. Internal reality thus replaced external reality.

The interpretation of this process disrupted his experience of continuous living in an ideal world and was felt by him to be a catastrophe. The awareness of the existence of another mind which saw things differently was experienced as a poisonous assault on his reality. His experience of the interpretation, then, might be understood as being violently ejected from his ideal world into a frightening world, reality, from which the delusional object provided protection.

The delusion of the poisoned drink, a belief held with firm paranoid conviction, is as Freud put it, "the application of a patch.... where originally a rent had appeared in the ego's relation to the external world." (Freud, 1924a p151) and so evades a much more devastating psychic catastrophe.

It is to this devastating catastrophe to which I now turn.

Clinical material from a schizophrenic patient

My patient is a twenty one-year-old man who started analysis two years ago. He had an acute schizophrenic breakdown when he was

18, which was characterised by hallucinations and delusions. His breakdown was followed by wanderings that took him to various places in England and overseas, finally being hospitalised. His state when I first met him showed mainly hebephrenic features with occasional, rather fleeting paranoid ideas.

He has one sister, born about one year after him, who has been of enormous importance to him. I am not clear whether they shared an actual incestuous relationship but much that he has said would indicate this. It has increasingly seemed as if he experienced the arrival of his sister as a catastrophic eviction from a phantasied paradise. However, this loss was dealt with by creating a new version of paradise where he and his sister had perfect understanding of each other and created an idealised union which was felt to function on a higher level than that which existed between his parents. This union was interrupted by the onset of puberty and subsequently by his sister finding a boyfriend, both of which appear to have had important aetiological significance for the overt breakdown.

When I first met him, I was struck by his effeminate appearance and his rather blank and other worldly attitude. He conveyed a profound sense of emptiness, having little capacity for conviction, and some degree of despair. He told me that when he was ill he caused a lot of trouble. He made reference to his travels in England and France; said that it was easier to get to my consulting room than he'd thought as his father had brought him; that when he talked he used other people's words; that he was suspicious of people who tell him he is ill.

I made the following suggestions to him: He felt emptied out and unable to think and felt that something had gone missing. I went on to say that his wanderings were an attempt to find lost parts of himself which though troublesome felt alive. His use of other people's words provided him with some structure within which to function, but left him feeling quite unable to feel any decision was his, and thus it would make no sense to ask him if he wanted analysis, though he had conveyed that he would come.

He responded by mentioning a hotel room which he had liked, a drawing room with lovely, coloured pencils. He then added that when he was in France he thought he was being taken somewhere to continue his travels but instead was put on medication and compulsorily detained under the mental health act, and transferred to a psychiatric hospital in London.

I suggested that he feared that I would rob him of the few pleasures he had left.

He then told me that there was a little girl whom he sometimes saw, that they had a drink together and that he enjoyed this. He added that he felt the fact that he missed his illness was a "guilty secret".

In his first session he conveyed very vividly both the sense of a destroyed inner world and the tenuous meaning he obtained from remnants of his delusions and hallucinations. He spoke of a voice that was becoming very fragile and is easily drowned out. He expressed surprise that he'd told me about it. It replaced a figure who he'd met when more acutely disturbed. He described it (this hallucinatory figure/voice) as "hanging by a thread". He appeared to obtain some relief from my suggesting that he felt the voice was what provided him with some sense of being alive, and also from my acknowledgement of his terror that I would use my words to drown it out.

He is not able to use the couch and is concurrently seen by a psychiatrist who manages his psychotropic medication.

As the analysis progressed, my patient brought a number of preoccupations which are related to my theme. He would arrive walking in a robotic way and, although usually talkative at the beginning, he would often spend much of the session in a silence interspersed with fragmentary speech and accompanied by stereotypic gestures (slowly turning his head from side to side). This created an atmosphere of utter deadness which I experienced as being trapped for ever, as if time had stopped. At other times he described hallucinatory relationships with magical figures who offered the possibility of being in control of the world so protecting him from a destroyed inner world which was described, affectlessly, as "full of carrion, rotting corpses and carrier bags full of rotting meat". This pictorial representation of a devastated world had its counterpart in the annihilation of psychic function where all distinctions are lost. In such a world nothing has significance for him and nothing can be believed. The hallucinatory figures,[4] derived from real people (such as William Burroughs and Timothy Leary i.e. representatives of 60s drug culture), lured him seductively into a world where "reality can be whatever you want it to be", "nothing matters" and "anything is permitted". These figures actively take pleasure in destroying belief and become particularly manifest when his conviction about analysis is most tested, namely at weekends and breaks. Though initially offering relief from a devastated world, this omnipotent organisation perpetuates the psychic catastrophe through its destruction of the distinction between internal and external reality. The link between a world where reality is defined by wish and a world where nothing matters shows a kind of insight, for if reality has no independent existence from the self then nothing can have any meaning. The activities of this internal organisation were originally described by Rosenfeld (1971) but here I wish to emphasise its effect on belief. This was illustrated very clearly by my patient's bringing to a session a particular aspect of the Orwell's novel "1984".

He described how the central character, Winston, having understood the way in which the authorities were controlling what people believed, wished to escape their grip. He went on to describe how Winston went outside the city to another place where history existed, ordinary human things were valued, such as a woman singing in the street; people wore ordinary clothes, not uniforms; a man in a shop showed him a piece of coal, highly valued as it was from "the old times". Winston was offered a room where he could go with his lover. He subsequently discovered that all the figures were actors employed by the State. The atmosphere in the room when he told me this was of horror.

For my patient, then, the world of 1984, where an omnipotent organisation dictates what is reality, very aptly mirrors his descriptions of the activities of the hallucinatory figures (Burroughs and other writers such as Timothy Leary), who advertised the world of no belief, figures with whom he had identified and idealised, but at this point dreaded. The world outside the control of the State, with its interest and respect for history, represented the world of analysis, and the horrifying denouement his fear that he would learn that I was being controlled by the hallucinatory figures.

A particular type of psychic catastrophe is lived out in the transference in the way that the patient experiences failures of the analyst to quickly understand his communications. He often talks with great urgency at the beginning of sessions telling me about events or dreams that have occurred since we last met. If there is no immediate response, there is a sudden dramatic transformation. The patient appears empty of thought, makes stereotypic gestures and the possibility of meaningful exchange is completely destroyed.

On one occasion, when he brought a dream at the beginning of the session which I was unable to respond to in any meaningful way, I interpreted this process to him. I suggested to him that when he brings such a dream he is bringing something lodged inside him which he wants to get rid of. If I speak to him and appear to understand him he feels I have relieved him of it, but if I say nothing, he sinks into despair (and turns towards hallucinatory figures).

He responded by showing that he at first experienced the interpretation concretely. He talked of his fear of the couch (which he has never used) and terrors of being unprotected and invaded by electricity.

However, he went on to tell me about an experience which occurred during the acute stages of his breakdown, which he called "a silent scream". He linked this to two newspaper headlines that had special significance for him at the time. The first read "John (his name) screams into space" and the second: "There is a blockage on the road", which he took as a warning.

I understood this as confirming my interpretation that he needed to get rid of something lodged inside him but that he was now making it clear that, if I did not respond immediately to certain communications, he experienced this as an obstruction inside me (the "blockage on the road").[5] This, in turn, precipitated a catastrophic situation, the patient being left screaming his thoughts, and with them his own psychic functions, out into infinite space. It was this process, I think, which underlay the sudden appearance, in the sessions, of states of utter emptiness, no belief, and only bizarre, disconnected thoughts and the repetitive stereotypic gestures.

I will now bring some more detailed material from two sessions on consecutive days, which illustrate the fragility of the capacity to believe and the interchangeability of psychic reality and external reality. The material also shows a recovery from the omnipotent manipulation of reality, albeit temporarily, accompanied by the development of the capacity to bring in representational form (a dream) the link between the delusion of controlling the world and the phantasy of invasion of the primary object.

Before presenting this material, I need to say that some weeks before the sessions to be presented, my patient had become interested in a picture in my room. This picture, though impressionist in form, clearly represents a particular scene. My patient told me he liked it as it could be whatever he wanted it to be i.e. **he** decides what is real (not the painter). Similarly, when staring at my symmetrically patterned rug he told me that by looking at, it he could alter the actuality of it, making it asymmetrical.

On the other side of my room, however, there is a photograph. On the Friday session before the Tuesday that I will describe, he commented that it was either a picture of a very large tree, taken from far off, or of a small plant, taken from very close up. I had suggested that his liking for the ambiguity of the photograph was linked to his wish to believe that he could feel either big or small in relation to the weekend separation, and thus bring it under his own control, so that it was of little consequence.

Session 1(a Tuesday):

The patient began by describing, with a conviction that was very unusual, his resentment at not having seen his sister. He went on to say that there is no eye contact between them when they meet. She could have invited him to see her at university but never did.

This was followed by a silence which rapidly became futile and empty as if the state of conviction had dissipated.

PT: I don't know if I believe what I am saying or if it's true.
AN: A moment ago you talked with real conviction as if appealing to me to know something important, then that feeling of knowing something, that you feel rejected, collapsed.

He talks of his sister and Paul (her boyfriend)

PT: She has Paul.... but it was like that beforehand

There was a boy at school called Brian. He had a brain tumour and had it removed. He has no feeling. If he laughed he would make a noise and force a smile onto his face.
Pause

PT: You are very calm in the session. Maybe you are cruel and violent in between. Maybe you have a wife and are violent to her.

He describes hearing a voice which says "pick up a new chapter'"

AN: "Pick up a new chapter" maybe refers to your making such a direct comment about me and also your wish to get away from it.

I went on to say:
You feel that I am full of your cruel and violent thoughts, trying desperately to hide them and remain calm.
(I later thought that maybe he sees me as Brian, the boy with the brain tumour, manufacturing the appearance of a friendly state, or alternatively, it was a way of pointing out that I was asking him to feel things he couldn't feel, and thus could only give an affectation of them).
I added that he locates himself inside his sister's attitude and rejects me.
I said something else and he thought I had said "John" (his name), which sent a shudder through him.
I said that he felt I was trying to make contact with him and force into his mind the violent sexual thoughts.
Silence (he seemed thoughtful).

AN: What are you thinking?
PT: I was looking at the photograph. There is a figure in it. That means it isn't ambiguous any more. The figure is man and so it must be a tree that is very big.
AN: How do you feel about that?
PT: Cheated.

AN: You started with a conviction that you felt rejected and isolated. That feeling of conviction collapsed and you turned it into me who was being rejected. You were then in a world in which reality could be what you want it to be. But the discovery of the tree, representing analysis, cheats you of being able to make things what you want them to be.

Discussion

So my patient started the session with a firm conviction that he felt rejected by his sister (she could not look at him), externally, and by me in terms of the coming weekend separation. This precipitated a feeling of being annihilated which was defended against by the destruction of his capacity to believe, in this state of affairs "I don't know if I believe what I am saying or if it's true." His recovery from this situation, however, was not replaced, as previously, by the creation of the omnipotent delusion of being in control of reality, but, instead, by accepting reality. Prior to this he had believed that he, not the photographer, nor the world which from which the photographic image derived, could define reality. The presence of the man fixed the perspective and so defined a reality independent of his (the patient's) existence. My patient's capacity to be aware at that moment of the objective world separate from himself, that is to see the man and register his significance "cheated" him of his own omnipotent manipulation of reality.

The man in the picture is also, psychically, the man who precedes him, who determines realities beyond his control, ultimately the father who existed in reality, before the patient entered the scene and who, with mother, determined his conception. From the patient's point of view, the man interferes with his possession of his primary object and robs him of access to it, with potential catastrophic consequences. (i.e. the man is "the blockage on the road" robbing him of access to his primary object and so leaving him screaming into space.)

Above I described how the patient treats external facts as if they are imaginative products and thus under his omnipotent control. What follows seems to be the same process, but in reverse; namely he treats what we would regard as products of his own psychic reality as if they are facts about the world, what I referred to earlier as the patient's "seeing" psychic reality in the functioning of the world around him.[6] What, for less disturbed patients, are unconscious phantasies underlying mental functions are, for my patient, aspects of his conscious experience.[7]

The session immediately followed the one described where he appeared to have accepted that the photograph fixed a perspective independent of himself.

Two weeks previously he, on arriving for his session, travelled in the lift with my female colleague which meant to him invading the primal scene. In that session he told me about a group of people he'd read about called the "illuminati" who believe they are controlled by a silica chip implanted in their brains. I will only bring the beginning of the session up to the point where he reported a dream.

Session 2(Wednesday)

The patient described himself as feeling a bit better. He went on to tell me that whilst he was waiting in the waiting room he heard me speaking on the telephone. He wanted to listen but didn't. He said that he would really like to know what I was like when I wasn't with him. He went on to tell me the following dream:

> *There was a woman who was 9 months pregnant who had a disease revealed by a rash on her arm which was the object of his considerable fascination. The rash was made up of oval white patches connected to red, blood coloured lines. The woman fell over.*

He associated the woman to a nanny or maid who has looked after the house for some years. He thought later that one of the white patches had within it "something like a silica chip or circuit".

Discussion

The beginning of the session suggests that he has maintained his capacity to recognise the existence of a world that is outside his own control and this is clearly related to the appearance of a vital ego function, curiosity (about my telephone conversation). His improved ego functioning has, in turn, created the capacity to give form, through his dream, to what "a world outside his own control" represents in unconscious phantasy, namely a pregnant woman. Historically of course it also refers to his mother's pregnancy with his sister. In the dream, the situation is, however, brought back under his control by his invasion of his object and controlling it from within, the silica chip installed in her arm, a violent procedure which destroys the woman. I would also like to suggest that the image of the pregnant woman gives form to a version of his object with an obstruction inside, robbing him of access to it "the blockage on the road". His "fascination" with the woman's illness suggests an identification with a me as someone disinterested and fascinated, a matter, however that I did not pursue.

Awareness of reality, that is a world that exists beyond his control, does not bring for my patient "dissatisfaction" but is instead a catastrophe. However, his attempt to regain control, through his penetration of the objective world, representing unconsciously a mother with a baby inside, creates a different catastrophe. His object is destroyed and he is left in a ruined world, akin to "the carrier bags of rotting flesh". It is this state which, I think, underlies that which Freud, in "On Negation" referred to as "the negativism displayed by some psychotics" (Freud, 1925 p238). This is the world that results when the basic psychic structures necessary for a sense of reality have been destroyed, brought about by the process that Bion described as -K, which breaks all links between objects, and between self and objects leaving "residues", a world of events without causes and a world in which there is no belief.

Klein (e.g. 1946) demonstrated that the need to invade and control the object arises from unconscious phantasies of entering the body of the mother to control her intercourse and destroy the baby within. My patient's material illustrates this very vividly. What I wish to emphasise here is that what, in a less ill patient, would exist as unconscious phantasies underlying the mechanism of projective identification, phantasies deduced from the material, are, for my patient, actual events consciously experienced, facts about the world. As I indicated earlier, he feels that he really does invade the analyst's mind who then in actuality **does** possess his cruel sexual thoughts.

Conclusion

In this chapter I have attempted to trace a theoretical development as to the distinction between neurosis and psychosis, from Freud's central papers concerning this theme to Bion's work. I have then added further considerations arising out of my work with a schizophrenic patient. In particular, I have emphasised the importance of Freud's paper "Negation" especially as regards the distinction he draws between ordinary negation and, what could be called the psychotic negation.

I have emphasised the disruption, in the schizophrenic, of the capacity or function of "believing" itself and suggested that this is a central component of the schizophrenic catastrophe. The clinical material has been used to illustrate the existence, in such a patient, of a devastated internal world where the capacity to believe was, as my patient put it in his first session, "hanging by a thread". I have, further, tried to show how the patient is lured by an omnipotent organisation into a situation where the world of "no belief" is replaced by a delusional world where reality can be whatever you want it to be. Internal and external reality are then felt to be under the omnipotent control of the subject and are treated interchangeably: psychic reality being experienced as concrete events, facts of the world, whilst external reality is treated as having the same ontological status as fantasy/imagination and therefore under the subject's control. Internal reality and external reality in this situation do not exist as separate entities that can be brought into the mind, but as categories that can replace each other. In this sense, to quote Bion (1962), the psychotic patient is "neither asleep or awake".

Mr. A, the schizoid patient, developed a belief that had the character of paranoid conviction. The schizophrenic patient showed the almost opposite difficulty in that for long periods he lacked the capacity to believe anything with any conviction whatsoever. This lack of conviction extended to his own delusions and is quite distinct from the sane capacity to doubt delusions. It reflects a disturbance in those functions that underlie what it is to believe something to be, or not be, the case (the function that Freud termed "judging").[8]

In the introduction I referred to the layering of psychic reality, drawing a distinction between experiential reality and unconscious phantasy. This distinction does not hold for the psychotic/schizophrenic situation where unconscious phantasy exists at the level of experience. The phantasy of projective identification, of entering objects and controlling them from within, for example, is part of my patient's experiential world. This is of course the reason why working with such patients, through the peculiar access they offer to unconscious phantasy, particularly those underlying mental functions (Wollheim (1984) calls this the mind's "iconic representation of its own activities"), has so enriched our understanding of the less disturbed, in whom these aspects of experience are less available.

I think it is this that Freud refers to at the end of the Schreber case where he describes Schreber's "rays of God" as "in reality nothing else than a concrete representation and projection outwards of libidinal cathexes....". He goes on to say:

> They [the rays] thus lend his delusions a striking conformity with our theory.

and adds:

> It remains for the future to decide whether there is more delusion in my theory than I should like to admit or whether there is more truth in Schreber's delusions than other people are, as yet, prepared to believe.
> (Freud, 1911 p79)

Notes

1 This is implicit in the work of Klein and of course, made most explicit in its development by Susan Isaacs (1948).
2 Freud's emphasis here seems to be on the reality of the external situation but, of course, psychic reality is also real. It will be suggested in the next section that Bion provides some important clarification of this issue. As outlined in the introduction, it is argued in this paper that the schizophrenic mind treats these realities as equivalent, even reversible.
3 In line with what has been discussed above, such delusions have, however, varying status. Sometimes delusional beliefs are held with firm conviction, but very often the schizophrenics "belief" in his delusions has a quite different phenomenological status, not because he is sane enough to question them but because residues of the schizophrenic catastrophe continue to wreak their effect on the capacity to believe.
4 These are not the only hallucinatory figures, there being others which have a quite different significance. He described the voice of a little girl who he felt had to be protected from violent forces. He felt he had to "clasp the image of her" to himself to save himself "from the void".
5 This illustrates the process Bion (1959) described as underlying the attack on the link between psychic objects.
6 Bion described these processes in the following way: "But the same patients who regard 'thoughts' as 'things' show every sign of regarding what I am use psycho-analytically to believe are phantasies as 'facts'" (Bion, 1977 p97).
7 For example my patient's stereotypic head movements which represent both the emptying out of "bad" thoughts (which are cruel and sexual), leaving them located in the consulting room, or in me, so that, in his view, I spend my weekends in cruel sexual activity (as referred to in the session just reported). These movements, I have learnt, also serve to recreate his idealised hallucinatory objects.
8 This is quite distinct from the manic depressive situation where the content of beliefs is bizarre but the function of believing remains intact, indeed is hypertrophied. Such patients talk with conviction about their grandiose delusions. They, so to speak, believe what others dream of, and so are much easier to empathise with. The schizophrenic patient, in the situation I am describing, lacks this capacity of believing with conviction. From a descriptive or phenomenological point of view the manic depressive feels he is in control of reality and changes it at will, whereas the schizophrenic patient experience reality as being altered.

References

Bell, D. (1992) *On Freud's "Negation"*. Unpublished paper presented to the British Psycho-analytic Society.

Bion, W.R. (1959) Attacks on linking. *Int. J. Psychoanal.*, 40: 308–315; republished in W.R. Bion (1967) *Second Thoughts*. London: Heinemann, pp. 93–109; and in Bott Spillius E., ed. *Melanie Klein Today: Developments in Theory and Practice, Vol. 1 Mainly Theory*. London: Routledge, 1988, pp. 87–101.

Bion, W.R. (1962a) A theory of thinking. *Int. J Psychoanal.*, 43: 306–310; Republished in W.R. Bion (1967) *Second Thoughts*. London: Heinemann, pp. 110–119; and in E. Bott Spillius, ed. *Melanie Klein Today: Developments*

in *Theory and Practice, Vol. 1 Mainly Theory*. London: Routledge, 1988, pp. 178–186.
Bion, W.R. (1962b) *Learning from Experience*. London: Heinemann Medical Books; reprinted 1984 Maresfield Reprints, Karnac.
Britton, R.(1995) Psychic reality and unconscious belief. *Int. J. Psychoanal.*, 76: 19–23.
Caper, R. (1988) *Immaterial Facts*. London: Jason Aronson.
Freud, S. (1950[1895]) Project for a scientific psychology. In: *S.E.1*.
Freud, S. (1901) The interpretation of dreams. In: *S.E.5*.
Freud, S. (1911) Psycho-analytic notes on a case of paranoia (dementia paranoides). In: *S.E.12*.
Freud, S. (1924a) Neurosis and psychosis. In: *S.E.12*.
Freud, S. (1924b) The loss of reality in neurosis and psychosis. In: *S.E.12*.
Freud, S. (1925) Negation. In: *S.E.12*.
Isaacs, S. (1952) The nature and function of phantasy. *Int. J. Psychoanal.*, 29: 73–97; also in M. Klein, P. Heimann, S. Isaacs and J. Riviere, *Developments in Psycho-analysis*, London: Hogarth Press, pp. 67–121.
Klein, M. (1946) Notes on some schizoid mechanisms. *Int. J. Psychoanal.*, 27: 99–110; republished (1975) in *The Writings of Melanie Klein, Vol 3 Envy and Gratitude and Other Works*, London: Hogarth Press, pp. 1–24.
Klein, M. (1952) Some theoretical conclusions regarding the emotional life of the infant. In *The Writings of Melanie Klein Vol 3, Envy and Gratitude and Other Works*, London: Hogarth Press, pp. 61–93.
Rosenfeld, H. (1971) A clinical approach to the psycho-analytical theory of the life and death instincts: An investigation into the aggressive aspects of narcissism. *Int. J. Psychoanal.*, 52: 169–178; republished in E. Bott Spillius, ed. *Melanie Klein Today: Developments in Theory and Practice, Vol. 1 Mainly Theory*. London: Routledge, 1988, pp. 239–255.
Wollheim, R. (1984) *The Thread of Life*. Cambridge University Press.

5 The *Negative* in Psychosis

Marie-France Brunet

Even though Freud's work germinated in a conceptual universe largely different from the present one, from a knowledge development point of view as well as the ideology of his time, we still consider that his ability to bring into play the diverse elements that constitute the psychic's order in a coherent manner, is still valid nowadays. Freud's thinking may be criticized or it could be considered that determined aspects of his work should be reformulated, but it seems difficult to surpass the articulation that he achieves from the heterogeneity that constitutes the human psyche.

Freud's thinking often emerges from the comparison between different entities. Thus, even though the emphasis of his theoretical building is referred to the study of neurosis, the latter is always put in relation to other modalities of psychic functioning (Green, 1990, 1995). His work had, on the other had, several turns, the most significant one being inaugurated in "Beyond the pleasure principle" (1920). The theoretical articles about psychosis follow this last turn, and thus belong to the late period of his work, when he already introduced the change on the drive theory, and formulated the second topic. Besides the two texts that seek to differentiate the structures of neurosis and psychosis, during the period between 1923 and 1925, Freud wrote a series of important papers about genital organization and the Oedipus complex as well as "The economic problem of masochism" and "Negation", which were expressions of his wish to go beyond clinical practice and settle new theorical horizons.

It is well known that Freud did not work clinically with psychotics, and that his most important approach to the analysis of a psychosis was through Schreber's autobiographical writing. This did not stop him from contributing, in the two articles on psychosis mentioned previously, some essential elements that have help in the understanding of the psychopathological and dynamic mechanisms of this entity in the light of his new hypothesis on the psychic apparatus, described in "The Ego and the Id" (1923). In "Neurosis

Psychosis"(1924), Freud distinguishes the different pathological entities according to the diverse vassalages of the Ego:

> We now see that we have been able to make our simple genetic formula more complete, without dropping it. Transference neuroses correspond to a conflict between the ego and the id; narcissistic neuroses, to a conflict between the ego and the super-ego; and psychoses, to one between the ego and the external world
> (Freud, 1924a, p.152)

The outcome will depend on the economic factor, that is, on the relative magnitudes of the drive forces. And he adds:

> In the second place, it will be possible for the ego to avoid a rupture in any direction by deforming itself, by submitting to encroachments on its own unity and even perhaps by effecting a cleavage or division of itself. In this way the inconsistencies, eccentricities and follies of men would appear in a similar light to their sexual perversions, through the acceptance of which they spare themselves repressions.
> (Freud, 1924a, p.152–153)

This quote contains already the relevance that the splitting of the Ego will take in Freud's later work, extending beyond the cases of perversion ("Fetishism" [1927]),it also anticipates the psychic configurations found in contemporary clinic. The first part of Freud's work presents neurosis as the negative of perversion, where repression is consider the most important mechanism, used to deal with internal psychic reality, more specifically with the drives demands emanating from the Id. In the late stage in Freud's work, the description of new defense mechanisms (denial, splitting, foreclosure) marks a turn these mechanisms acquire greater importance in post Freudian authors. Shifting the importance of these defense mechanism implied that neurosis be put in contrast and in relation to psychosis. At the end of the paper "Neurosis and psychosis", Freud questions which mechanism would be analogous to repression, through which the Ego disconnect itself from reality. This questioning continues in his paper written shortly after "Neurosis and psychosis", "The loss of reality in neurosis and psychosis" (1924b). Here, Freud points out:

> In psychosis, the initial flight is succeeded by an active phase of remodelling; in neurosis, the initial obedience is succeeded by a deferred attempt at flight. Or again, expressed in yet another

way: neurosis does not disavow the reality, it only ignores it; psychosis disavows it and tries to replace it.

(Freud, 1924b, p. 185)

So, we can see that denial (*verleunung*), which is different from repression (*verdrängung*), appears as the defense mechanism used in psychosis to disavowal the perception of external reality.

In his 1927 article, "Fetishism", Freud introduces a modification, regarding the ideas he put forward in the paper just mentioned: he now points out that in regards to aspect of reality that was denied, two simultaneous currents exist: "The attitude which fitted in with the wish and the attitude which fitted in with reality existed side by side". [...] I may thus keep to the expectation that in a psychosis the one current – that which fitted in with reality – would have in fact been absent (Freud, 1927, p.156). This same topic is summarized in his unconcluded article from 1938 "The Splitting of the Ego in the Process of Defense":

> He replies to the conflict with two contrary reactions, both of which are valid and effective. On the one hand, with the help of certain mechanisms he rejects reality and refuses to accept any prohibition; on the other hand, in the same breath he recognizes the danger of reality, takes over the fear of that danger as a pathological symptom and tries subsequently to divest himself of the fear. It must be confessed that this is a very ingenious solution of the difficulty. Both of the parties to the dispute obtain their share: the instinct is allowed to retain its satisfaction and proper respect is shown to reality. But everything has to be paid for in one way or another, and this success is achieved at the price of a rift in the ego which never heals but which increases as time goes on. The two contrary reactions to the conflict persist as the center-point of a splitting of the ego.
>
> (Freud, 1938, p.275–276)

The denial of reality encompasses certain areas, no psychotic breaks from it in a radical way, which would be incompatible with survival. This notion of the splitting of the ego is highlighted by most authors whose psychoanalytic work has been centered in psychosis (Searles, Bion, Aulagnier).

In the same article, Freud resumes his thinking on the role on fantasy's in neurosis and psychosis, and about this last one, he points out:

> In a psychosis, the transforming of reality is carried out upon the psychical precipitates of former relations to it – that is, upon the memory-traces, ideas and judgements which have been

previously derived from reality and by which reality was represented in the mind. But this relation was never a closed one; it was continually being enriched and altered by fresh perceptions.

(Freud, 1924b, p.185)

Here we recognize the value of Freud's theory of representation. While reference is generally made to the notion of object and word representation, it is fecund to broaden it, to include, like in this paragraph, the representation of reality, and even the psychic representative of the drive (Green, 2013), as Freud defines it in 1915: "the psychic representative of stimulus that come from the body's interior and reach the soul" and he adds: "as a measure of the exigency of work that is imposed to the animic as a consequence of its interlocking with the bodily". Even though the statute of the psychic representation is very different from the representations as such, it must be recognized that between the somatic stimulus and their psychic representatives there is already a transformation that give them the quality of the psychic. The surge of the psychic representatives of the drive must be considered an emergent, that is, as a movement that emerges (Castoriadis, 1974), and as such, it can be conceived that it suffers alterations from its beginning, where there may not be any representation like is the case in severe autism (Haag, 2005) to lower levels of representation, like in adult's psychosis. Despite the differences in basic theory, diverse authors agree to different degrees in regards to the fact that psychotic disorders have their origin in early stages of development, we see it in Aulagnier's pictogram (1075), in Searle's infantile symbiosis (1959a), in the Alpha function deficit in Bion (1962). In fact, psychoanalysts interested in the theory and practice of psychosis usually explore and theorize the origins of the psyche. This interest is understandable because psychosis leads to posing the question of the etiology of psychotics, but also the reverse side of the question: what psychic events need to occur so that a subject does not develop psychosis? Freud's conceptualization proposes an origin, which, anchored in the soma, is already of a psychic order, "in a way unknown to us". However, he did not consider enough the participation of the object in the dawn of life, which becomes increasingly evident in cases where the participation of the object fails. This is one of Freud's open questions in the conceptualization of psychosis. The second one attains to the notion of thought disorder which is central in psychotic structure. Contemporary authors have attempted to shed light on these two aspects.

The theories of origins and the object's role

The first topic proposed by Freud revolves around the notion of conscience, with the instances of the unconscious, preconscious and conscious, the drives were found "outside" the psychic apparatus, they were "neither conscious nor unconscious", and only their representatives were admitted to consciousness. When Freud, in 1923, formulates the second topic, he divides the instances of the psychic apparatus into Id, Ego and Superego, in this new model, the category of unconscious corresponds to a psychic quality. The drives, unlike what happened in the first model, are within the psyche, in the Id. The second drive theory now divides them in life and death drives, and destructivity is thus situated within the apparatus. This entails that now the libido or sexuality is limited on various instances by the Ego, the superego, and the destructive drives.

The second topic gives account of a more heterogenous psychic apparatus, given that it incorporates the biological component of the psyche in the Id, and includes the cultural dimension in the new instance: the superego. To complicate things even more, the Ego, including its defense mechanisms is largely unconscious. The representation (of object and word) is no longer a starting fact, but a result of laborious acquisition of the psyche. In his later writings, Freud emphasizes the drives' place and role, that is strongly anchored in the soma, but that is of the psychic order, and imposes on it a work that involves the transformation and representation of the drives on account of its link to the body. This continuous work will however always leave a place for the unrepresentable, that which does not succeed in being transformed and remains in the mind in its most primitive forms.

Post Freudian psychoanalysis wanted to shift from the emphasis given by Freud to the intrapsychic, giving more importance to the object and object relationships. Later theoretical developments develop in good measure, as a response to the excessive solipsism of the Freudian theory. However, in regards to this issue, towards the end of his work, Freud introduced two elements that must be considered. The first is the description, in "Mourning and melancholia" (1917) of an object of different order from the contingent object, interchangeable. In "Mourning and melancholia" the object is irreplaceable. The second element to consider refers back to the fact that, by changing his drive theory, sexual drives come to be named as life or love drives. The reference here is to the shift from pleasure organ in order to favor the development of links with an object. But, despite these two elements, Freud did not sufficiently develop the object's place, nor the role it plays, because of its failures and the pathology that ensues. The broadening of the field and clinical work of patients with non-neurotic pathologies forced post-Freudian psychoanalyst to review the function of the object in the structuring of the psyche.

Bion's theorization formulates an α function (Alpha function), "intentionally, devoid of meaning" (Bion, 1962, p.3) and considers that this function is first exerted by the mother through her rêverie capacity. She receives through projective identification, the infant's undigested sensory impressions and emotions or β (Beta) elements, transforming them into α elements. The child will have to reintroject the transformed projections alongside with the α function model, which will allow him to become a thinker. So if this whole process is carried out properly, the infant will be capable of tolerating frustration and emotions, otherwise the evacuation mechanisms would become excessive, impeding the retention of emotional material necessary to form a thought. The passage of β elements to α elements starts a progressive process of abstraction, allowing the evolution of concrete thought to abstract thought. This will never be complete, persisting in the mind, along thoughts with a thinker, the β space, that contains β elements. These are unthinkable because they correspond to a period in which there was not yet an apparatus to think the thoughts; they are thoughts without a thinker. These thoughts, typical of the primordial psyche, will only be apt for discharge or expulsion. We must insist, however, that not all β elements will be evacuated, and that in determined circumstances, they may alter the thought processes. It can be considered that this is one of the aspects that influences the predominance of the psychotic part of personality. Without ignoring the aspects inherent to the child, Bion's theorization incorporates an intersubjective aspect, taking into consideration that each individual has a different capacity to tolerate frustration. If this capacity is too low, the projective identification mechanisms will be excessive, hindering the development of psyche and thought. Both components, the maternal rêverie and the child's tolerance to frustration can be considered as an example of the complementary series (Bion, 1962, chap. 12).

Searles, whose clinical work was predominantly with chronic psychotic patients, put an emphasis on the failures of the symbiotic period (1959). Be it because of difficulties of the mother or the child, the symbiotic stage could either not have taken place properly, or on the contrary, the members of the pair could not renounce to the symbiotic tie when further individualization was needed. Searles highlights the integration and differentiation processes, which must act in a complementary and harmonic manner in order to achieve a healthy personality. One of Searle's a great contribution is what he considers can be observed in a privileged – although not exclusive – way, in relation to inpatient psychotics, who dissociate and project different aspects of their personalities on the diverse members of the treating team, parts that will have to be reunified in order for the patient to achieve a total vision of himself. This can allow him a relatively larger integration of his personality in as much as the treating analyst shows him his own dissociated and projected aspects of his personality. Particularly interesting is his article "The Effort to Drive the other Person Crazy – An Element in the Aetiology and psychotherapy of Schizophrenia" (1959), where he studies the effort by one of the parents or the whole family to drive the subject crazy, an element that can take part in, alongside others, a pathogenic relation that acts in a predominantly unconscious way – a relation that tends to promote emotional conflict in the child, while activating opposite aspects of his personality. The motives behind this effort cover a large spectrum, from an intense hostility, to almost, at the opposite end, the desire to have a closer relationship with the other person as well as wishes of self-realization.

With different theoretical bases, Aulagnier (1975, 1984) proposes an earlier mode of operation in the infant's psyche that helps him in the process of metabolizing what he receives from outside the psyche different from the primary process, for she considered that these could not account for the psychotic phenomena. From her conceptualization of representation as a central activity of the psyche, she formulates a primal representation form, the pictogram, that arises at the moment of the encounter between mouth and breast. The pictogram ignores the duality that composes it. The pictogram will leave a mark, a fracture in the subject that will leave the subject with a psychotic potential, given the lack of an experience of pleasure and fusion that accompany the satisfaction of the need. But this postulate of the pictogram by itself would once again imply ignoring the primary object's role both in normal states and in the diverse psychopathological structures. The spokesman discourse, generally the mother, will be added to the pictogram, which registers the inaugural encounter between the child's body and its erogenous zones, that is the breast or complementary object. The spokesman will deliver the first identificatory referents. The spokesman, in normal conditions is a subject in which the repression has already been exerted, and the "Je"[1] constituted. The action the spokesman exerts in the infant, needed for the "Je" of the subject to emerge (the *infans*), is referred by Aulagnier (1975) as the necessary "primary violence", For Aulagnier, the "secondary violence" is different in that it always involves something excessive and generally deleterious to the development and the acquisition of the child's autonomy, predominantly in his capacity to think.

It must be added that the child will be able to take ownership and transform the identificatory referents that are assigned to him, to historize the initial moments of his life before the advent of his "Je", if these referents were given by their primary object. For Aulagnier, psychosis would emerge above all from the absence of the maternal discourse towards the infant. This absence would have originated in her relation to her own mother. Thus, more than one generation is webbed and needed in order to stop the child from representing something new, something that will be the result of the child's work of historization something not yet lived, that is not just a repetition of something experienced in the history of the mother in particular, or in both parents. The mother would have a foreclosed death wish towards the child, that is not evidenced as explicit hate, but through an affectless discourse and a care. The articulation of both of these qualities, the failure of the experience of fusion in the primal form of representation, the pictogram, and the characteristics of the parental discourse described above are responsible for a failed process of historization, central to understanding the configuration of psychotic potentiality. The emergence of psychosis as such will depend on certain events or encounters in the subject's life.

Green (1995, 2013), proposes another way of conceiving the object's contribution to the psychic development of the infant. He considers that during pregnancy and in the first months after birth, a transformation composed of two aspects operates in the mother: on the one hand, she is subject to a regression which increases her capacity to identify with the child, and on the other, she recenters all her cathexis on him. Green names this process "motherly madness", which will grant the mother a feeling of omnipotence regarding everything happening to the infans: she will assign to him a subjectivity, giving meaning to his experiences of pleasure as well as displeasure even if the infant does not have any yet. This passage through the motherly response will provide her child's experiences not only with sensorial qualities but with physical quality as well. Green describes, via the mechanisms of double return (turn to the contrary and towards the own person), previous to repression, a circuit of stable cathexis, oscillating, between the infant and the mother, each having very asymmetrical levels of psychic development. The circuit that determines the mutual libidinal investiture of the pair, will allow the child to take in the maternal response that responds to his needs, not only physical, but also psychical. At a certain moment, this circuit will be interrupted, which corresponds to what Freud calls the loss of the object, and this interruption restores the normal narcissism in the mother and establishes in the child the primary narcissism as an identificatory pole which brings together centripetal investitures to give rise to the identity of the subject. This juncture also coexists with the creation of what Green calls the framing structure, an internal container that will serve as a base for future representations and from which will objectal investitures emerge. The whole process involves what the author denominates "the work of the negative" (negative hallucination), that allows the representation of the container which is prioritized over the mother's representative characteristics. Moreover, it later favors the erasure of the representation of the object in favor of the word representation, that is the emergence of language, a phenomenon essential to the passage that goes from concrete thinking to abstract thinking. For this author, these two developments are lacking in the psychotic individual, for whom the words are invested as things, which implicates a severe alteration in thought. On the other hand, the absence or failure of an internal container has as a consequence a lack of limits of projection mechanisms which prevents the transformation of psychic material.

None of these authors fall in the trap of considering that the difficulties found at the origin of psychosis originate only in the environment, as it is the case with some other theorizations. They have the virtue of considering external factors, without discarding the existence of others coming from the child. Both vertices, the intersubjective and the intrapsychic are strung together to give place to the understanding of complex pathologies such as psychosis.

The two times and the negative

In the paper "The loss of reality in neurosis and psychosis", Freud points out that psychosis takes place in two steps: in the first, a rupture happens between the I and reality, and in the second, a neo-reality is built, which is constituted by the positive aspects found in psychotic patients' clinic (delusion, hallucinations). The rupture with reality, for its part, has been addressed by contemporary authors among the so-called clinic of the negative or work of the negative:

Thus we might expect that in a psychosis, too, two steps could be discerned, of which the first would drag the ego away, this time from reality, while the second would try to make good the damage done and re-establish the subject's relations to reality at the expense of the id. And, in fact, some analogy of the sort can be observed in a psychosis. Here, too, there are two steps, the second of which has the character of a reparation. But beyond that the analogy gives way to a far more extensive similarity between the two processes. The second step of the psychosis is indeed intended to make good the loss of reality, not, however, at the expense of a restriction of the Id – as happens in neurosis at the expense of the relation to reality – but in another, more autocratic manner, by the creation of a new reality which no longer raises the same objections as the old one that has been given up (Freud, 1924b, p.184–185.).

There is a significant tendency in clinical work to emphasize the second step described by Freud, leaning towards the analysis of the contents of delirious reconstruction. For my part, I will prioritize the approach of the negative aspects, which we can link to the first step, that is the rupture with reality.

In his paper, "Differentiation of the psychotic from non-psychotic personalities", Bion, (1955) takes up Freud's contributions as well as Klein's, and particularly, the description of projective identification. He highlights, in psychotic personality, that hate is not only directed towards external reality, but also internal reality and towards everything that enables the experience of consciousness of the external and internal reality which leads to the fragmentation of the personality, and in particular of the apparatus that allows for the perception of reality. The psychotic part would attack the sense organs, projecting the parts of these by projective identification on external objects, giving rise to what Bion called bizarre objects. This process of attack will interfere with the passage from the schizo paranoid to the depressive position described by Klein (1946), which will be different to that of normal development. It must be highlighted that this functioning will alter in a negative manner from the beginning, from the outlines for verbal thought development. Bion has, from the start of his work granted a great importance to the study of thought and its alterations in psychotic patients. He re-considered the idea that learning and knowledge could not be explained only through the two emotions so emphasized by Freud and Klein, love and hate, and proposed a new category, K (knowledge). For the K link to exist, the presence of a container (the mother) capable of receiving the child's contents is needed, and this container will be characterized by a commensal relationship that does not imply damage but growth for both members of the couple. A destructive tendency may prime if paranoid anxieties or fear of annihilation are too intense. Frustration and anger can also make the projection mechanism predominate, and the projection will be followed by a return of the projected which will reappear with increased persecutory characteristics.

In their 1973 book, *L'enfant de ça*, A. Green and J.-L. Donnet describe what they called white psychosis, or navel of the psychosis. This book is part of one of Green's major investigation interests, that is, the clinic and theory of the negative, that was initiated in 1967, with the article "Primary narcissism: structure or state" (1967) and reached its higher elaboration point in the book "The Work of the Negative" (1993). *L'enfant de ça* is a book that articulates theory and clinical aspects, and it is the result of a research project that is built on the base of long interviews carried by the authors in a psychiatric service, which gradually centered in one case, that of Z's. The interest of this clinical case's lies on the fact that it takes psychoanalytical listening as well as psychoanalytic theory to its limits since the patient's discourse presents a historical and symbolic reality so charged that it tends to erase psychic reality. The interviewers as well as the attendees seem to reach the conviction that the only way out for Z's psychic dilemmas was psychosis; a conviction that they could only question a posteriori. Even though the interview, fully transcribed, was a failure because the interviewer ended up reinforcing the patient's narcissistic defenses, it gave the opportunity to the authors to reflect deeply on the phenomena of psychosis. What is shocking about Z's story is that he was conceived as a result of a relationship between the mother and her son-in-law, which, despite not being strictly incestuous, mobilized defenses against prohibitions, and contributed to the confusion of generations.

For Z, the overwhelming presence of his mother contrasts throughout his life with the dispersion of the father figure (in three different men), which hindered the differentiation and separation from the mother figure, as well as the oedipal triangulation. The difficulty to achieve a separate identity constitutes the axis of the pathological process. The splitting of the Ego will attempt to keep the two paternal identifications separate, separating, in this manner, that which should never have been united.

The thinking theory developed in *L'enfant de ça* is inspired by Freud as well as Bion's theory. In both, thinking is not derived directly from the drive in that there is a need for a processes of drive excess negativization and successive transformations that require an object sufficiently present so that the subject can later on tolerate its absence and create a representation. Thus, the notion of absence must be considered as an achievement of the psychic apparatus. In white psychosis, absence cannot be constituted, which obeys to the characteristics of oedipal objects. Even though both parental objects are represented in the oedipal structure, they are not differentiated by sex nor by the function they accomplish. They are differentiated by the criteria of good and bad, that correspond to that of the inaccessible object and the invasive object. Therefore, in white psychosis, a true triangulation has not been achieved, what exists is what Green call a bitriangulation: the subject relates to objects that are symmetrical opposites and because of this, they do not constitute anything other than a double-sided object. The relevant consequence of this is the negative implications it has over the capacity for thought, because in both cases, the necessary absence for representative work cannot be constituted. The bad object, intrusive, is never absent, and mobilizes massive counterinvestitures that explain the psychism's attempt to evacuate it. The good object, on the other hand, is inaccessible. There is idealization of the good object, and persecution of the bad object, from which the subject, paradoxically cannot be separated. If it did, the experience of emptiness would be even more unbearable, so the subject returns to the bad object. In white psychosis, this situation does not lead to a manifest psychosis, but the subject experiences a paralysis in his ability to think, which is usually described as having a blank mind, an incapacity to think or to memorize. An erasure of representations and of thoughts is constituted, caused by the presence of destructive drives. A disinvestment of one's own thinking has happened, which is not followed by a reinvestment. This results in the emptiness of thought, its negative hallucination, a hole in which the subject can lodge in psychosis, with or without delirious restitution.

Though *L'enfant de ça* refers to only one case, Green will reference white psychosis in several moments in his later work. His reference to whiteness explains the low intensity of symptomatology but that whiteness is the presence of psychosis because of the presence of a thought disorder that hinders the capacity to elaborate conflicts and its appropriation by the subject.

Clinical case

I will briefly present a patient (Joanne) who was evaluated, by request of the treating team, by a clinical group in the main psychiatric center of Santiago. The interview took place three months into her hospitalization, during which the patient had been broadly studied. There was at first a suspicion of some organic component, which was ultimately ruled out. During this period, J had not experienced major changes or variations in her clinical state, which was the motive for the consultation.

J was 42 years old who lived with her two sons (a 16-year-old son and a 5-year-old daughter) in her parents' house. She had had two previous hospitalizations, with use of electroshock therapy in 2012. In the last months she showed constant and broadened suicidal ideation: she wanted to "*go*" with her daughter, had tried to choke and stab her, and then throw herself and the girl into the river she also attempted multiple overdoses of medication.

The first contact with J was when she came into the room, an obese woman, somewhat disheveled, with very few movements, which were ungraceful. Throughout the interview, she kept staring pointedly at the analyst. Her gestures were scarce. Her speech was constantly interrupted; as if it was influenced by an invisible force, it got immobilized, it seemed her speech kept being extinguished, having to be "re-ignited" and started over by the questions asked by the analyst.

I will transcribe some extracts of the interview, which started, as they usually do, with an open question regarding the reasons why she had been hospitalized, pointing out to her that the interviewer had no previous information:

J: *"Because my body is totally anesthetized, I pull out my hair and it doesn't hurt at all... this has been happening for five years, but the worst was since two months ago"... "when my daughter was four months old I stopped sensing smells, I didn't sleep, my hair was falling out, I pulled it out and it didn't hurt"...* She worries about not feeling, and states that she did feel before, love, tenderness, sadness. When asked if anything similar had happened with her older son, she point out: *"No, on the contrary".* In the first four months with her daughter, she says that *"I felt her skin, her cries and her laughter" I cried when she cried, laughed when she laughed"... "The day after she turned four months old, I stopped being able to sleep. I didn't sleep for two months. Not sleeping and not feeling started together, at the same time"...* And she adds *"I felt immortal, because I think if I don't feel anything I won't die. Because I don't get restless, nothing scares me".* She states that that same year she was living with her husband, after having been apart for years, but he drank a lot, he was always drunk, so she separated from him again... Of her parents she doesn't talk much, she says they are both good, but then adds that the father drank and hit the mother, leaving the children to stand between them. He stopped drinking before the patient's first child's birth. The maternal grandfather passed away a few months before she was born. She has an older brother, and a younger sister. About the mother, she only says she is caring, *"she bathed us, fed us, breastfed us and made us sleep"* but that until two years ago, the date in which she rekindled with a sister, she was sad, very sad.

Her older son was desired, but about her daughter, now 5 years and 6 months old, she says: *"I didn't really want to have her because I was working and I wanted to give the best to my older son, and another child meant more expenses"... "I started living with my husband when my older son was 8 years old... he didn't want any more children either".* The desire to kill her children came after her daughter's birth, and seemed to be stronger towards her, even though she sometimes states she has wanted to kill them both. In that period, she points out she started walking like a robot. From some time she was a little better, after taking alternative medicine, she says: *"I started getting up early, I felt everything in my body, I felt cries, I felt laughter".* At the moment of the interview, when asked if she felt something now, she refers: *"No, if you want I'll show you and pull out my hair, I don't feel anything, I don't feel pain".*

Joanne presents a clinical picture that could be catalogued as having a psychotic potentiality, a psychotic structure or a white psychosis. There is no delirium; what predominates throughout the interview and makes it difficult is the paralysis of thought, that stops the patient from thinking about her conflicts and establish for them a causality that would make them subjectivable. This work must be carried on by those who listen to her speech, which continually tends to extinction, as if when talking about experiences that shock the rest of us, she had nothing else to say. During the group discussion, it was highlighted how different this clinical picture was from what we usually see in the hospital where we generally interview patients who were more productive in their speech. What stood out in Joanne was the element of repetition in her family of origin and her own family: the patient is the second daughter, a woman, of a couple where the father is an alcoholic and violent with the mother, which is the same in her story about her own being part of a couple and her second daughter, a female. Both daughters were unwanted. In the patient's story, we are under the impression that her upbringing seems to have been more operative, meaning that she would take care of the physical needs but was not emotionally involved: a devitalized mother, emotionally absent. In Joanne's experience the rejection towards her daughter is more apparent, despite the great difficulty she shows when talking about her emotions. These emotions seemed to be related in a mirror-like manner (she cried when she cried, she laughed when she laughed), or have a "somatic" character rather than being felt as internal experiences (she felt cries, she felt laughter). We can appreciate in this patient a progression of a process of deobjectivization (Green, 1995, 2010), which would have been activated at her daughter's birth. From this event, that seems to have faced her with the unthought and unthinkable – that of the forclusion or the exclusion from the Ego – of her own childhood, leads to hate which in consequence leads her to attempt infanticide and suicide. If that were the case, both daughters would be murdered simultaneously. She progressively disinvests other objects, like her son, with whom she seemed previously to have a closer and more loving relationship. At the same time, she seems to disinvest her own internal experiences, her emotions, as well as her body and its functions (she walked like a robot).

It is of interest to consider "the negative" in normal development as well as in pathology. Similar mechanisms, used with variable intensities, finalities and combinations lead to very diverse solutions. The work of the negative and the negative hallucination, are indispensable for the structuration of the psychic apparatus and for the rise of thought, but their use acquires a pathological dimension when it is associated with destructivity. The latter becomes operative and predominates when the unpleasant and painful experiences are such that they overcome the subject's capacities to tolerate them either because of the child's vulnerability or due to the object's failures. In any way, when this happens, the destructivity will not only be directed to breaking bonds with the object and reality, but it will also operate in erasing its imprints inside the psyche. In extreme pathology, we must even consider the possibility of the erasure or destruction of representations besides their exclusion within the Ego. As stated by Green, the "white", which has a place in normal thought, is broadened, and extends in the psychotic and severe borderlines cases beyond what would be the thought's process breaths, it can lead to a thought paralysis, as described by Green and Donnet (1973), and as can be appreciated in the clinical case.

The study of psychosis without restitutive symptoms allows a look into that which is "before" or "behind" the delirium or the hallucinatory. Surely, there are several simultaneous processes operating here. To the denial of reality are added disinvestitures of thought, another way of avoiding contact with painful aspects, but these are not followed, as in neurotic configurations, by reinvestitures. The projection mechanisms become excessive in an attempt to expel the bad object, and, as a consequence it empties the mind of the elements that would eventually allow it to deal with conflicts and establish a causality that would give meaning to the subject. Because the space as well as temporal experiences are altered, there is less limit to the process of expulsion. The return of the violently expelled content will cause varying degrees of persecution.

The void or blank will attract or rather induce a fill, be it with drives in a brute state, or with the remains of the imprints the subject manages to create before the surge of psychosis. Even when considering, as has be done by most authors including Freud, that the delusion contains a nucleus of historical truth, it will not be directly manifested. The origin of any of these conceptualizations will never be made directly visible. What the analyst will perceive, through the patient's speech, will constitute a derivative of it, with all the elaborations and deformations the Ego of the subject has imprinted on it. As a matter of fact, it is wrong to think that the primary processes will be visible in the psychotic. Instead, what is visible to us are altered primary processes, deformed, transformed. The analyst that embarks to navigate alongside the psychotic patient will try to discover, in that neo-reality, that nucleus of truth. Which is not clear will be of aid to the psychotic. The psychotic finds in delusion a sense from which he was previously deprived, and will hardly renounce it to accept our neurotic fantasies. One of the great paradoxes that inhabits the psychotic subject is constituted by him trying to get rid of an invading object from which he seems to have been unable to renounce. This object preserves the primal omnipotence in the internal word, persecutory omnipotence that did not achieve to be the object of any displacement. Searle's (1959,

1972) work probably has particular impact not only for having treated chronic patients, but because his way of understanding them reveals the psychotic attempt at reproducing, or rather allowing the subject to experience in a delusional manner that which he expected of the primary object. Perhaps our possibilities are more humble in that we can offer a containment model which includes the availability to, alongside the patient, be able to think not only what he directs to us through a discursive listening, but also what we are able to catch through our countertransference and what we can create by means of our imagination.

Note

1 We have kept in the text Aulagnier's denomination of "Je", that the author differentiates from the notion of Moi, which corresponds to the Ego instance described by Freud. As Piera Aulagnier points out, the "Je" is an instance linked to language, and anticipated by the motherly discourse, which grants it the first identifiying statements that introduce the child in a historized and symbolic order. This concept, linked to Lacan's theorizations, is however distanced from his perspective, in that, for Aulagnier, the "Je" doesn't remain captured in the ignorance nor in the passitivity in relation to the Other's discourse.

References

Aulagnier P (1975). *The Violence of Interpretation: From Pictogram to Statement*. London/New York: Routledge, 2001.
Aulagnier P (1984). "*L'apprenti-historien et le maître-sorcier*". Paris: Puf. [*The Apprentice Historian and the Master Sorcerer*].
Bion WR (1957). Differentiation of the Psychotic from the Non-Psychotic Personalities. In: *Second Thoughts: Selected Papers on Psycho-Analysis* (p.43–64). Northvale, New Jersey, 1993.
Bion WR (1962). *Learning from Experience*. London: Tavistock.
Castoriadis C. (1974). *The Imaginary Institution of Society*. Cambridge, Massachusetts: The MIT Press, 1998. [(1974) L'Institution imaginaire de la société. Paris: Points, 1999].
Freud S (1917). Mourning and Melancholia. In: *SE 14*.
Freud S (1920). Beyond the Pleasure Principle. In: *SE 18*.
Freud S (1923). The Ego and the Id. In: *SE 19*.
Freud S (1924a). Neurosis and psychosis. In: *SE 19*.
Freud S (1924b). The Loss of Reality in Neurosis and Psychosis. In: *SE 19*.
Freud S (1924c). The Economic Problem of Masochism. In: *SE 19*.
Freud S (1925). Negation. In: *SE 19*.
Freud S (1927). Fetishism. In: *SE 21*.
Freud S (1938). The Splitting of the Ego in the Process of Defence. In: *SE 23*.
Green A (1967). Primary Narcissism: Structure or State? In: *Life Narcissism, Death Narcissism*. London: Free Association Books, 2001.
Green A (1990) *Introduction on Private Madness*London: Karnac, 2005.

Green A (1993). *The Work of the Negative*. London: Free Association Books, 1999.

Green A (1995). *Propedeutique. La métapsychologie revisitée*. Paris: Ed. Champ Vallon.

Green A (2009) *Pourquoi les pulsions de destruction ou de mort?:* Ithaque, 20010.

Green A (2013). *Penser la Psychanalyse avec Bion, Lacan, Winnicott, Laplanche, Aulagnier, Anzieu, Rosolato*. France: Ithaque.

Green A, Donnet J-L (1973). *L'enfant de ça*. Paris: Ed. de Minuit.

Haag G (2005). Temporalités rythmiques et circulaires dans la formation des représentations corporelles et spatiales au sein de la sexualité orale. In: François Richard & Fernando Urribarri (Dir.), *Autour de l'œuvre d'André Green Enjeux pour une psychanalyse contemporaine* (p.181–192). Paris: PUF.

Klein M (1946). Notes on Some Schizoid Mechanisms. *International Journal of Psycho-Analysis*, 27: 99–110.

Searles H (1959). Integration and Differentiation in Schizophrenia: An Over-all View. *Brit. J. Med. Psychol.*, 32 (1): 261–281.

Searles H (1959). The effort to drive the other person crazy – An element in the Aetiology and Psychotherapy of Schizophrenia. *Brit. J. Med. Psychol.*, 32(1): 1–18.

Searles H (1972). The function of the patient's realistic perceptions of the analyst in delusional transference. *Brit. J. Med. Psychol.*, 45(1): 11–18.

6 The Object of Psychosis

Paul Williams

Psychosis, for many, remains an enigma eluding interpretation or amelioration. A considerable literature has emerged since Freud's formulations on psychosis (Freud, 1911b, 1915, 1924a, 1924b) yet psychoanalysts seldom take psychotic patients into treatment and the psychoanalytic therapy of psychosis is today virtually unavailable in hospital settings. With regard to the treatment of schizophrenia, one psychoanalyst recently suggested:

> Psychoanalysis has no more special relevance to schizophrenia than it does to multiple sclerosis or cancer or homelessness.
> (Michels, in Lucas, 2009 p30)

This indictment, perhaps concerned with separating speculation from the "pure gold" of evidence-based medicine, cannot be confined to psychoanalysis. It is applicable to every approach to schizophrenia given that the etiology of the disease is unknown. An exception to the dearth of psychoanalytic input has been the recent development of early intervention and need-adapted treatments that use stress-vulnerability models designed to address first episode psychosis to prevent relapse and admission (cf. Cullberg, 2001, Martindale, 2001, in Lucas, 2009 p3). A small number of psychoanalysts in various parts of the world, usually psychiatrists working in in-patient settings, also bring a psychoanalytic perspective to bear on the treatment of psychotic individuals. Notwithstanding the limitations of psychoanalysis, we do know that psychotic, including schizophrenic, individuals try to connect and disconnect from internal and external figures in confused, self-defeating ways. Their frustration lies in *being in a world of others* who are experienced as terrifying, destructive objects from which they must shrink. Hallucinated, dreaded objects are accompanied or replaced by seductive, perverse "siren" objects whose protection the patient believes is needed if they are to survive. In fact, a line of inquiry into this chaotic object world is evident throughout the history of engagement by psychoanalysts with

DOI: 10.4324/9781003384120-6

psychosis, from Freud onwards. This paper traces that line and suggests that objects and part-objects are a primary preoccupation of the psychotic individual.

Contemporary psychiatric treatment of psychosis relies on pharmacological interventions to control delusions and hallucinations and "therapeutic training" of consciousness to adapt to external reality and social norms, with little or no inclusion of a dynamic perspective. Suppression of symptoms and "community care" is the treatment most widely employed in the western world. Individuals with psychosis are understood theoretically to a degree that exceeds improvement in their condition. Attempts to integrate medical and psychological knowledge of the illness have failed. Within psychoanalysis, progress has slowed in part due to psychoanalysts who emphasize preservation of the purity of the discipline rejecting adaptations needed to treat psychosis, which discourages innovation. This may be in part a legacy of Freud's view that instatement of a positive transference fails in the treatment of psychosis, something clinicians now know to not be the case. Jung's parting of ways with Freud was to some degree a consequence of the former's experience treating psychosis, a subject with which he had more familiarity than Freud. Ferenczi's attempts to treat severely disturbed patients were met with hostility, and he was not alone. Valon observes:

> ... analysts from the heroic period who faced these questions [of the treatment of psychosis by psychoanalysis] *along with those from the following generation (Reich, Reik, Rosen, Fromm-Reichmann etc) all evidently encountered difficulties with the orthodoxy of the psychoanalytic "establishment".*

He adds:

> *The wish to draw a firm line between what is psychoanalytic and what is not or what no longer is, is naturally the temptation. Thanks to this border, the border separating psychotic and neurotic could thus be resolutely established and, beyond it even, the border separating illness and good health. One would then overlook Freud's insistence on the fact that the psychic mechanisms featured in heavily magnified form in mentally ill individuals, be they perverse, neurotic or psychotic, actually exist in human beings of the most normal kind, the difference pertaining to quantity and not essence.*
> (Valon, 2020 p170)

Whatever the limitations of engagement with psychosis, *fear of the illness*, in one form or another, is likely to underly these anxieties.

Bearing psychotic anxieties

Family, caregivers, even clinical staff are intimidated by the force of psychosis. Its unintelligibility can evoke heightened alarm and fear. Phantasmagorical ideas, overwhelming anxiety, lack of insight and opposition to ordinary human interaction arouses aversion, helplessness and, finally, disapproval. Freud was open about his angry reactions to psychotic individuals who he found to be lacking in humanity (Dupont, 1988, p251). Anyone can be horror-struck. Familiarity with the territory of psychosis is essential if mobilization of extreme defenses is to be checked. Psychoanalysts tend to find it difficult to accept that they themselves are vulnerable to psychotic anxieties, as though this might imply they are "psychotic". This is rarely discussed and has little or no place in trainings where evidence of psychotic anxieties in a candidate or analyst might be construed as unfitness to practice psychoanalysis. Unusual levels of tolerance of psychotic anxieties, embrace of doubt and a growing familiarity with psychotic processes are required of the analyst treating psychosis. Given the fear psychosis generates, it is not surprising that psychoanalytic treatments can be seen as misplaced, cavalier or "heroic". Richard Bentall views fear of psychosis as a product of categorical psychiatric distinctions between sanity and madness which stigmatize patients with psychosis, intimidating everyone. He suggests:

> *Why not help some psychotic people just to accept that they are different from the rest of us? Fear of madness may be a much bigger problem than madness itself.*
>
> (Benthall, 2003 p511)

Received classifications of insanity and "normality" risk subverting clinical work by dehumanizing interaction. Defensiveness in hospital staff undermines relationships with patients. Menzies-Lyth's classic study of hospital nursing first portrayed this dilemma (Menzies-Lyth, 1960). Although the treatment situation is fraught, psychoanalysis of psychosis under appropriate conditions can yield considerable benefits. Many patients report longstanding improvements in mental health deriving from a reduction in psychotic confusion. This yields a marked improvement in the quality of life, prevents readmission, and facilitates maturation of the personality (Jackson and Williams, 1994 p. xviii, pp 5–8).

Conran, on the unique contribution of psychoanalysis to psychosis, writes:

> *Much of the business of psychoanalysis is to help the patient find a story in the first place, and then one with which he can live... The*

> quotation I most cherish is that of Isaac Bashevis Singer who said "The story is everything. If the Iliad had come to us as a commentary by Marx or as an interpretation by Freud, nobody would read it". In another context he [Bashevis Singer] wrote "A story must be a love story. Many writers have attempted to write a story which is not a love story and they have always failed."
>
> (Conran, in Williams Ed., 1999 p27)

The most tragic story of loss of love is psychosis, and assistance in writing this tragic love story is the analytic task. Psychotic patients are the best psychoanalytic educators. Their need for and aversion to trustworthy objects produces a depth of relational complexity that yields insights not only into psychosis but into all psychoanalytic work.

Freudian and post-Freudian objects in psychosis

Freud's formulations of psychotic functioning developed not from clinical experience but theory. His study of Schreber's memoirs confronted him with a world catastrophe – a breakdown repression could not explain (Freud, 1911). In repression, instinctual energy connects to a significant unconscious memory, then to a substitute conscious object. In psychosis, instinctual energy is withdrawn, a disaster for the ego. "Disavowal" was employed to explain this withdrawal. Without a patient, Freud was unable to elaborate the symbolic meaning of Schreber's delusions but he studied their form and the early events and relationships in Schreber's life, particularly the role of men in relation to a horror of "enforced homosexuality". Schreber's delusions offered clues to the early collapse of his mind and object world ("object" being employed in its early Cartesian, dualistic form). His suffering in childhood at the hands of an authoritarian father has since been widely discussed (Niederland, 1951, 1959, 1960, 1968, MacAlpine & Hunter , 1953, Lothane, 1993, Israels, 1989) and Freud concluded that his illness derived from projection of homosexual libido which gave rise to paranoid delusions of persecution – a negative Oedipus complex. He noted that such unconscious conflicts occur in neurosis. From this, Freud developed a theory of delusions as a defense against homosexuality and as a form of restitution. He also thought that Schreber's attempt to cure his emasculation – a fantasy of becoming a woman in a voluptuous relationship with God – derived in part from the privation of not having had children of his own. Freud's landmark paper on narcissism (1914) underscored the view that in schizophrenia, libido withdrawn from external objects is connected to the self or ego via regression from object love to a narcissistic stage of development. Psychosis is a "narcissistic neurosis" employing "ego-libido" in contrast to "object-libido" in neurosis. Fixation points denote the scale of regression, schizophrenia being its most radical manifestation. Freud's explanation of Schreber's illness pointed to a primary masochistic tie to the object *for the sake of survival*. Subsequent developments in the psychoanalytic understanding of psychotic states, not least in object relations theory (which began in Hungary with the work of Ferenczi, Balint and Hermann) have explored forms of dependence upon the object, including masochism and the desire for/terror of annihilation of the object.

Many investigations into delusion formation followed Freud's papers on Schreber and narcissism (cf. Abraham, 1924, Tausk, 1919, Van Ophuijsen, 1920, Staercke, 1920, Nunberg, 1920, 1921, Laforgue, 1926, 1929, amongst others). Introduction of the structural model was followed by Freud's two short, major papers on psychosis in which he turned again to the problem of reality in psychosis (Freud, 1924a, 1924b), from which subsequent psychoanalytic investigations into psychosis developed. In psychosis and neurosis there is a conflict between the ego and reality. In neurosis the ego applies repression to detach from id impulses, preservation of the relationship to the external world being the priority. In psychosis, the ego forsakes reality, allying itself with id impulses. The neurotic distorts reality whereas the psychotic inflicts damage on reality, creating a gap or fissure bridged by a hallucinated reality. Collapse of the relationship to reality undermines the capacity to symbolize and brings about the well-known loss of distinction between words and things, the former now equated with the latter under the sway of primary process.

Continuity, discontinuity?

Freud placed psychosis on a theoretical continuum with neurosis (the "continuist" view) and this has been widely accepted. In recent years it has been questioned. Some consider psychosis to be a discontinuous entity, possessing mental processes unlike neurosis and requiring a different form of investigation (London, 1988, De Masi, 2020). As De Masi puts it:

> *... by postulating a clear divide between neurosis and psychosis, discontinuous theories maintain that withdrawal is a dissociated experience that is neither integrable nor transformable in the psychic world. Even when a degree of awareness seems present in the patient, it makes no contact with the delusional belief.*
> (De Masi, ibid, pp 11–12)

Seen from a discontinuity perspective, dissociation between non-psychotic and psychotic thinking makes links harder, if not impossible, to establish (Freud regarded dissociation as a defense, not a nosological category – part of his disagreement with Jung). The discontinuous or dissociationist perspective raises important questions: for example, at the schizophrenic end of the psychotic spectrum, damage to non-psychotic thinking is inflicted to an extent that some patients appear untreatable. Is being untreatable due to non-psychotic thinking having been mutilated beyond repair by a separate, distinct mental process? To what extent does the patient retain a need for the object and is this revivable, or is the delusion "complete'? Is psychosis a dissociation from the object world into some kind of "objectless" world? Marcus, reporting on a panel discussion of psychosis, notes the technical difficulty these questions pose:

> *A technical issue remains, however, whether we approach psychotics only with words and concepts or mainly non-verbally with intuition and tuning in to the emotions between analyst and patient. Should we combine both of these approaches and, if so, how?... The panelists mostly chose to ignore these charges, focusing, as panelists on this topic usually do, on their particular sub-interest and experiences with patients. Whether this is because we lack a common conceptualization, we lack the data, or we refuse to hammer out an agreed language of terms and concepts, is sometimes debated but often ignored. And it may be that the phenomenon is not unitary. If so, then of course such patients are dealt with differently at different times by different analysts.*
>
> (Marcus, 1996 p565)

Freud's insights during the fertile period 1911–1924 remain germane to contemporary inquiries into the destructive power of psychosis. Hinshelwood lists these areas of inquiry as: "symbol formation; psychotic and non-psychotic parts of the personality; primary process and ego weakness; omnipotence and identity; the existential problem; interpersonal relations" (Hinshelwood, 2004, p59). Whichever line of inquiry is undertaken, the psychoanalyst is faced with an intensity of relationship between the ego/subject and object unlike any other. This is conveyed by patients as a struggle to determine *the nature and condition of the object and its whereabouts*. [1] Actual or imminent loss of the object or obliteration of the subject by the object (or vice-versa) are ongoing events; two minds yielding different, contradictory responses frequently in unrepresented form. The analyst is required to *experience in the present* these contradictory communications, from which deduction of links to non-psychotic thinking and restitution of symbolic meaning can, in this writer's view, become imaginable. Bion puts it thus:

Memory and desire exercise and intensify those aspects of the mind that derive from sensuous experience... Psychoanalytic "observation" is concerned neither with what has happened nor with what is going to happen but with what **is** happening. Furthermore, it is not concerned with sense impressions or with objects of sense... awareness of the sensuous accompaniments of emotional experience are a hindrance to the psychoanalyst's intuition of reality of which he must be at one. Every session attended by the psychoanalyst must have no history and no future.

(Bion, 1972)

The clinical encounter is forbidding in terms of claims made on the emotional reserves and psychological resolve of the clinician. Then there is the analyst's hatred of the patient. The opening lines of Winnicott's paper "Hate in the Countertransference" could not be clearer:

In this paper I wish to examine one aspect of the whole subject of ambivalence, namely, hate in the counter-transference. I believe that the task of the analyst (call him a research analyst) who undertakes the analysis of a psychotic is seriously weighted by this phenomenon, and that analysis of psychotics becomes impossible unless the analyst's own hate is extremely well sorted-out and conscious.

Winnicott (1949)

It is not difficult to see why many disciplines take an arm's length approach to psychosis. Fear and dread of our own reactions to the illness can be paralyzing. However, recognition of psychic and external reality remains contingent upon the relationship with the object, including in psychosis, which is why psychoanalysis is better placed than any other discipline to address this matter.

Pursuit and destruction of the object

Following Freud, Federn's theory of the ego was influential in understanding the object world of the psychotic individual. He addressed the lived experience of the ego and the distinction between the subjective self and object world (Federn, 1926, 1934, 1953). The fluid ego boundary is a sensory organ of awareness that fails in schizophrenia, producing a false (internal) reality that usurps external reality. Federn advised that negative and psychotic transferences be handled with great care until the ego can tolerate awareness of them. Klein, in positing an immediate relationship between infant and object from birth and of commensurate defense mechanisms, viewed projection and introjection of objects, good and bad, and of part-objects (cf. Abraham, 1924) as structuring perception of external reality (Klein, 1932, 1945, 1946, 1958). Projection of destructive impulses can be so intense as to induce persecutory anxieties which threaten the ego with dissolution. The role of introjection and projection in Klein's account of delusion formation is close to Freud's formulation. Klein's core view is that the infant must imagine they have unconsciously created the (chaotic) world inside and outside before they can address a world they have not created. Contemporary Kleinians have extended these insights, yet Kleinians, like other psychoanalysts, today rarely undertake the analysis of psychotic patients. Segal and Rosenfeld were perhaps the foremost exceptions in recent years.[2] Segal (1950, 1957, 1972) and Rosenfeld (2003, 2018) deepened the understanding of excessive projective identification, its persecutory consequences, and the splitting processes implicit in the destruction of symbolization and creation of psychotic states.

The interpersonal tradition in the US, deriving from the work of Fromm-Reichman (1950) and Sullivan (1962), revised the treatment technique for schizophrenia away from reliance upon interpretation towards emphasis on the analyst's emotional sensitivity to the relationship. The task, as they saw it, was to *enter into* the experiences of the patient's disturbed world. Given the sensitivity of the psychotic patient to transference experiences, the analyst is required to accept his or her (inevitable) misunderstandings, errors and failures to a degree that far exceeds the treatment of a neurotic person. The quality of the relationship between analyst and patient supplants the primacy of interpretation of intra-psychic states. Searles (1956) strove to accommodate the interpersonal relationship and interpretation of intra-psychic states through transference and countertransference experiences, which were often shared with the patient to achieve "personification" of the relationship. His, at times, dramatic interventions were not, he believed, experienced by the patient as persecutory so much as alive depictions of experiences the patient recognized, including accurate perceptions of Searles' character.

Hinshelwood, commenting on the impact of the interpersonal movement, notes:

> *Sullivan's inspirational influence on American psychoanalysis was eventually overshadowed in the 1940's by the émigré European analysts, who set out to eradicate American psychoanalysis*
> (Hinshelwood, 2004 p81)

The interpersonal movement evolved in different forms, however, most importantly into the school of relational psychoanalysis. The divide between adherents of an intra-psychic model of the mind and those who view the relationship between analyst, patient and environmental conditions as mutative continues to this day, perhaps no more so than in debates on the origins and treatment of psychosis.

Radical revision of the theory of psychopathology in severe disturbance occurred with Fairbairn's view of libido (drive) theory as secondary to the primacy of object-seeking (Fairbairn, 1944). The reality of the actual object and the internal perception of the object are central for Fairbairn, and the role of unconscious fantasy is downplayed. Over time, the primary identification is relinquished in favor of mature dependence, self and object having been differentiated. For Fairbairn, psychosis arises during the earliest (oral) phase of infantile dependence when the emotionally conflicted infant faces an impossible predicament – to decide whether or not to engage with the breast/mother. Introjection of a bad object leads to fear of destroying the object by loving this (fragile/dangerous) object, and so the infant attempts to abandon object relating leading to schizoid or psychotic illness.

Winnicott linked Freudian and Kleinian thinking (Winnicott, 1958b, 1965c) whilst developing his own concept of the transitional object that bridged internal and external reality (1958c). From this he constructed an influential conceptual system of object relations and object usage and a sophisticated developmental model of the self that included impact of impingement on the "true self" leading to psychosis.

The most significant contribution to the understanding of psychosis since Freud is held by many to have come from Wilfred Bion (1967). Bion stated that we employ consciousness as a type of "sense organ" to manage psychic and external reality. Tolerance of frustrations and confusions occupies the contained non-psychotic, or neurotic, personality. But in adverse circumstances (where containment fails) radical evasion of reality and deployment of massive projective identification rid the mind of unbearable experiences via a psychotic personality (Bion *ibid*). His distinction between psychotic and non-personalities in relation to the object is central to the analysis of psychosis.

There is no space to comment on many further contributions to the understanding and treatment of psychosis, such as the work of Sechehaye (1947), Pichon-Riviere (1952), Pankow (1968, 1977), Laing (1960), Benedetti (1987), Jackson (2001), Rey (1994), Boyer (1998), Rosenfeld D (1992), Freeman (1965, 1998), Pao (1979), Arieti (1974), De Masi (2021) and Robbins (2019). The list is not exhaustive.

Psychotic and non-psychotic personalities in psychosis

Pursuit of the object is an essential, healthy activity of the non-psychotic mind. It follows that the quality of the analytic relationship is critical to the outcome of treatment of psychosis. In psychosis, the psychotic personality of the patient reacts violently against the pursuit of the object but does not itself pursue the object directly. It pursues the ego and the non-psychotic personality with the aim of attacking the need for an object and by destroying symbolizing activity. Apprehension of reality by the ego is thus impaired. Psychotic organizations – psychic structures in the mind – utilize perverse, cruel fantasies to disable the ego's functioning and intimidate the non-psychotic personality (Williams, 2014). They attack both libidinal interest in the internal object representation and qualities in the actual, external object, striving to render external reality catastrophic by undermining both ego and object. Perverse predictions of disaster arise particularly when the object is needed or reality is faced. Compelling, seductive promises of sensuous gratifications are applied to produce autoerotic isolation. Articulation by the analyst of two separate worlds is needed – psychotic and non-psychotic, inner and outer – that have become confused. This is a precondition for resuscitation of links between subject and object. Careful, systematic observation and discussion of confusion between internal and external realities, and how these realities have become confused, at all times led by the patient's immediate concerns, give rise over time to faith in the analytic process. With enough evidence to vindicate the patient's faith in the process, some trust in the object may begin to emerge. Winnicott describes the task as precarious, requiring great patience:

> *In the clear-cut psycho-neurotic case there is no difficulty because the whole analysis is done through the intermediary of verbalization. Both the patient and analyst want this so.... More dangerous, however, is a state of affairs in an analysis in which the analyst is permitted by the patient to reach to the deepest layers of the analysand's personality because of his position as a subjective object, or because of the dependence of the patient in the transference psychosis; here there is a danger if the analyst interprets instead of waiting for the patient to discover. It is only here, at the place when the analyst has not changed over from a subjective object to one that is objectively perceived, that psychoanalysis is dangerous, and the danger is one that can be avoided if we know how to behave ourselves. If we wait, we become perceived objectively in the patient's own time, but if we fail to behave in a way that facilitates the patient's analytic process (which is the equivalent of the infant's and the child's maturational process) we*

suddenly become not-me for the patient, and then we know too much, and we are too dangerous because we are too nearly in communication with the central silent and still spot of the patient's ego-organization.
Winnicott (1963)

An approach of the kind cited above employs a continuist model of psychosis. But we know that psychotic ideation and speech can appear highly discontinuous. The limits of the continuist model might be thought of as (a) the extent to which the ego and non-psychotic thinking have been mutilated and (b) the analyst's capacity to identify and articulate these limits through intuitive awareness. Freud (1938) posited a "kernel of truth" in delusional thinking. The patient's communication of this "kernel" via distorted variants is best considered, in this writer's view, as a "matrix of mutilation". This mutilation combines frantic attempts to find an object and repeated vitiation by defences against an unthinkable devastation of object relationships in infancy. As the psychotic story unfolds, approaches to this "matrix of mutilation" reveal more clearly protective "ways out" or "hubs" denoting the individuals primitive responses to their impossible crisis – what Green refers to as *"plaques tournantes"*. These are defensive knots of confusion reflecting different traumatic lineages stemming from the catastrophe in infancy. The intersection of these defensive strategies generates phobic terror in the transference (Williams, 2000 p1046). Green revised our understanding of free association by revealing how these phobic knots of "anticipatory terror" involuntarily bring together multiple traumatic experiences in condensed form as the analysis deepens – a vortex of trauma – which must be analyzed in all its non-linear forms. Trauma expresses itself in the analytic setting through recurrent strivings towards and collapses in the relationship with an object. Like tendrils or shoots that are cut down before they can grow, strivings appear according to prevailing anxieties and needs, only to be savaged. Anticipatory anxieties intensify to become terror as these conscious and pre-conscious states coalesce in the deepening transference. The living out of these confusing experiences in the transference and their interpretation in detail is necessary (Green, 2000). The process is not linear in a developmental sense, as these strivings and assaults are not bounded by temporal awareness. They erupt continuously and simultaneously, manifesting themselves in confusing psychotic accounts of oppression. It is here that the analyst's role is critical: the unravelling of confusion and the mental state of the analyst in doing this work are of incalculable value to the patient. The concept of psychotic and non-psychotic parts of the mind (or "personalities') is, in this writer's experience, essential in understanding these confusing, traumatizing concatenations.

Psychotic and non-psychotic parts of the mind is an idea that was first introduced by Moritz Katan, who extended Freud's concept of regression in psychosis. He suggested that in the pre-psychotic phase there exists a highly conflicted, narcissistic form of the Oedipus complex. The psychotic individual, unable to traverse the Oedipal phase, in effect abolishes it. The pre-decompensatory conflict continues to exist and can be accessed at different times allowing the analyst contact with both psychotic and non-psychotic mental states (Katan, 1954). Bion's contribution to psychotic and non-psychotic personalities appeared not long after Katan's work and became the basis for a theory of technique that has influenced psychoanalysts worldwide. Bion addressed both discontinuity in psychosis and its links to non-psychotic experiences from early life. He describes the disastrous formation of the two worlds in which the patient lives:

> *The differentiation of the psychotic from the non-psychotic personalities depends on a minute splitting of all that part of the personality that is concerned with awareness of internal and external reality, and the expulsion of these fragments so that they enter or engulf their objects.*
> (Bion 1957a, p43)

Lucas paraphrases his formulation:

> *From early on in life, Bion suggests that there exists a separate psychotic part that attacks all the aspects of the mind that have to do with registration of awareness of internal and external reality. In consequence of this attack, the individual's developing awareness of sense impressions, attention, memory, judgement and thought are fragmented and projected into objects outside of the self. The projected fragments engulf the objects so they take on the characteristics of the projections. Bion called these creations "bizarre objects" and saw them as developmentally early examples of delusional formations.*
> (Lucas ibid., p85)

Clinical implications

What follows are illustrations of the coexistence of psychotic and non-psychotic parts of the mind in psychosis. Psychotic attacks on non-psychotic thinking are immensely destructive, but when contained may reveal tracks in the sand of how and where the disaster arose. When the analyst intuits the aim of delusional thoughts and the deformed expressions of reality used to protect against experiences felt to be unbearable, differentiation of non-psychotic from psychotic thinking may become possible.

In Bion's Sao Paolo seminars, an analyst presents a disturbed patient. The patient frequently says "I have brought you some dreams, Doctor". Bion asks the analyst why he says they are dreams. The analyst replies that the patient tells him so. Bion imagines himself saying to the patient: "Where were you last night? What did you see?" (Bion, 1994 p142). Bion's benign question, "where did you go when you went to bed?" takes into account a concrete experience of dream-as-reality, and a willing individual trying to talk in a way he imagines a patient in analysis might talk.

An encounter with a psychotic woman provided by Lucas reveals the suffering that can erupt when awareness of the psychotic side becomes conscious:

> *While on the ward, for months, [a young woman] kept denying any problems. One weekend, she went home to her mother and jumped out of her bedroom window, fracturing her leg. While still on the orthopedic ward she came to see me in my out-patient clinic. She was in a frightened state and asked to be readmitted to the mental hospital, on medical discharge. When she returned to the mental hospital, she reverted to a denial of any problems. Antipsychotic medication was having no effect on her mental state. I then realized that she hadn't jumped out of the window in a state of despair, she had been pushed out by an intolerant [psychotic] part. When I put this to her, her mental state suddenly changed. She made out that she was religious and that I was a bigot and intolerant of religion.*
>
> (Lucas, 2003 p6)

Hinshelwood states that "the choice of which part of the patient to link with is influenced strongly by a wish on the part of both [psychotic and non-psychotic parts] not to engage too deeply with the psychotic terror, omnipotence and destruction" (Hinshelwood, 2004 p85). When psychotic reality is addressed, the outcome is fierce and sometimes excruciating. It is therefore not possible to address psychotic activity directly, but only through the medium of the non-psychotic personality. In Lucas' example it is possible that his intervention stressed the psychotic component at the expense of the patient's non-psychotic anguish at being with her mother and being in a mental hospital, leading to a psychotic response to Lucas's comment.

The following encounter with psychotic and non-psychotic experiences leads to examples of collaborative engagement through the use of intuition, awareness of transference and countertransference and delineation of non-psychotic from psychotic processes.

Paranoid schizophrenia: "the radio loves me"

The interview with Sally occurred on an in-patient ward at the Maudsley Hospital, London (cf. Jackson & Williams, 1994). Sally is the second child and eldest daughter of a large catholic family. The parents' marriage was unhappy and Sally's relationship with her mother conflicted. She decompensated in her late teens believing the town was filming her masturbating. It became apparent over time (beyond reasonable doubt) that she had had an incestuous relationship with her father, as had other siblings. Sally believed her mother abandoned her to her father whom she viewed as a maternal figure. The father viewed Sally as a maternal figure. A longing for a mother drew Sally into relationships with women leading her to fear she was homosexual. She also feared she might turn into a man. Between 21 and 30 she became chronically psychotic and was eventually admitted, broken down and clutching a photo of two church spires which she said were needles put up her bottom by doctors. She complained her abdomen was inflated, cut her wrists, smashed crockery, was violent, smelt gas and accused the nurses of turning her into a paraffin addict. Medication was paraffin and food poisoned with gasoline. The delusions were felt to be attempts to survive the consequences of incest and to defend against severe depression due to a sense of abandonment by her mother. She was interviewed by Murray Jackson, a psychoanalyst on the ward. Video-taping interviews of patients was customary and considerable advance discussion took place amongst staff in light of Sally's traumatic history. The staff could not be entirely sure whether Sally would feel intruded upon, or whether she was now sufficiently contained on the ward to deal with it. It was decided she was probably capable of deciding for herself and would be given the opportunity to decide or change her mind at any time. What follows is the first 15 minutes of the hour-long interview.

MJ: I thought I'd like to tell you that we have a couple of people attached to the unit, and we put them behind that mirror there, so there aren't too many people in the room. There's a room behind there.
SALLY: Is there someone behind, looking in?
MJ: That's correct. There's a small room on the other side of that mirror.
SALLY: I'd rather see them.
MJ: Certainly. Would you like me to introduce you to them, or would you want them to come and sit in the room with us?
SALLY: I think I'd rather they stay in that room.

MJ: I see. The other thing is that we take a video recording of our interview, which is so that we can discuss our interview afterwards. This enables us to see more clearly what we can do to help you, but you don't have to have this recording happen if you don't want to.
[Pause]
Can you tell me what you're thinking about?

SALLY: I've already been recorded so… it's alright…I've been on television. I don't mind. It's a while since it happened.

MJ: You speak as though my making a recording might be a relief in some way.

SALLY: Yes, it would. It means that you have got…you want to protect the privacy of this interview, and you've got a copy of it, so it means it belongs to you.

MJ: I would have a copy, and I would make sure no-one would see it who wasn't authorized by me. I will ask you again about it later, because you may change your mind. [Pause] I wonder whether the relief might also be because in the past you felt you were being spied upon. This camera is watching you and we both know it is, but sometimes you feel uncertain as to what is going on.

SALLY: It comes and goes. I haven't been thinking about it for a while. I think about…more about…the way I'm cut off on that ward. I'm on a lot of drugs, I feel dizzy…I think you're playing around with my head.

MJ: Playing around with your head.

SALLY: Putting me in front of mirrors and…videos and stuff like that…I just find it quite frightening.

MJ: Although in one way it might be a relief, it feels frightening, because you feel something is being done to your head. You feel you are being influenced in ways that might harm you.

SALLY: Things of mine…I just…I don't care about space any more…I want to be with somebody who loves me…I feel as if people don't care. The radio doesn't work, and that frightens me a lot. Every time I phone people up…that frightens me… they answer, or they don't answer and the phone seems to be phoning.

MJ: The phone is phoning. In what way is the phone phoning?

SALLY: You phone up and they answer, and then…you…they ask you if you're going to put more money in…and then it goes…it cuts off and …I think they come back again as well.

MJ: Yes. [Pause] You feel that nobody loves you. [Pause] Do you think that's a feeling you had before you came into hospital?

SALLY: I felt looked after a little bit on the other ward…my privacy was respected.

MJ: I understand that one of the doctors who you felt cared about you was about to go away.
SALLY: Yes, he did go away. Dr L went away as well. I saw him quite a lot, and then I got into a state. Then I got used to Dr R.
MJ: You get close to someone and they go away and you lose them...[Pause]. Do you think you've had the feeling that anybody loved you really?
SALLY: I thought that the radio loved me...[begins to cry].
MJ: You thought that the radio loved you, but it's not working. It must feel like a great loss to you.
SALLY: It does...[crying]
MJ: What was it like when you felt the radio did love you?
SALLY: It was like...it was just like...being nursed...sweet music coming out of the headphones and nice voices. I trusted them.
MJ: You trusted them. They are there all the time when the radio is working.
SALLY: I didn't think I was listening to programs on my own...a lot of people were listening as well as me, and...it was if you knew a broadcast...a DJ had his own type of humor, and...he used to get people to phone him up...I could never do competitions... his listeners could...and you just felt part of a gang.
MJ: You felt you belonged.
SALLY: Yes.
MJ: And then the radio ceased to work?
SALLY: It sort of works...the records are out of tune...I can't hear the interviews properly. There's buzzing...and...the news... seems...all I know is my reception...is badly...is in a bad way.
MJ: Have you ever felt that you belonged to a gang, felt loved? Apart from the radio?
SALLY: Yes, I have. I felt loved by my boyfriends...it's a long time since I saw them. They didn't want me. Except the last boyfriend, Helmuth...[Yawns]...I was unfaithful. He...he...and myself decided I wasn't going back to Germany with him. We split up that way, and he...and he found another girlfriend quickly.
MJ: The feeling that nobody cares about you sounds as if that's a problem you had before you came into hospital. You feel you're not really loved, except by boyfriends and the radio. [Pause]...I wonder, do you think your mother loves you?
SALLY: I think she must have done, but not any more...not much... but it doesn't mean to say that I don't love her ...[Becomes distressed...cries]...I'm scared my mum's going to go to prison.
MJ: Then you would lose her.
SALLY: [crying] Yes, I would. I don't want her to go to prison.
MJ: What would she have done to go to prison?

SALLY: I'm being filmed...things that...get sort of...go round and round in my brain...I thought my brothers and sisters were going to go to prison, my mother, Jane, Erica, Helmuth... something to do with blood...I thought it had to do with sex...I thought a radio DJ I used to go and see when I was little, when I was 16, well...I...I mean the thing I felt most secretive and brokenhearted, wasn't a secret any more. I got this dog to lick me sexually. It was in front of one of his programs. Because it was illegal...everybody was saying that I'd done it as an exhibitionist thing...and that he'd split up from his family because I wrote to him and told him I loved him, but it was before I realized about the dog...

MJ: You got the dog to lick you sexually in front of the program, you thought. And that was illegal?

SALLY: [distressed, crying] It was horrible...I didn't want anyone else to know about it. I thought that I was being filmed. Afterwards I thought somehow ever since I've been little everything I've done has been done with cameras, and...there's something else that talks about being alive and being dead, which I refused to...to...you know. You can say if you punch yourself you feel dead because you can't feel the punch...but not that you're dead...oh, I don't know.

MJ: You feel the punch, and you remain feeling dead?

SALLY: Yes.

MJ: But if you could do something that you could feel, you might feel more alive.

SALLY: [calmer] Something wicked happened to do with blood... I get periods... I slept with men with my period... they were penalized. I thought it because my mother kept asking what drugs I'd been taking – I've taken LSD and cocaine and... marijuana... I thought my mother was penalizing my friends who took drugs... I just thought it was terribly unjust, because... it had been done in private.

MJ: This seems to be what you are most concerned about: private things secretly done that shouldn't come out in the open but do. It upsets you so much that things come out in the open, and then people will get sent to jail or penalized for it. The dog licking you should have been kept private. Nobody should ever have found out about that.

SALLY: No.

MJ: Can you tell me, who is the most important person in your life, including since you were little?

SALLY: I always used to love my father [cries].

The relevance of this vignette is to illustrate first the importance of containment, then the holding in mind, using intuition, of both psychotic and non-psychotic communications. For example, Sally's non-psychotic longings for a mother were concretized into a delusion that the radio loved her. By articulating the patient's crisis with the object and her non-psychotic need, the analyst is able to appreciate, with her, the delusional "solution" of locating people in the radio itself, as though these were real. Delusional systems can appear discontinuous to the point of preventing access to non-psychotic thinking, but this is not immutable. When first admitted, Sally was overwhelmed by confusion. After careful containment, she, like the majority of psychotic patients on the ward, voiced concerns about the whereabouts, nature and condition of the object. Pursuit of her concerns over time, in the manner depicted above, led to significant improvements in her thinking and her life. Eventually, she became able to embark on an out-patient analysis.

Conclusion

Whether the treatment model employed is continuous or discontinuous, it is argued in this paper that (a) treatment of psychosis cannot succeed without suitable and adequate containment (b) identifying the limits or otherwise of continuity of psychic functioning is critical (c) once containment is established, the communication of clinical links between psychotic and non-psychotic mental states in the transference-countertransference relationship is necessary and is the single most effective therapeutic tool available to the clinician.

Notes

1 When talking with hospital admission staff I learned that psychotic patients tend to make two initial demands. The first is for relief from the pain of their suffering and the second is for someone to talk to – frequently but not necessarily hospital staff. Grotstein paraphrases this as: "There are no atheists on psychiatric wards" (Grotstein: personal communication).
2 Rosenfeld created consternation amongst his colleagues for his advocacy, late in life, of a measure of technical flexibility with regard to "thin-skinned" narcissists, in order to avoid re-traumatization (Rosenfeld, 2003). His credibility regarding the analytic treatment of psychosis suffered as a result.

References

Abraham, K (1924) *A Short Study of the Development of the Libido, Viewed in the Light of Mental Disorders.* In Abraham, K (1973) pp 418–501.

Abraham, K (1927) The Process of Introjection in Melancholia: Two Stages of the Oral Phase of the Libido. In D Bryan and A Strachey (Trans.). *Selected papers of Karl Abraham, M.D.* (pp. 442–452). London: Hogarth.
Arieti S (1974) *Interpretation of Schizophrenia.* New York: Basic Books.
Benedetti G (1987) *Psychotherapy of Schizophrenia.* New York: New York University Press.
Bentall R P (2003) *Madness Explained: Psychosis and Human Nature.* London: Allen Lane.
Bion W R (1957a) "Differentiation of the Psychotic from the Non-Psychotic Personalities" *The International Journal of Psychoanalysis* 38: 266–275.
Bion W R (1967) *Second Thoughts: Selected Papers on Psychoanalysis.* London: Routledge.
Bion W R (1972) "Notes on Memory and Desire" *The Psychoanalytic Forum* 2: 272–273.
Bion W R (1994) *Clinical Seminars and Other Works.* London: Karnac.
Boyer B (1998) *Countertransference and Regression.* Jason Aronson.
Buckley P (1988) *Essential Papers on Psychosis (Essential Papers on Psychoanalysis),* 17, NYU Press.
Conran M (1999) Sorrow, Vulnerability and Madness. In *Psychosis (Madness)* ed. P Williams, London: Institute of Psychoanalysis/Karnac Books.
De Masi F (2020) *A Psychoanalytic Approach to Treating Psychosis. Genesis, Psychopathology and Case Study.* London: Routledge.
Dupont J (1988) *The Clinical Diary of Sándor Ferenczi.* Harvard University Press.
Federn, P (1926). Some Variations in Ego-Feeling. *Int. J. Psycho-Anal.* 7: 434–444.
Federn, P (1934). The Analysis of Psychotics. *Int. J. Psycho-Anal.* 15: 209–214.
Federn P (1953) *Ego Psychology and the Psychoses.* Imago Publishing.
Freeman T with J L Cameron and A McGhie (1965) *Studies on Psychosis: Descriptive, Psycho-Analytic and Psychological Aspects.* London: Tavistock Publications.
Freeman, T (1998) *The Psychoanalyst in Psychiatry.* London: Karnac.
Fromm-Reichmann, F (1950) *Principles of Intensive Psychotherapy.* Chicago: University of Chicago Press.
Freud S (1911b) Psycho-Analytical Notes on an Autobiographical Account of a Case of Paranoia (Dementia Paranoides'). In *SE12*: 9–79.
Freud S (1914) On Narcissism: An Introduction. In *SE14*: 73–102.
Freud S (1923) The Ego and the Id. In *SE19*: 12–66.
Freud S (1924a) Neurosis and Psychosis. In *SE19*: 149–153.
Freud S (1924b) The Loss of Reality in Neurosis and Psychosis. In *SE19*: 183–187.
Freud, S (1938). Constructions in Analysis. *Int. J. Psycho-Anal.* 19: 377–387.
Green, A (2000) The Central Phobic Position: A New Formulation of the Free Association Method. *International Journal of Psychoanalysis* 81: 429–451.
Hinshelwood R (2004) *Suffering Insanity. Psychoanalytic Essays on Psychosis.* London: Brunner Routledge.
Israels H (1989) *Schreber: Father and Son.* New York: International Universities Press.
Jackson M (2001) *Weathering the Storms: Psychotherapy of Psychosis.* London: Routledge.

Jackson M & Williams P (1994) *Unimaginable Storms: A Search for Meaning in Psychosis*. London: Karnac Books.

Katan M (1954) The Importance of the non-Psychotic Part of the Personality in Schizophrenia. *The International Journal of Psychoanalysis* 35: 119–128.

Klein M (1932) 1975*The Psycho-Analysis of Children. The Collected Writings of Melanie Klein, Vol. 2*. London: Hogarth.

Klein M (1945) The Oedipus Complex in the Light of Early Anxieties. *Int. J. Psycho-Anal.* 26: 11–33.

Klein M (1946) Notes on some Schizoid Mechanisms. In *The Collected Writings of Melanie Klein 3*: 1–24.

Klein, M (1958) On the Development of Mental Functioning. *Int. J. Psycho-Anal.* 39: 84–90.

Laforgue R (1927) Scotomization in Schizophrenia. *The International Journal of Psychoanalysis* 8: 473–478.

Laforgue R (1929) The Mechanisms of Isolation in Neurosis and Their Relation to Schizophrenia. *The International Journal of Psychoanalysis* 10: 170–182.

Laing R (1960) *The Divided Self*. London: Tavistock.

London N J (1988) An Essay on Psychoanalytic Theory: Two Theories of Schizophrenia. In *Essential Papers on Psychosis*, P Buckey ed., pp 5–48. New York University Press.

Lothane Z (1993) Schreber's Feminine Identification: Paranoid Illness or Profound Insight? *Int. Forum Psychoanal.* 2(3): 131–138.

Lucas R (2009) *The Psychotic Wavelength. A Psychoanalytic Perspective for Psychiatry*. London, New York: Routledge.

Macalpine I, Hunter R A (1953) The Schreber Case – A Contribution to Schizophrenia, Hypochondria, and Psychosomatic Symptom-Formation. *Psychoanal Q.* 22: 328–371.

Marcus E R (1996) Panel Report: Psychic Reality In Psychotic States: Chaired By Ramon Ganzarain. *Int. J. Psycho-Anal.* 77: 565–574.

Menzies-Lyth E (1960) A case-study in the functioning of social systems as a defence against anxiety: a report on a study of the nursing service of a general hospital. In *Containing Anxiety in Institutions: Selected Essays, Vol. 1*. London: Free Association Books, 1988.

Niederland W G (1951) Three Notes on the Schreber Case. *Psychoanal Q.* 20: 579–591.

Niederland W G (1959) Schreber: Father and Son. *Psychoanal Q.* 28: 151–169.

Niederland W G (1960) Schreber's Father. *J. Amer. Psychoanal. Assn.* 8: 492–499.

Niederland W G (1968) Schreber and Flechsig – A Further Contribution to the "Kernel of Truth" in Schreber's Delusional System. *J. Amer. Psychoanal. Assn.* 16: 740–748.

Nunberg H G (1921) Der Verlauf des Libidokonfliktes in einem Falle von Schizophrenie. *Internationale Zeitschrift fur Psychoanalyse* 7(3): 301–345.

Pao P N (1979) *Schizophrenic Disorders: Theory and Treatment from a Psychodynamic Point of View*. New York: International Universities Press.

Pankow G (1968) *Gesprengte Fessein der Psychose*. Muchen: Reinhardt.

Pankow G (1977) *Structure Familiale et Psychose*. Paris: Aubier Montaigne.

Pichon-Riviere E (1952) Quelques observations sur le transfert chez des patients psychotiques. *Revue Francaise de Psychanalyse* 16: 254–262.

Rey H (1994) *Universals of Psychoanalysis in the Treatment of Borderline and Psychotic States*. London: Free Association.
Robbins M (2019) *Psychoanalysis Meets Psychosis: Attachment, Separation, and the Undifferentiated, Unintegrated Mind*. London: Routledge.
Rosenfeld D (1992) *The Psychotic*. London: Karnac Books.
Rosenfeld H (2003) *Impasse and Interpretation: Therapeutic and Anti-Therapeutic Factors in the Psychoanalytic Treatment of Psychotic, Borderline, and Neurotic Patients*. London: The New Library of Psychoanalysis.
Rosenfeld H (2018) *Psychotic States: A Psychoanalytic Approach*. Routledge.
Searles H (1956) *Collected Papers on Schizophrenia and Related Subjects*. New York: International Universities Press.
Sechehaye M (1951) *Symbolic Realization*. New York: International Universities Press.
Segal H (1950) Some Aspects of the Analysis of a Schizophrenic. *The International Journal of Psychoanalysis* 31: 268–278.
Segal H (1957) Notes on Symbol Formation. *The International Journal of Psychoanalysis* 38: 391–397.
Stärcke A (1920) The Reversal of the Libido-Sign in Delusions of Persecution. *Int. J. Psycho-Anal.* 1: 231–234.
Sullivan H (1962) *Schizophrenia as a Human Process*. New York: Norton.
Tausk V (1919) On the Origin of The Influencing Machine in Schizophrenia. *The Psychoanalytic Quarterly* 2: 519–556.
Valon P (2020) Gisela Pankow (1914–1998): Towards a psychoanalytic treatment of the psychoses. *The International Journal of Psychoanalysis* 101 (1)L 169–185.
Van Ophuijsen J H (1920) On the Origin of the Feeling of Persecution. *Int. J. Psycho-Anal.* 1: 235–239.
Williams P (Ed.) (1999) *Psychosis (madness)*. London: Psychoanalytic Ideas Series, Institute of Psychoanalysis.
Williams P (2000). "The Central Phobic Position: A New Formulation of The Free Association Method" By André Green. *Int. J. Psycho-Anal.* 81(5): 1045–1060.
Williams P (2014) Orientations of Psychotic Activity in Defensive Pathological Organizations. *International Journal of Psycho-Analysis* 95(3): 423–440.
Winnicott D W (1949). Hate in the Counter-Transference. *Int. J. Psycho-Anal.* 30: 69–74.
Winnicott D W (1958b) *Collected Papers: Through Paediatrics to Psycho-Analysis*. New York: Basic Books.
Winnicott D W (1958c) Transitional Objects and transitional phenomena. In *Collected Papers: Through Paediatrics to Psycho-Analysis*. London: Hogarth.
Winnicott D W (1963). Communicating and not communicating leading to a study of certain opposites. In M Masud Khan (Ed.), *The maturational processes and the facilitating environment: Studies in the theory of emotional development*. London, UK: The International Psycho-Analytic Library.
Winnicott D W (1965c) *The maturational process and the facilitating environment: Studies in the theory of emotional development*. New York: International Universities Press.

7 Psychosis and Neurosis
Which reality?

Dominique Scarfone

Freud begins the first of his two papers of the years 1923–24 on neurosis and psychosis with the following general outlook:

> neurosis is the result of a conflict between the ego and its id, whereas psychosis is the analogous outcome of a similar disturbance in the relations between the ego and the external world.
> (Freud, 1924 a, p. 149)

But he adds immediately: "There are certainly good grounds for being suspicious of such simple solutions of a problem" (*ibid.*)

And we must be thankful for his theoretical and clinical integrity. For indeed, things are not that simple and, moreover, if they were so, this would add little to our understanding of psychosis that the understanding of neurosis had not already provided. Hence we would remain totally puzzled regarding what difference runs between the two ailments.

In the first paper, "Neurosis and psychosis", Freud seems to be simply putting the newly formulated topography (a.k.a the "structural model") of ego, id and super-ego to the test of nosography. Can we use the second tripartite model, he seems to ask, to account for the major clinical forms encountered in our practice, namely neurosis and psychosis?

The answer is at first a positive one, with the advantage that the second model introduces a new player, the super-ego. A player that complicates, by enriching it significantly, the metapsychological description of the pathologies involved. So that, while he started with the two classes of pathology mentioned in the title, Freud ends up describing three classes: transference neuroses, psychoses and narcissistic neuroses. The latter are not really a newcomer: the name "narcissistic neuroses" is given to "neurotic" pathologies (melancholy, for instance) where the super-ego plays center stage, so to speak, whereas in transference neuroses it played more in the wings. But Freud is well aware that this new player is in fact always part of the drama.

DOI: 10.4324/9781003384120-7

Freud recaps the paper by writing:

> Transference neuroses correspond to a conflict between the ego and the id; narcissistic neuroses, to a conflict between the ego and the super-ego; and psychoses, to one between the ego and the external world.
>
> (*Op. cit.* p. 152)

And, again, he immediately adds:

> It is true that we cannot tell at once whether we have really gained any new knowledge by this, or have only enriched our store of formulas; but I think that this possible application of the proposed differentiation of the mental apparatus into an ego, a super-ego and an id cannot fail to give us courage to keep that hypothesis steadily in view.
>
> (*Ibid.*)

Freud's skepticism seems even better illustrated by the fact that he felt the need to write a second paper under the title "The loss of Reality in Neurosis and Psychosis" (Freud, 1924b). The move here is just as interesting: while the first paper was a celebration of sorts regarding the super-ego, this second paper gives a large place to the relation to reality. We get a sense that Freud was not quite satisfied with what the first paper was able to achieve:

> I have recently indicated as one of the features which differentiate a neurosis from a psychosis the fact that in a neurosis the ego, in its dependence on reality, suppresses a piece of the id (of instinctual life), whereas in a psychosis, this same ego, in the service of the id, withdraws from a piece of reality. Thus for a neurosis the decisive factor would be the predominance of the influence of reality, whereas for a psychosis it would be the predominance of the id. In a psychosis, a loss of reality would necessarily be present, whereas in a neurosis, it would seem, this loss would be avoided.
>
> (p. 183)

One can almost see him repeating the second sentence quoted from the first article – something like: This is too simple to be true. So, once again, he relativizes things:

> But this does not at all agree with the observation which all of us can make that every neurosis disturbs the patient's relation to reality in some way, that it serves him as a means of

withdrawing from reality, and that, in its severe forms, it actually signifies a flight from real life.

(*Ibid.*)

The solution Freud comes up with can be summarized as stating that yes, both neurosis and psychosis entail a loss of reality. The decisive difference between the two losses is what happens next. In neurosis, the loss – now reworded as the "loosening of the relation to reality"– is only apparent since the psyche maintains – by the compromise formation obtained through fantasy – the relation to the part of reality that had to be avoided due to the repression of the corresponding instinctual impulse.

> The neurosis consists rather in the processes which provide a compensation for the portion of the id that has been damaged – that is to say, in the reaction against the repression and in the failure of the repression.
>
> (*Ibid.*)

What Freud seems to be saying, then, is that neurosis *avoids* but a limited parcel of reality, and it does so in order to compensate for the refusal the subject had opposed, through repression, to the id's pressure. It's the price the subject has to pay for rebelling against the drive impulse. Only the elements in reality that resonate with the repressed desire are subjected to a certain distortion in the relationship to the subject. In psychosis, however, there is a radical break with reality which is directly caused by the pain it causes to the subject. Except that in this case there is no possible compromise through fantasy. The loss of reality is brutal and uncompensated for except through the construction of a new reality. We thus come to realize that while neurosis and psychosis may have *seemed* to have a common feature in the loss of reality, they in fact are not at all the mirror image of each other. Neurosis allows for a *quid pro quo* compensation between the Id and reality; psychosis does nothing of the sort. Reality cannot be paid back for the damaged relation through some renunciation of parts of the id. Quite the contrary! The holes in the damaged reality – i.e. the relational blanks left by the break-up with the parts of reality that cannot be tolerated –, are filled-in by a neo-reality that obeys all the more easily to the requests of the Id since the reality testing itself has been knocked-out by the subject's retreat from the scene of pain.

So the difference between the two pathologies lies in the "second step", for while: "(b)oth neurosis and psychosis are (...) the expression of a rebellion on the part of the id against the external world, of its unwillingness –or, if one prefers, its incapacity – to adapt itself to the exigencies of reality, to Ανάγκη [Necessity]". (p. 185), they are different in more than one way. For one thing, "in neurosis a piece of reality is avoided by a sort of flight, whereas in psychosis it is remodeled" (p. 185), but more precisely, "in psychosis, the initial flight is succeeded by an active phase of remodeling; in neurosis, the initial obedience is succeeded by a deferred attempt at flight" (*Ibid.*)

So here we are, with a new presentation of the dynamics between the psychic agencies interacting with each other. Freud's second tripartite model has been put to task to account for the major classes of pathology through the interplay of three new agencies, but in so doing he has let *reality* sneak in as a fourth agency. Except that, whereas ego, id and super-ego possess a genuine metapsychological status, reality is not as clearly qualified in metapsychological terms. Reality plays an agentic role in psychosis where it is said to conflict with the ego, while in neurosis it looks more like the stage onto which the neurotic drama takes place. In all cases, reality is synonymous with "external world" i.e. it supposedly refers to the same surroundings that are shared by everyone. Granted, it can be painful, but it is still a reality that others can observe and comment upon. It is something the subject can rebel against and lose contact with in a limited or extended way. This loss of contact may be due to the repression of a drive representative – which requires a renunciation to a part of reality (neurosis)–, or because reality itself is so painful that the subject needs to retreat from it more radically and put a new reality in its place (psychosis).

The Trouble with Harry

Addressed in such manner, reality ends up reminding us of Hitchcock's film *The trouble with Harry*, where Harry is the name of a dead man found in the outskirts of a village and whom we progressively learn that many a villager has had a difficult relation with. Hence, the corpse is interred, unearthed and interred again many times over, depending on whose interest it is to have it hidden away or left in the open. At a certain point the situation becomes untenable, no one (especially, we, the moviegoers) really knowing who Harry really was, let alone who might have killed him and why. On the one hand, you could say that it was always the same "Harry" – the corpse –, and yet each of the persons concerned had had a different experience with him. The materiality of Harry may have been one, but his relational reality was quite varied!

In the Freudian papers we are examining, our problem with the notion of reality – our own "trouble with Harry" – is that Freud seems to ask implicitly of us readers to accept a supposedly universal definition of the reality in question. At one point in the second paper, however, he is a little more nuanced: this is when he mentions "the memory-traces, ideas and judgements which have been previously derived from reality and by which reality was represented in the mind." (185–86). We thus get a sense that the reality Freud speaks of is in fact a *picture* of reality obtained through perception and/or reconstructed thanks to the memory traces of ancient perceptions. Still the impression lingers on that he is also thinking of an objective reality, the same for all. As if Freud had not heeded his own lesson, that the choice is not between material reality or a mere image thereof, but that a *psychic reality* exists besides material reality, *just as real as the latter*, and creating an inflection in the subject's experience with what we keep calling "reality" in general. Though generally true, this fact is most compelling in the case of the construction of the psychotic's neo-reality, so it is strange to see that Freud does not heed at this point his long-established view: that pathology is a magnifying glass for the understanding of normal processes. As for the neurotic, Freud presents him/her as merely *avoiding* a small piece of the same, generally defined reality, as if the rest of their external world remained untouched. I will now try to show that another take on the issue of reality is possible while staying true to Freud's own lesson that pathology instructs us about normal processes.

Material vs Psychical Reality

Our clinical experience, and Freud's own discussion of President Schreber's memoirs, signals to us that it is not just any reality – and certainly not a generally shared reality– that is at stake, whether in neurosis or in psychosis. I remember from the years of my psychiatric practice how currently hallucinating schizophrenic patients whose social benefits checks were administered by personnel in the outpatient clinic – who gave them out to the patients in weekly installments – were perfectly punctual each Monday morning when the time came to get their week's money. Their relation to material reality (space, time, quantity of money) was not the least disturbed when it came to the administrative form of interaction with other humans. What a closer look at the psychotic's problem with reality clearly reveals is that it concerns the *relational* reality, one involving the significant others of primeval times (parents and family members) or those others who occupied a similar significant place in later life. But then again, it's not the *material* aspect of the relation that poses a problem, but the *psychical* reality they were confronted with through the reality of the "messages" that the future patient received from these others. This is congruent with Laplanche's

(1992) proposal that psychic reality is actually implemented and conveyed through the *reality of the message*. In normal/neurotic cases, the differentiation and structuring of the psyche happens in the infant through the process of translation of the adult's messages, a translation that partially fails because it does not possess any code to deal with the unconsciously emitted sexual charge in the ordinary messages of attachment and care. Translation thus yields a more or less coherent ego structure on the side of the translated message, whereas the untranslatable elements get implanted in the body-psyche as foreign bodies, as the primal sources of the drives (Laplanche, 1987). In the case of psychosis, the translation of such messages is either imposed or impeded by the emitters who violently intromitted themselves in the subject's psyche (Laplanche, 1990; Scarfone, 1992/2003), abusively intruding upon the subject's effort at achieving their own translations, their subjectivity, or, as I prefer to say, their subjectality (Scarfone, 2021). This entails a less differentiated psychic structure where a fragile ego is, so to speak, constantly harassed and taken apart by the impossible task of making sense when the translational function itself has been thwarted by the violence of the message.

The reality that the psychotic subject needs to put in place of the lost one – however distorted in the eyes of "normal" people it may feel – is a genuine effort at constructing a meaningful discourse on the basis of the crazy psychical situation that he/she was put in by the violent intrusion (Aulagnier, 1975). Irrational as they may seem, delusions and hallucinations are indeed attempts at *meaningful* reconstructions of the psychical reality that was badly deviated from its more personal, idiosyncratic form, hijacked and to a certain extent *formatted* by the violent impingements of the other in the service of this other's narcissistic needs. As Winnicott (1952) clearly saw, psychosis is an illness involving a failure in the environment.

Roch's Example

"Roch", was a schizophrenic patient with whom I met twice weekly for more than fifteen years. He was tortured by what he thought was his mission to save humanity from the negative "cosmic forces" that "threatened us all". Roch did not embrace this messianic mandate triumphantly, but rather as a personal tragedy that he could not escape from even as he knew that it sounded totally crazy to most people. After having put an end, at his request, to our 15-year long therapy, Roch would sometimes phone me, he explained, so that he could listen to my voice, as most of the time this sufficed to calm his episodic bouts of anxiety. When anxiety was too strong, however, he would leave a message asking me to call him back. In those instances, a thirty minute phone chat would suffice to make his anxiety tolerable, after which I would not hear from him for months.

One day Roch called me even though his anxiety crisis was already over. He said he wanted to check something with me. While visiting family in a distant city, he had grown anxious beyond the usual. So, he went into a walk-in clinic of general medicine to ask for the renewal of his prescription of tranquilizers. He had, he explained, spent the pills he had brought along, and given the distance, was unable to reach the psychiatrist who still treated him pharmacologically. The doctor in the walk-in clinic inquired on why he was treated in psychiatry to begin with, so Roch told him of his delusions about the cosmic forces and his mission to combat them and save the world. To Roch's dismay, the doctor commented that those were not delusions, that such things really existed, along with UFOs and visitors from other galaxies. At that point, Roch folded the prescription sheet in his pocket and hastily left the GP's office. Back in town, he called me to check if I agreed that the GP was himself delusional and actually crazier!

I believe Roch was able to hold such a critical stance towards his delusions because over the fifteen years of our work together we had endeavored to examine all the imposed distortions he had endured in his experience as a subject. We had directed our efforts at delimiting a mental space that the patient could claim as his own; a space, in Aulagnier's (1975) words, for the advent of the "I". Though this did not make the delusions totally disappear, they were certainly pushed somewhat to the margins. It is worth mentioning that before entering our fifteen-year long therapy, Roch was a case of "revolving door" hospitalizations, but was never hospitalized again after having found someone who would listen to him and attend to his efforts at making sense of a crazy experience. As the therapy went on, he became progressively able to elaborate his personal theory of mental functioning and of what had gone wrong in his mental life – a theory that I could genuinely subscribe to, despite some minor peculiarities in his vocabulary (Scarfone, 1993). To give but one example, when Roch asserted that during his childhood his father had "ejaculated in (his) brain", it was not clear if he was using a metaphor or reporting an actual experience of sexual abuse, only displaced from the sexual area to the brain. Whatever the case, everything Roch recounted over the years suggested indeed that the father had *f...ed* with his mind – and with that of two other brothers, one of whom had committed suicide while the other was badly addicted to masochistic whipping rituals. In my view, this converged with the idea that, whether or not there had been a material sexual abuse, what really mattered was that the patient had indeed been violently intruded upon, penetrated by the father's "messages" which took the form of diktats that Roch was unable to either obey or disobey.

One thinks here of what Morton Schatzman (1973), quoting president Schreber, dubbed "soul murder". The delusional "mission" that Roch felt weighing on his shoulders was the more or less viable third way he had found, relegating the "dangerous forces" to outer space, hence far from the more painful surroundings. His delusional reconstruction of reality, i.e. his effort at producing a shareable account of his painful reality, was therefore a form of compromise, although different from the neurotic compromise formations. Delusions, here, occupied the place that, in neurotics, belongs to fantasies. All the same, Roch's father was thus carefully spared any direct confrontation; the combat was displaced onto another, far away battleground. The difference with neurosis is that while Roch knew of the damage caused to him by his father's own paranoia, he could not impede his psychotic *experience* – the new version of reality – from happening; he could not relegate it to the domain of fantasy. For him, the neo-reality was of the order of certainty. He was not different, in that regard, from president Schreber whose "commerce" with God was all the more real to him, he said, since he was not a religious person, so that the story with God was not the object of his *belief*! It was rather his *experience* that God really wanted to transform him into a woman and copulate with him (Freud, 1911, p. 24).

A Matter of Freedom

Bu what about the neurotic's reality? Freud says that the neurotic also rebels against reality, but in the end attempts a partial flight rather than a reconstruction. However, we could here again object that the neurotic's psychic reality certainly interferes with any pretense at a universally valid conception of external reality. The reality that truly matters for anyone's psychic life is a *relational* reality. A reality where, even in the most ordinary context of attachment and mutual attunement with the caring adults, the infant's psyche nevertheless encounters "compromised messages" whose translation is doomed to partially fail; a failure due to the enigmatic, untranslatable sexual elements within the otherwise ordinary communication (Laplanche, 1987). Hence, the neurotic-to-be is exposed to certain elements in the environment that are not so different, as to their nature, from what is met by the future psychotic: in all cases, the enigmatic components encountered and dealt with are the expression of the other's unconscious desires. What is truly different for the future neurotics, however, is the degree of freedom they enjoy in translating the other's messages and therefore in elaborating *their own* infantile theories and fantasies. In other words, the relative freedom to enjoy a space for the "I" to exist (Aulagnier, 1975). A psychotic patient like Roch, on the contrary, saw his psychic efforts totally hijacked as he was forced to respond to his father's demands for total mental obedience. His father would indeed repeatedly assert his own worldview, while discouraging his children from listening to their schoolteachers if they taught anything that challenged his theories, and stating that he'd rather commit suicide than be proved wrong.

The difference between psychosis and neurosis then seems not to rest so much on whether the subject avoids reality (neurosis) or radically breaks away from it (psychosis). As mentioned earlier, this would be a workable hypothesis if there existed but one universally shared reality. We saw earlier, however, that there are solid grounds for asserting that the reality at stake in psychopathology is not plain material reality, though of course material things and events *can* be recruited and play a role in the communicational drama of neurosis or the tragedy of psychosis (or, for that matter, in the so-called borderline states), by way of displacement onto them of the unmanageable relational difficulties. In psychosis, these are hard to deal with directly because of the subject's entrapment in an inextricable relational nexus. Roch's displacement of his father's violence onto "cosmic forces" is an example in kind. The resulting delusions may *seem* to suggest that material reality is also at stake, but this merely reflects the displacement and projection onto it of the psychic tragedy.

It follows that psychosis and neurosis differ by the sort of relationship that can be entertained with the irreducible, enigmatic, untranslatable core at the heart of the subject's encounter with the other's message. Neurotics can wrap around that core a layer of fantasy that insulates, to a certain extent, the subject's relation to this core from the rest of his/her discourse. Neurotic/normal subjects can therefore share their world view with a plurality of people because their pathological compromise formation is private and, most importantly, their capacity to translate – or their psychic apparatus as a whole – is not itself at stake. They were left relatively free to put into a subjective form their experience of meeting otherness and its sexual enigmas. Their unavoidable partial failure did not bring down their whole thinking process. Psychosis, on the contrary, results from the impossibility of adopting a unique subjective stance, inasmuch as this would mean that – like Roch's father clearly stated – someone else's subjectivity would have to be radically challenged. In both cases we are in the realm of communication, but what matters is if, and to what extent, a violence is exerted on the psychic apparatus itself. Primal violence (Aulagnier,

1975) and implantation of the Sexual (Laplanche, 1987) are unavoidable facts in anybody's infantile experience; they are in fact structuring events. Secondary violence (Aulagnier) and intromission (Laplanche), on the contrary, pertain to pathogenic subcultures of adult-infant relations. The other's narcissistic needs and impositions take precedence over the needs of the infant. In such conditions, the effort at making sense of the world – and the violence experienced within it – can still be attempted, a discourse can still be held, except that it lacks the private layer where a fantasy is, well... a fantasy. The psychotic patient can simply not afford the luxury of fantasy; he/she feels accountable to others for whatever thoughts form in his/her mind, and is actually strongly driven to share them, or even to proselytize about them, because his/her very thinking capacity must be constantly verified. Psychotic discourse, as Lacan (1976) once said, is an effort at rigor.

References

Aulagnier, P. (1975) *The Violence of Interpretation. From Pictogram to Statement.* (Transl. Alan Sheridan), London: Routledge, 2001.
Freud, S. (1911) Psycho-Analytic Notes on an Autobiographical Account of a Case of Paranoia (Dementia Paranoides). In: *The Standard Edition of the Complete Psychological Works of Sigmund Freud* (hereafter *SE*), Volume XII, p. 1–82.
Freud, S. (1924a) Neurosis and Psychosis. *SE*, Volume XIX, p. 147–154.
Freud, S. (1924b) The Loss of Reality in Neurosis and Psychosis. *SE*, Volume XIX, p. 181–188.
Lacan, J. (1976) *Conference given at Yale in 1975, in Scilicet*, n°6–7, Paris: Le Seuil, p. 9.
Laplanche, J. (1987) *New Foundations for Psychoanalysis* (Transl. Jonathan House), New-York: The Unconscious in Translation, 2016.
Laplanche, J. (1990) Implantation, Intromission. In: *Essays on Otherness* (Edited by John Fletcher, Transl. by Luke Thurston), London: Routledge, 1999, p. 135–139.
Laplanche, J. (1992) *Seduction, Persecution, Revelation, in Between Seduction and Inspiration: Man* (Transl. Jeffrey Mehlman), New-York: The Unconscious in Translation, 2015.
Scarfone, D. (1992/2003) "It Was Not My Mother", From Seduction to Negation, *New Formations*, n° 48, Winter 2002–2003, p. 69–76.
Scarfone, D. (1993) La plainte psychotique et sa modulation, *Nouvelle revue de psychanalyse*, n° 43, "La Plainte", p. 83–92.
Scarfone, D. (2021) Trauma, Subjectivity and Subjectality, *American Journal of Psychoanalysis*, 81, p. 214–236.
Schatzman, M. (1973) *Soul Murder: Persecution in the Family*, New York: Random House, p. 173.
Winnicott, D.W. (1952) Psychoses and Child Care. In: *Through Paediatrics to Psychoanalysis (1975)*, The International Psychoanalytic Library, p. 219–228.

8 Possessiveness and its Relation to Some Youthful Follies

Carlos Moguillansky

Introduction

When Freud studied the link with reality, he had in mind the role that infantile sexuality and the castration complex played in it. This vision proposes a complete and flawless creature, with omniscient knowledge and unlimited power. God, the phallic mother or the combined object are expressions of the belief that this creature's nature transcends castration. The link with reality has a close relationship with knowledge and with the illusory security that it brings to the integrity of the *Self*'s conception. The human being created unreal myths to locate that absolute knowledge in magical or supernatural characters. And that purpose is present in current beliefs and modern religiosity. Knowledge and possessiveness provide an illusory shelter. And in their extreme form, these shelters are transformed into a madness made full of certainties. In youth some follies are unleashed, generally transitory. Their defensive purpose illustrates the human desire to create the unreal in order to avoid contact with the unknown. This painful contact with the unknown is inevitable every time an adolescent faces the risky tasks and the gestures that are necessary for assuming his own life and deciding his path. That crossroads demands that he put his psychic resources into play. Psychoanalytic theories studied this fact under the chapter of introjective phenomena that arise in late adolescence. And linked them with the youthful reactivation of the complex of emotional experiences and logical operations that, as a whole, we call the *Oedipus Complex*, to locate the sexual and generational differences that preside over psychic structuring. Those processes culminate in the introjection of an internalized agency with ethical and moral functions. Psychoanalysis called this agency the adult *Superego* (E. Jacobson, 1969[1]) or *Ego Ideal* (P. Blos, 1979[2]), to differentiate it from other expressions of moral functions present since childhood. D. Meltzer (1972[3]), from the Kleinian theory of object relations, pointed out the importance of introjective identifications at

DOI: 10.4324/9781003384120-8

the end of adolescence, to distinguish these functions from other types of previous identifications.

If that process stumbles, it is replaced by a bond presided over by possessiveness. Because the introjective disorder prevents the due and necessary support to embark the risky gesture it forces the individual to find refuge in the possessive relationship with a person or an object. The peer group relationships simply replace the child dependence and their miscarried functions derive into a dysfunctional attribute.

Some youth addictions and the attachment to a couple, a group, the family or an institution illustrate the defensive and prosthetic role that possessiveness plays in this case. This situation triggers, at its extreme, the severe loss of reality of madness. The hallucinations and delusions of madness are the transitory refuge in the unreal of those who cannot face the rigor of their life, when parental control falls or vanishes.

Possessiveness transforms the sexual object into a practical one – what we usually call an object of the *Ego*. The possessiveness in adolescence intends to manipulate the object and, in extreme cases, to exercise omnipotent control over its sexual menace. The adolescent debut focuses on the sexual problem at the center of the clinical experience. And it threatens the framework of personal and family narcissistic defenses that, as a whole, we describe as possessiveness. Theories of adolescence have emphasized the role of loss and grief and have relativized the sexual character of the debut of adolescence and the intensity of uncertainty and its associated castration anxiety. This generated confusion regarding the role of manic defenses, especially in addictive behaviors, since they react against the loss of parental support. And, only through these lenses, they are regarded as defenses against the threat that sexual debut promotes.

Unreal creation needs the support of a partner. *Echo* supports *Narcissus*. As we will see, this bond of complicity is present in many different clinical situations. *Echo* enjoys by transitive effect the unreal world of *Narcissus*. And, while *Echo* grasps him possessively, *Narcissus* surrenders to her to avoid the confusing sexual threat of his debut. No adolescent can initially differentiate his own sexuality from what he remembers from his childhood seduction, which still contains cues of the passion language of adult sexual desire. This confusion brings about a reactivation of the *Oedipus complex* which reestablishes the differences between the adult and infantile positions.

The unreal is an imperious creation in a desperate situation. In this text I will study the role that knowledge and the unreal play in the defensive building of juvenile follies. I want to anticipate that these juvenile follies, in general, adopt a possessive form. The histories of Neven, a young man of 17 years old, and of Mitay, a young woman of 15 years old, are described at the end of this text. They illustrate in their follies the power of an omnipotent creature God, a phallic woman – who knows all that is necessary to know. In their hallucinations and fantasies, Neven and Mitay submit to that creature and declare she is the owner of their wishes and persons. Possessiveness and knowledge gave them an illusory shelter against the uncertain and the unknown.

I cannot address, for reasons of space, the issue of femicide, which is closely associated with this subject. I imagine that the observations made here can be applied to it. Possessiveness confuses the alliance of desires with a possessive agreement, which grants an illusory right of dominion over the freedom of the others, and which lowers their human condition to the simple role of a possessed object. This agreement has its counterpart in the illusory protection that is received from an idealized agent. On one hand, the agent owns the freedom of his victim in a pact that has little to envy to a mafia agreement. On the other hand, the victim owns the protector agent with the power of her feebleness. That pact challenges the rule of freedom that presides over any action that claims to be human action.

The relationship with the unreal

Reviewing Freud's texts *Neurosis and Psychosis* and *Loss of Reality in Neurosis and Psychosis* – both written in 1924 – requires an in-depth study of his contribution and, at the same time it requires a review of current ideas about reality and its loss. A hundred years after these ideas, today it is argued that the psychic relationship with reality is an interpretation. The logos carries out a transduction of what is manifested in it. It tries to objectify the data, but it cannot avoid being the invention of the person who makes it. No psychic action escapes this loss of reality. And in all of them there is a creative fraction. David Hockney argued that he needed to see today's sunny morning if he wanted to paint yesterday's misty morning. The memory of him from yesterday required the realistic limit of his today's perception. And his memory qualified his perception. This invention is built on beliefs, learned knowledge, traditions and also, why not, on a dose of delirium. The perceived reality is in a permanent productive interaction with psychic reality. And for this reason, the production of reality coexists with its consequent loss. Daydreaming is just as dangerous as not dreaming at all. Whoever is linked to reality needs to live in it, without this process subduing or annulling his subjectivity. Nevertheless, creation is never totally original. It is installed on an object that "is already there" that gives this reality a practical form or confirms its reality as a psychic invention. This applies both to creative illusion and unreal deliria.

The link with reality is related to the oscillations between the emotional climate and the struggle that the different psychic motives unfold for the control of consciousness and motility. This struggle, described by D. Meltzer in *Claustrum* (1992), has several factors: a) the difficulty to grasp psychic events, which, because of a defensive maneuver, becomes imperceptible to the individual; Freud showed the loss of words as consequence of repression, in the "Forgetting proper names" of his *Psychopathology of Everyday Life* (1901); and Freud (1917) and Bion (1959) pointed out the denial impact of negative hallucination; b) the discovery of psychic determinism has shown that the naturalized relationship of the "possessor" with the exercise of his will is reversed when an unconscious desire takes over his will, his conscience and his actions. The inversion of the possession relationship is eloquent in *A 17th century demonological neurosis* (1923), but there are many examples where fantasies, ideas or emotions – of hysterical, obsessive, paranoid or depressive origin – take over the individual; and c) the lack of symbolic boundaries, which distinguishes the sexual and generational differences proposed in the notion of the *Oedipus Complex*. This last factor has raised a current debate, due to the positions that see in this symbolic failure the explanation of the supposed non-existence of the oedipal efficacy. This point is not minor since these "modern" theoretical positions have a different impact in clinical work. While some emphasize the symbolic failure as the responsible for that structuring of the personality, others see the cause of the structuring of the personality as a result of the lack of the relationship with the primary object. Whereas the former remained in the field of logos, the latter explained the events from the deficit of an experience of love. Without wishing to elaborate on those arguments, I only underline the importance of this crossroads.

Based on these arguments, the loss of reality is associated with the failure to record the data that allows it to be recognized as such as well as the control of consciousness shaped by a dominant psychic factor. Another factor, as important as the previous two, resides in the stability of self-esteem. J. Maltsberger (2001) indicated:

> ... *Integrity of the self depends on the stability of the self-representation, narcissistic balance ensured to the self-representation by the interaction of Ego and Superego systems, and the comparative maturity of that aspect of the Superego we call the ego-ideal. From the Ego Ideal issues, a representation of the self as it ought to be; narcissistic stability requires reasonable correspondence between the ideal*

self and the self-representation. Too much disparity between the two gives rise to those states of tension that may result in disruption in relations between the superego and self, resulting in superego attack, as in melancholia, or in abandonment of the self by the disappointed superego.

The same disparity could occur between the *Ego*´s expectation and the representation of the object. This conflict is linked to the construction of myths and beliefs, which provide coherence and a hostile defensive support to a social group. This factor is as effective in the youth group as it is in the entire society, contributing in the creation of catastrophes, wars and ethnic prejudices. J. Sémelin (2005) and V. Klemperer (1947) illustrated the role that myths and linguistic expressions play in the creation of ideologies of extermination. This massive irrational phenomenon arises with the projection of a stigmatized enemy on a minority, which serves as an undesirable scapegoat. And thus, it contributes to sustaining the narcissistic balance of the dominant group. The same idea arises in the femicide action of homicide followed by suicide. In it, mutual death appears as the bizarre solution of a problem defined as impossible, from an unreal and omnipotent point of view. In some patriarchal societies, endemic femicide is an act endorsed by cultural tradition. We still do not know the reasons for the epidemic femicide phenomenon. At present, its frequency has increased and the social or ideological factors that trigger these events should be sought.

Negative hallucination and repression electively affect psychic representation. The emotional factor adds to its efficacy. Emotional storms trigger a self or straight aggressive or passionate act. Suicidal and murderous attempts are usually impulsive acts that respond to intense confusion (Maltsberger, 2001; Laufer, 1995; Moguillansky, 2006). Emotion also takes larval forms, in which resentment, hatred or jealousy trigger the final act. The storm of emotions affects the perception of the psychic quality: it relativizes the facts that contradict it or makes them invisible. The tormented person is blind and deaf to what escapes to his design and performs an impulsive, determined and confused act (Moguillansky, C. *Ibid*.). He believes that his *Ego* is not in the body attacked by the suicidal attempt (Maltsberger, J. *Ibid*.), or he sees in that act the solution for his no way-out situation (Laufer, M. *Ibid*.). Although these episodes are not a picture of insanity or psychosis, their transitory loss of reality is conspicuous.

Knowledge and the building of the unreal

Borges (1957) wondered why the Sphinx was necessary. What necessity induces man to create an unreal creature? Why are weird creatures everywhere in our artistic creation, our churches, our monuments or our museums? This question redefines the issue. It is not about the loss of reality, but about a creation. Psychic reality impels man to create the unreal because, without the unreal, a part of his subjectivity remains without expression.

The being in contact with reality and the experience of insanity are subject to an intersubjective agreement. Therefore, it depends on each family, each town and each era. Bion helps us not to forget that, like the brilliant idea, madness is presented as a thief that alters the natural relationship of possessiveness. The issue has a particular meaning in the transition to exogamy. This journey is not linear and admits countless comings and goings and resignifications of reality. The adolescent discovers that he is a foreigner from the familiar and the exogamous world. He does not even belong to anyone. This conflict illustrates the transformation that adolescents experience with their own body and with their ideas about themselves and about the world where they choose to live. As in other life crises, uncertainty and ignorance prevent knowing how and what are the facts and the decisions to be taken. In that case, the agents of an illusory certainty appear: the gurus, the know-it-all, magic. And especially the groups of belonging. As we will see, they offer a possessive solution, they become a shelter to belong to or where to live in.

The *Sphinx* and *Phyton* allude to knowledge. Both creatures appear in the *Oedipus* myth. They invite us to think about the supernatural and esoteric knowledge that frames the life of man and precipitates it in his destiny. Is *Oedipus* marked by the tragedy of the oracle or does it refer to the ineluctable and future repetition of it? Knowledge is stunned by the unusual chance of events. And the esoteric myth of absolute knowledge defensively seeks to solve that point of anxiety. The absolute knowledge attributed to the *Sphinx* eludes the anxiety implicit in the risky gesture of the debut – as the inaugural decision to take charge of one`s own life. It is curious that the characters, to whom absolute knowledge is attributed in the *Oedipus* myth, are female or participate in the women`s knowledge: *Tiresias*, the *Sphinx* and the *Python* serpent. These characters live in the divine world and, therefore, lack castration. In fact, castration would remove them from their esoteric position. The tragic myth proposes that the hero stumbles over the stones that *Moira* – the fate – puts in his way and suffers the necessary consequences from *Ananke* – he cannot avoid any pain or any shame.

The *Sphinx* and *Python* know. Their knowledge of man is inaccessible to *Oedipus*, who stumbled on both. *Python* prophesied in the oracle of *Delphi*, where she dwelled: *"you will kill your father and take his place."* *Oedipus* could not help but kill his father in a hazardous dispute. On his way to Thebes the *Sphinx* challenged him:

"Who is the animal that walks on all fours at dawn, at noon walks on two and at dusk walks on three?" Oedipus knew the answer: *"the man, Myself"*.

Oedipus' response could not have been more accurate. Man is the only animal that solves his faults using a tool: the cane. Man is unique for being able to create an artifact. The ability of men`s art depends on his relationship to reality. He is capable of changing it. The history and the art of *Oedipus* were not natural. Man's surprise at his own art and his history warned him of his smallness in the face of the universe. He then created the supernatural, as an unreal way to overcome it. His art is a way of solving his smallness: he solves it by creating the unreal. Unnatural art is human, but man cannot bear his smallness and builds the supernatural. Even though he is capable of learning and knowing something, he needs to believe in a supernatural and esoteric creature that knows everything.

The supernatural knowledge of *Python*, of the *Sphinx* and the art of *Oedipus* gives him an anomalous dimension. In the end, *Tiresias* – condemned for his knowledge about woman nature – alerted Oedipus to what he ignored: *"you have taken your mother for a wife"*. They were heroes on the frontier of what man should not know. By having access to this transgressive knowledge, *Oedipus* surpassed his fundamental reference, that conveyed to him who he was: *"you are the son of Laius and Jocasta and, by not having awareness of that truth, you will have a tragic destiny."* The myth gave *Oedipus* his well-known destiny: first he had the privilege of being more than the others and then he must be the victim of what he had been. *Oedipus* paid his guilt for knowing what others did not know and for ignoring what he should have known. This knowledge about him plunged him into tragedy: he was tied to the obligation of being the husband of his mother and transgressing the reference that marked him as who he is. The incest taboo is nothing more than that and *Oedipus* could not bear to have known it – to have lived it and to have been that. He found his who, that which has been. That which can only be known in the experience of having been and experienced that.

Man created the *Sphinx* to locate in her the forbidden knowledge, which defines who he is. Man respects a shared cult: the law of incest. That law determines who the man is and what is the limit between his desire to be the owner of his life and the anomalous path that he adopts if he transgresses the law. The only law that defines him as who he is. Human law coexists with possessiveness. While the law respects the human condition of each person, possessiveness denies the human condition of the other. Marina Abramovic, in *Rhythm 0* (1974), showed how the lack of a human response triggered inhuman violence. She literally made herself available to the public, along with 72 instruments of different functions – from a pencil, through a Polaroid, to knives, whips, chains and a loaded pistol –, offering her body to an interaction without scripts. Her immobility allowed the public to expose the wildest fiber of themselves. The capacity to judge human reality is built on the respect for the human condition. When it fades the worst of man appears.

In this text I discuss the clinical manifestations that take place during the crossroads in which the adolescent Oedipus – crosses paths with his father – *Laius*. Winnicott taught us that the adolescent finds himself in the metaphorical alternative of killing him, without killing his parental symbolic function. At this junction, an adolescent makes his debut, appropriates his desire and defines a personal path for his life. In his journey, he dismisses his father and personally assumes his function. However, the decline in affiliation with the primary figures is transformed into a filiation that links his desire with the wishes of those who, from then on, are his ancestors (Moguillansky, 2019). Affiliation is characterized by the directive influence of the parents' will on the child. Filiation is the reverse path, which goes retroactively from the son to the tutorial figures – parents or not – who inspire his wish. The relation between filiation and affiliation is the same as that between the unconscious wish and the conscious will.

The crossroads of the debut puts each adolescent in the middle of a topical and dynamic change in him. The creation of his own path is original and, like every human act, tries to avoid unnecessary pain. However, at that same crossroads there are teenagers who cannot make their debut. They remain prisoners of the possessive family bond. This possessive bond is a defensive move against the underlying pain – of confrontation with the uncertainty – with what is still meaningless. Here I will refer to possessive experiences, which trigger responses that they are not in contact with reality and often border on madness.

Possessiveness gives ample evidence of its dramatic and often deadly effect. The femicide, in which *Othello* and *Don José* murder *Desdemona* and *Carmen*, are replicated throughout the generations. They are extreme incidents of a phenomenon common to all ages, which presides over the disorders of adolescent development. These disorders related to individuation are the result of a possessive pact, where guilt for abandoning a parent or both is coupled with fear of loneliness or the unknown. Possessiveness is usually mutual, although the formula of the jealous partner and the victim predominates. In this unstable and stormy bond, the intensity of mutual intrusion coexists with the need for mutual abandonment. And the crime of passion occurs when the victim breaks the pact of fidelity unleashing in this way the helpless impotent anger of the murderer. The mad solution of murder, sometimes followed by suicide, is a response to impotence. Behind this impotence, one can see the impossible purpose of a possessive and ambivalent love. Perhaps *Medea* gives the measure of that ambivalent impotence, when she unloads her anger on her children to hurt her husband. By killing *Jason*'s sons, she denies that they are also hers. In the paroxysm, *Medea* admits: "*A woman is usually full of fear and is cowardly to contemplate the fight and the iron, but when she sees the rights of her bed injured, there is no other mind more murderous ...*" (Euripides, 431 BC). Maltsberger would add that *Medea* could not know who she had really killed.

Narcissus and Echo

Beyond the vengeful anger we see what today would be called narcissistic pain. The facts can be seen from the neutral reference to the myth of *Narcissus* and *Echo* in *The Metamorphoses* of Ovid (8 AD). The characters in the myth have a subtle and impossible mutual dependence. Death is the "solution" to this impossible mutual dependency, by proposing the solution of the end of life to a paradoxical relationship. Death castrates, breaks the illusory completion that *Narcissus* pursues in his desire to proclaim himself in his image and that *Echo* pursues in his desire to possess *Narcissus*. The two imaginary illusions transform sexual difference into the level of possessors and dispossessed, into the terrain of narcissistic confusion: fear of castration and envy of the penis. The symbolic role of the phallus is personified in the penis object and, from this imaginary transformation, it becomes a concrete object that is given and taken, can be lost and be possessed. Possessiveness arises from the concretion of the symbolic attribute of the sexual position in an object that could be possessed.

Freud developed the theme of possessiveness in his papers on Communication of a case of paranoia contrary to psychoanalytic theory (1915) and on Some neurotic mechanisms in jealousy, paranoia and homosexuality (1921). Jealousy is a form of paranoia. And psycho-analytical studies saw homosexuality as the cause and also the defense of paranoia. After this transposition of jealousy and sexuality, narcissism plays a central role in the scene of the loved one and in that of the lover who wishes to possess him. Although their attitudes are different, *Narcissus* and *Echo* are attracted to each other. *Narcissus* looks to *Echo* for the mirror to confirm his supreme figure, his beauty and his love; and *Echo* seeks to possess *Narcissus* and complete himself with him. If *Echo* is the necessary witness to *Narcissus*'s beauty, *Narcissus* is *Echo*'s missing piece. Both are involved in their mutual exchange of demands. This exchange has the value of a functional complementation. Each fulfills the mental and vital functions of the other.

Complementarity generates an essential bond and its loss is a mutual catastrophe. For each requires the function of the other. That love does not speak of sex, but of the complementarity in being; to fill up a lack in being. In the myth, *Narcissus* dies drowned by his own enchantment with himself, and *Echo's* passion reaches the same possessive limit, when she wishes that *Narcissus* only wants her. The destinies of the scene – the one proposed by *The Metamorphosis* and the one illustrated by psychoanalysis – show the same impossible, deadly and ambivalent love. *"I killed her because she was mine"* sang the poet Eduardo Galeano. The oxymoron of that jilted love exposes the denial, of whom he sees as mine the woman that has already left him and stopped loving him. It opens the way to an idealization; whose lack of limit and measure is only comparable with the ambivalent persecution that accompanies it. When Meltzer taught us the effects of projective identification, he argued that the intensity of its certainty was correlative to the intensity of the claustrophobia it generated (Meltzer, 1973).

The third as a bystander and the rules that work behind him

Not without reason, love is defined as a great benefactor and as a possible murderer. If the human being learned the difference between the freedom of desire and the possession of an object, much suffering would be saved and the horror of femicide would have no meaning.

André Green (1983: 40) rightly pointed out that current psychoanalysis has slipped from the study of the *Id* towards the observation of the *Ego* and the *Self*. And the idea of a bystander lost his forbidding role and gained an operative and mediating role, without taking into consideration the unconscious effect on the others. The study of adolescents and their families illustrates the production of reality that each of the participants generates around the same incident. These differences – like a *Rashomon* effect – are the result of the projective defenses that each member prints to who he coexists with. Of course, the loss of reality that exists in usual disagreement differs from the gross rift, installed when each member´s versions are extreme. In this case, the misunderstanding is enormous because of the intensity of the projections.

The bystander offers only a symbolic place. His third position allows a symbolic distance that, in turn, establishes the validity of a generic law on the violent local rule of the conflicting positions. The rule located in the third has essentially a discursive nature. The role of the adolescent gang resides in it, and it has its effect when an adolescent suffering from a possessive bond can accept and share the spontaneity and desire of the group´s rules. Nobody imposes the rule, but the realm of the group installs the freedom of desire, which prevails over the possessive cloister. This formula marks the difference between the law of the possessive tyranny and the desire of law.

If this symbolic role is confused with an operative function – a concrete set of rules-, clinical observation slides from the logos towards a superficial empiricism. Even worse, if an ideologization of the debate is installed on the clinical observation, one falls into a biased look that loses sight of the interplay that involves all the characters in the clinical scene. We need to find this blurred border between ordinary discrepancy in the clinical observation and the gap between sanity and insanity and to discover the rules governing intersubjectivity in this matter.

Clinical material

P. Blos studied the case of Nancy in his book *On Adolescence* (1962). Her compulsive sexual behavior was reactive to her mother's homosexual seduction. In order to underline the marginal aspect of Nancy´s heterosexuality, Blos defined Nancy as a case of sexual delinquency. The sexual seduction of her mother`s narcissistic possessiveness threatened to lock Nancy in a dead-end cloister. Guilt for her sexual behavior was a defense against her claustrophobic anxiety and homosexual panic.

There are two other interesting cases reported in the literature. M. and E. Laufer (1995) described their experience with the case of Jane. And P. Aulagnier (1986) described her contact with her patient Philippe. With her provocative behavior Jane literally managed to be sexually harassed. She repeated her childhood story with her seductive father who, whenever Jane sought him to feel his protection, he passively offered himself as a sexual object. Jane being the target of repetitive harassment ended in a serious suicide attempt. In the case of Philippe, he had a delusional and hallucinatory crisis on his trip to Peru. P. Aulagnier remarked on the absence of representations of his childhood, despite the fact that Philippe and his family replied to Aulagnier: "we were a happy family".

These two adolescents presented an acute episode of serious loss of reality that evolved favorably thanks to a usual analytical approach. In both cases, the experience of lack of genuine emotional contact with significant others, was solved through the reiteration of a harassing relationship in the case of Jane and through the notorious denial of Philippe`s emotions. The episodes of sudden loss of reality of these young people coincided with their desperate loneliness, which left them in a situation with no way out. Could we say that they lacked a love figure? Or was it a problem in the construction of their representation of themselves? They lose their personal point of reference to indicate who they were for whom. Both Jane and Phillipe were caught in a possessive agreement. And they repeat this implicit and unconscious agreement in every act of their current life. The paradox of the possessive agreement is that it leaves those who need to fend for themselves without emotional resources, in the ambiguous position of possessor or possessed. Therefore, this pact supposes the extreme functional dependence of a symbiotic agreement: each member is the depository object of the unlimited fantasies of the other. Mutual surrender requires being unconditional. Thus, we arrive at the main thesis of this text:

> *Therein lies the key to the implicit insanity of that silent pact. In this context, the object is not absent. It is a functional absence: the discriminative symbolic boundary that defines each one's desire as their own is missing. None of the participants wishes to respect the desire of the other. The forced absence explains that, later, in the solitude of a separation or abandonment, the silent madness of that pact turns into the explicit madness of those who were left without resources. The noisy violence that accompanies the explicit madness should not take away the importance of the silent violence that characterizes the mute period of insanity. These are two different phases of the same possessive situation. In both one notices the same lack of human contact that Marina Abramovic showed in her performance.*

The possessive, fearful and reactive world contrasts with the experience of growth, which occurs in usual adolescent life and in the psychoanalytic office. This reality is plastically described by D. Meltzer in Claustrum (1992 [1994]: 111):

> *In the events of the consulting room, two unique mentalities are locked in love and war... they also find themselves in an interest, both for themselves and for each other; And, certainly, there are moments when the intensity of that interest holds together the love of each other and the struggle to initiate a truly passionate conjunction. It may not last long each time, but its promising growth quality is unmistakable.*
> (Ibid.: 111)

I underlined the topic of *interest*, because it is a remarkable clinical finding. Interest transcends love and hate. Bion's imprint is seen in Meltzer's vision of a passionate threesome on their way to mental growth. These psychic links – L, H and K in the terms of W. Bion

(1965) – are united in a knot that limits their intention: that is the germ of passion, which distinguishes human action from any other act.

Arendt had the same idea as Bion. Unlike the possessive pact, human interaction proposes a circulation of human interest that takes place in the actions and speeches of those who participate in it. Interest in others transcends their individual work. Human production focuses on who is who in each of the individuals who live together. Arendt (1958: 206) defined the interest as what exists between the people: an *inter est – written in Latin*. Its premise of freedom excludes any arbitrary fidelity and opposes the privilege of a possessive covenant. The spontaneous *inter est* and the natural free activity of a group of adolescents may prevent possessive tyranny, because the group naturally follows the rules of freedom and rejects any coercion. This idea fits with the usual social isolation observed in the cases of adolescents, who have been captured in the nets of a possessive claustrum.

This interest is glimpsed with greater intensity in the realm of intimate life. Intimate emotional life is interested in the development of spontaneity, safe from the risk of harassment, derision or indifference which is typical of public anonymity. In the intimate sphere it is possible to wait and offer a tender treatment. Respect for the pain of others is perhaps the most important motive for emotional intimacy. Pain stands as a subtle boundary between tender love and possessive love. In the intimate realm, possession is limited by the partner's right to pain and surrenders to respect for pain. That limit is subtle, but it is effective when it can be made explicit.

It is understandable that pain intolerance interferes with access to consciousness and motility. Bion (1957) insisted on the role of intolerance to frustration and on the intolerance of linking one psychic element to another. Pain intolerance should be added as a specific factor of attacks on the painful reality. Freud recognized this fact in his works *Mourning and Melancholia* and *Metapsychological supplement to dream theory*. Pain awakens a denial of perception, which supports the manic mechanism as a specific defense against loss and break-in pain.

Possessive insanities: Silent insanity and explicit insanity

A few years ago, I described a fertile rupture in a relationship in adolescence, what I called: the *debut*. In it, each adolescent had revealed her/his singular answer, about who s/he really was. That revelation and his effective response have an effect on their speech – their way of being able to express themselves – and action. They turn their lives upside down, as the discovery of who they are offers them the opportunity to assume an autonomous and independent attitude. Their speech and action transcend the previous infantile dependency. As the debut is the expression of their singular position, the adolescents' behaviors lose their character as a simple copy of the attitudes of the group or their superiors. Sexuality occupies a central role in psychic motivation and prints its mark on this rupture. This means that the debut is sexual because it involves a change in sexual position, regardless of whether or not it arises at the beginning of genital experience. This idea was exposed as follows:

> The Self generates the false illusion of continuity on the discontinuous succession of events of its experience, in the way that a succession of photographs merges in the action without interruptions of a film ... The interpretation that each person makes of his life is assisted by the interpretive tradition in which it participates and by the emotional support of the family and the group. This framework generates a continuous and illusory establishment. From time to time, however, a more noticeable discontinuity than usual occurs, when personal invention or a new experience breaks the discursive tradition and dislodges the subject from his habitual institution (Moguillansky, 2012).

The ideas of affiliation and filiation made it possible to differentiate two modes of construction of the usual identification in adolescence and in adult identity. Affiliation focuses on group membership and each member's adherence to the group's emblems and rules. On the contrary, filiation arises as an unconscious act, a desire that reveals a personal tendency to be someone special. And, from there, this desire finds antecessors in people or characters in the individual's story. They will then become the ancestors. The debut is clearly linked to filiation, as it is its most visible event. And possessiveness is an extreme and unhealthy form of affiliation. Possessiveness and debut are opposite phenomena which, in a certain sense, exclude each other.

The evolution of some adolescents leads to a debate on the status of insanity. Some cases have an hallucinatory or delusional disorder – an *explicit insanity*. It alternates, before or after these episodes, with mute periods of a somehow functional disorder something more serious than a vulgar characteropathy – a *mute insanity*. These adolescents show a severe introjective disorder and a family claustrophilic relationship with a mutual possessive attachment. Due to their difficulty in understanding the emotions of human relationships, they copied the modes of that interaction, with a superficial and instrumental attitude. H. Arendt distinguishes operational work from action, which requires an understanding that brings personal and human motives into play. In action, human beings reveal themselves as who they are, express themselves through a speech – a way of expressing themselves – and offer an interlocution that transcends what they are. In short, they put who they are at stake. Contrary to this notion of action, work, as described by Arendt, is a patterned activity, with pre-defined and institutionalized exchanges. This operative pact gives shape to external support for people who have an introjective disorder and need to take refuge in a bureaucratic rule. Instead, action debut marks a before and after in adolescence and defines the later course of adult life. Without the debut, life's experience loses its depth and uniqueness and slides into psychological responses that range from character pathology to extreme possessive insanity.

Let's look at these ideas in the light of two clinical vignettes.

I met Neven when he was 17 years old. His parents were worried because he had had hallucinations a few days before the consultation. In his hallucinations, he had dialogued with a resplendent figure, dressed in white, with white hair and beard. That man had gently suggested that he should bring people together. The parents added that they were going through a bad time and had thought about divorce. The parents told me that the paternal grandfather had suffered from a severe celotypic disorder and that Neven's mother was extremely possessive of her children and her husband. Neven had severe contextual disorders. His being original in central Europe accentuated his problem in adapting to the customs of his peers at school. He did not understand the meaning of jokes, he fantasized romantically with one of the students or took refuge in the company of a young homosexual, whom he protected. It was difficult to decide what was the precipitating factor in his crisis. His young friend offered him the security of being the one who helps someone who is weak and in need. And it also indicates the homosexual position which, for Freud, is not a cause, but a libidinal condition, that can precipitate somebody into madness. I was inclined to think about the unconditionality of the fragile need of his friend that meets the conditions that will later be present in the other Neven relationships. But the persecutory fears that followed his hallucinations made me think of homosexuality as an effective concurrent reason for his crisis. Except for that first moment, homosexuality did not return to present itself as an active topic. Although it has a mutual connection with the celotypic attitude, as seen below.

Our first meeting was difficult. He firmly believed in his hallucinatory experience. God had really called him to help him in his beneficent endeavor. He was in an ecstatic state of grace and did not accept that his hallucinations could be linked to his parent's problems. But a brief ray of intelligence flashed in his eyes when he heard my ideas about the connection between his parents' troubles and his hallucinations. The hallucinatory disorder quickly subsided and we began a traditional psychoanalytical treatment without the need for further psychiatric medication. Neven's evolution was satisfactory. He had no further hallucinatory episodes, but his revelation had a profound impact on him. And it took him many months to carry out a complete critique of that mystical experience. Although he was able to complete his studies and finish his law degree, his contextual disorder remained evident. He was unable to get out of the expected lines and restricted himself to being who he was expected to be. Behind that restriction was his fear of disobeying his mother.

Only few months after starting treatment, Neven fantasized about a classmate from his school and he talked to me about his love. One day, he spent many hours waiting for her at the door of her house and, when she arrived, he declared her passionate love for her, with great detail. The young woman responded politely that she was very grateful for his feelings, but she was not the person he believed he loved. He did not know her and she was not interested in meeting him. Neven was stunned by that answer. And he confessed that he never imagined that something like this could happen. He seemed to live in a parallel world, without noticing the contextual cues provided by his life. His mother supported his infatuated attitude with omnipotent promises and compliments. Moreover, she criticized the analytical task because her son came in a euphoric state to his sessions and left the sessions depressed. We can see *Echo's* support for *Narcissus*.

Two years after starting treatment, he decided to stay at home in the summer holidays without his parents and met Meg, his current wife. That was his first act of independence. But, as we saw, Meg was a very pretty young woman, very possessive and absorbing. The possessive circle closed again and became an insurmountable barrier to analytical influence. Neven began to follow Meg's ideas about everything as he used to do with his mother. The situation became more complex because there was an arm wrestling between two mistresses. Even though Meg's possessiveness must have caused him some discomfort, she won the fight. Neven´s passive surrender to the woman's desire is illustrated by the following fantasy: *"He was asleep and a woman began to fellatio him while she was masturbating. Then she inserted his penis inside her. He tried to touch her breasts, but she rejected him. Finally had a frantic orgasm while continuing to masturbate with his penis inside her."* She did not want to be with him, but with his penis. He was very excited watching the scene. Meanwhile he no longer knew who owned that penis ... It was and it was not his and maybe it was hers. That ambiguity was the most exciting of all the experience and he masturbated with this fantasy. The delivery of his penis to the woman was both a sexual fantasy and a way of bonding with a woman. She appropriated him and his wishes, while he watched her being away from himself. He was ecstatic with the experience of having a complete woman who possessed him and let him possess her in secret. The exchange was a sexual game and the shared possession of an object that completed both and avoided the experience of a painful castration. *Echo* and *Narcissus* danced together. Nobody knew who is who or has what.

The treatment lasted seven years and Neven has led a normal life as far as I know. His link with reality improved. He phoned me a couple of times to say hi and he told me that he did not need further treatments. My impression from a distance is that the acute picture of his explicit hallucinatory insanity occurred as a consequence of the breakdown of the family balance and was eventually offset when he reestablished a possessive bond with Meg. The two phases of possessive madness can be seen in the explicit hallucinatory break and in the mute modes of his possessive bond with a tutor, who was supposed to guide him in an incomprehensible world. I guess that even now, despite the fact that Neven's clinical situation improved, a pathological possessive nucleus remained effective throughout the treatment and beyond.

Neven's story shows that possessiveness is a tough nut to crack, even with intensive analytical treatment. This situation of possessiveness occurs when the debut is frustrated if an indiscriminate and possessive bond is installed between the parents and the children during latency. This relationship creates a private cloister where public law is replaced by a rule of exceptions, freedoms and slavery that create a peculiar local tyranny. The cloister annuls the public law. Freud (1916) described this fact in *"exceptional patients"* who claimed their right to different treatment. The exceptional situation proposes a private agreement. It takes for granted a possessive bond between the adolescent and one of his parents and in some cases with both. Possessive loyalty cannot be broken. The punishment is guilt and fear of freedom to choose. That break is classified as a severe betrayal of the quasi-mobster family pact. Fidelity of possessiveness restricts the freedom and requires compliance with this loyalty: *"if you don't do it, you don't love me"* or *"you're not one of us."* A pact far removed from usual affiliation.

Mitay suffered a similar hallucination experience at the age of 15. She felt haunted by a multitude of eyes that floated on the wall and in the air. Her parents were a wealthy family from the province. Soon after starting treatment, her father asked me for an interview. He emphatically pointed out to me that he was not going to allow his daughter to kill his wife. I asked how he imagined she could do it. He replied: *"a sister of my wife had killed his mother-in-law. She had made her sick of cancer with his mistreatment"*. The treatment had a traditional format and Mitay received medication only the first months of it. She and her father fought every day. No matter what Mitay had done, she received her daily beating from him. That situation changed abruptly when I was able to point out that they were very excited about each other. Although Mitay got very angry with my intervention, the beatings disappeared after that. Instead, the intense almost celotypic attachment of both parents to her became apparent. She could not establish any love bond. Mitay finished her university degree, finished her treatment and migrated to the USA. She came to see me after a few years. She was working in her profession and had not suffered any further episodes. She had been unable to raise a family, but she considered she had a happy life.

In both cases, the hallucinatory crisis was an omnipotent answer to a desperate situation. These adolescents needed to know what they did not know – they could not tolerate uncertainty and meaningless experiences. God and the persecutory eyes were the expression of their need to have a response coming from supernatural creatures to their uncertain world.

Discussion

The possessive pact is confused with desire and even with love. This confusion is not a naive mistake; as it is part of the possessive pact's unconditional nature. The traitor becomes a serious enemy of the group and threatens the family cohesion. Their betrayal is punishable by a severe sentence, which usually entails death, as indicated in femicide or in some cultures, for having broken a pact: not following the family culture or loving a member of another ethnic group. The local rule denies the effects of the Oedipal rule and results in an introjective disorder. The ability to discriminate against the different subjects of the family or of a couple fails to clearly define the ties of love, hate, and possession that affect them unite. This disorder is an inadequate solution to the Oedipal conflict, in favor of a possessive binding organization, far beyond usual affiliation.

The possessive pact isolates the adolescent from public social life. This is a key point of the whole problem and, perhaps, is also its possible solution. Generally, society offers public spaces where social life proposes new ways of associating to people which has a random format, with no more preformed privileges than those that personal differences provide. This way of associating does not presuppose equality in principle, but it requires a certain equity among the members of the group. Nobody has privileges. And if that happens, the group establishes antibodies or defines the situation as an injustice. J. Mc Dougall (1978; 1994) described a similar defense in psychosomatic disorders. The predominance of the adhesive response generates an operative act, which solves the daily urgency of their lives without emotional contact, neither with one's own response nor with that of the other. Operational efficacy hides the underlying disorder and does not elicit alarm about emotional deficits or lack of empathy with the other. Although there is no who at stake, the indifferent treatment complies with the explicit rule of coexistence. This rule creates the most important emotional support for these disturbed adolescents and supersedes mutual *inter est*. These operative acts exceed the range of characteropatic reactions, although they are often confused with them. The lack of emotion is mute, as it is supplied and disguised by courtesy and by the desire to please or to be approved. We do not yet know why in some cases these difficulties manifest themselves sometimes through hallucinatory disorder and through somatic pathology in others.

The narcissistic modality, implicit in the cloister, replaces the sexual – tender and sensual – emotions. And, in many cases, it is solved by a crude opportunistic will, centered on selfishness or practical interest. The apparent deficit of emotional interest is the result of an attack on the emotional bond, derived from the intolerance of pain that could arise. It is not a deficit. The absence of a capacity to register pain installs an empty operative action. The manic nature implicit in this emotional attack triggers a simultaneous adhesiveness to a supporting object. It establishes an emotional complicity that sustains self-esteem. The object may have dissimilar characteristics. It can be a relative, an animal, or an inanimate object. It is credited with an idealized and animistic, almost supernatural power of healing. Naturally, emotional tyranny leads to highly attached ties, bordering on celotypic, indiscriminate relationships and addiction.

Although these are not isolated individuals, they behave as marginal and pseudo-integrated members of the group. They adopt the tips and norms of the group, but lack the emotional valence that would make them full users. The loneliness of their marginalization is covered with pharaonic and omnipotent defenses or with the attachment to machine strategies – TICs, video games. Mute insanity can remain unchanged over time and circulate as somewhat strange behavior. Or trigger an episode of explicit insanity. In all cases, it is difficult to establish which comes first, whether indiscriminate family ties or fringe insanity. Although it should be noted that such attachment does not imply emotional concern, in the usual sense in which it is understood, since possessiveness generates another type of affectivity and is accompanied by severe emotional myopia, incapable of emotional rapport. The breakdown of explicit insanity usually occurs due to a trip, a separation, or a life crisis, such as an emotional debut or vocational crisis. They require the response of the deepest who – the response from where the individual actually is – of the adolescent and the lack of coherence of his response awakens the crisis. The emotional storm has different expressions: it can go from just a picture of great anxiety to a storm that has the character of a hallucinatory episode – only visual or eventually accompanied by a dramatic dialogue, or the character of a delusion – pharaonic, persecutory, passionate – of short duration. One can find a variable combination of these three modalities. In the few cases I observed, the adolescent retains emotional contact, although he denies the unreal and problematic nature of his crisis. The adolescent is willing to make verbal contact with whoever intends to help him. I always felt that I could understand what was happening, unlike what I experienced when faced with a schizophrenic condition. This quality of my countertransference has been of singular help and clinical importance. That specific contact was expressed by the patient, who somehow gave indications of some spark of light in his relationship with me. Somehow a celotypic, claustrophilic or possessive bond was always present. And I consider that this type of link seems to have some causal value, at least in its condition of preventing a genuine emotional contact between the adolescent and her/his most important emotional relatives. To say it all, adherence – typical of introjective disorder – replaces emotional contact.

Notes

1 Jacobson, E. (1969): *The Self and the Object World*. International Universities Press, New York.
2 Blos, P. (1979): *Adolescent Passage. Developmental Issues*. International University Press, New York.
3 Meltzer, D. & Harris, M. (1972): *Seminario de Novara*. Quaderni di psicoterapia infantile. Borla, Novara.

References

Arendt, H. (1958): *The human condition*. Chicago: Univ. of Chicago Press.
Aulagnier, P. (1986): *Aprendiz de historiador y el maestro brujo*. Bs. As. Amorrortu. 2003.
Bion, W. (1957): Attacks on linking. *International Journal of Psycho-Analysis*, 40(308). 1959.
Bion, W. (1965): *Transformations*. London: Routledge, 1984.

Blos, P. (1962): *On adolescence. A psychoanalytic interpretation*. New York: Free Press.
Borges, J. L. (1957): *Manual de zoología fantástica*. México: F.C.E.
Euripides (431 a de C.): *Medea – Μήδεια – tragedy presented in the 87ª Greek Olympiad*.
Freud, S. (1901): The Psychopathology of everyday life. In: *The Standard Edition of the Complete Psychological Works of Sigmund Freud (SE), Vol. 6*. Strachey, J. (ed.) London: Hogarth Press.
Freud, S. (1915): Communication of a case of paranoia contrary to psychoanalytic theory. In: *The Standard Edition of the Complete Psychological Works of Sigmund Freud (SE), Vol. 14*.
Freud, S. (1917): Metapsychological supplement to the theory of dreams. In: *The Standard Edition of the Complete Psychological Works of Sigmund Freud (SE), Vol. 14*.
Freud, S. (1921): Some neurotic mechanisms in jealousy, paranoia and homosexuality. In: *The Standard Edition of the Complete Psychological Works of Sigmund Freud, Vol. 18*.
Freud, S. (1923): A seventeenth-century demonological neurosis. In: *The Standard Edition of the Complete Psychological Works of Sigmund Freud (SE), Vol. 19*.
Green, A. (1983): *Les chaines d´Éros*. Paris: Odile Jacob.
Klemperer, V. (1947): *LTI – Lingua Tertii Imperii: Notizbuch eines Philologen*. [*LTI, La lengua del tercer Reich. Notas de un filólogo*. Barcelona, 2001]
Kurosawa, A. (1950): *Rashomon*, film based in two tales of Ryūnosuke Akutagawa.
Laufer, M. (1995): *TheSuicidal Adolescent*. London: Routledge.
Laufer, M. and Laufer, E. (1995): *Adolescence and Developmental Break-Down*. London: Routledge.
Maltsberger, J. (2001): *Psychoanalytic Studies of Suicide in English*. IPA Congress Suicidality. Hamburg.
Mc Dougall, J. (1978): *Plaidoyer pour un certain anormalité*. Paris: Gallimard.
Mc Dougall, J. (1994): *Teatros de la mente*. Madrid: Yébenes.
Meltzer, D. (1973): *Sexual States of Mind*. London: Harris Meltzer Trust. Karnac. 2008.
Meltzer, D. (1992): *The Claustrum*. London: The Roland Harris Library. Claustrum [1994], Bs. As. Spatia.
Moguillansky, C. (2006): *Diálogos clínicos en psicoanálisis*. México: ELEIA.
Moguillansky, C. (2012): Las instituciones latentes y el debut adolescente. *Controversias en psicoanálisis de niños y adolescentes*. Vol. 10. controversiasonline@apdeba.org.
Moguillansky, C. (2019): La función de la afiliación y de la filiación en la adolescencia. *Controversias en psicoanálisis de niños y adolescentes*, Vol. 24. controversiasonline@apdeba.org.
Sémelin, J. (2005): *Purifier et détruire. Usages politiques des massacres et génocides*. Paris: Seuil. [Ed. Español. *Purificar y destruir*. San Martín, UNSAM EDITA. 2013].

9 The Regulation of Psychic Reality Through Sensory Perception

Elisabeth Skale

In this chapter, I present detailed material of a 4-times-a-week analysis of a young man, "Paul", which will help discuss how the patient used sensory perception in the service of neurotic and psychotic defences. Paul's defensive processes were mainly manifested through a distorted sense of smell and taste and sometimes changes in his visual perception.

Loss of reality is a term Freud first used in his paper "Formulations on the Two Principles of Mental Functioning" (1911) and does not mention again until his essays of 1923 and 1924. In his writings, he states that the loss of internal reality is a clinically proven phenomenon, which he implicitly presupposes in many cases of neurosis and explicitly describes in detail as the process in psychosis of substituting a delusional world for outer reality. Perceptual changes in the form of hallucinations or illusions are characteristic and pathognomonic of psychotic loss of reality. In the context of neurotic symptomatology, too, sense organs can be put in the service of defence and cause interferences and disturbances of perception.

Paul is a 26-year-old man who dressed like a student, he is tall, slim, has delicate, slightly effeminate features and very untidy brown hair. He first came for an interview with me after a first interview process with a colleague at the Vienna Psychoanalytic Society's clinic. At the clinical conference of the outpatient-clinic, this colleague had given a vivid description of her first impression: Paul came in for the appointment and spent a long time in the bathroom. This colleague later realized that he nearly clogged the toilet with paper, and left behind a very strong odour. When he finally entered the consultation room, he took off his pullover, claiming it was because he was hot because of the heat, and sat down in front of her in his T-shirt.

So, when he came to see me, I was expecting all sorts of diversions, but Paul managed to start his first session right away. His remark at the very beginning – that he needed to know he had at least two hours of time so he could start talking – seemed

DOI: 10.4324/9781003384120-9

comparatively harmless compared to the idea I got from the colleague's presentation of the patient. Still, he managed to turn me into someone who sets limits: I had to tell him the session would last no longer than 50 minutes.

In spite of the limitation of time, Paul was still able to give a vivid description of his difficulties and symptoms that were at the origin of his request for psychoanalytic treatment. A "perfection neurosis", as he called it, was the reason it took him hours every day to clean his flat. It prevented him from advancing in his studies and interfered with him getting in contact with his friends and his girlfriend. Over the past three years, his mental state had slowly deteriorated, and he felt his life had come to a complete standstill. Up until our first session, he had been able to keep up with all demands of his studies, just like he had at school, by studying very hard. But now, towards the end of his studies (i.e. at the beginning of his analysis), he felt unable to keep up with the demands of his inner orders placed on himself. At the same time, he was unable to ward off his compulsion to be perfect. But he knew he had to, because whenever he managed to almost live up to his standard of "perfection", he started to sweat – and everything went wrong from there on. For instance, when he was cleaning the flat, he always ran the risk of having a "perfectionistic fit" that caused him to sweat profusely. As a result, he felt he needed to take a shower, which caused him to sweat some more which was something he could not stand at all. It was extremely difficult for him to get himself out of this "state".

Paul recounted that he had slowly withdrawn from his friends over the past three years, especially in wintertime. He was no longer able to clean his flat or wash his clothes. He also refused to contact his family and even sent back packages sent by his mother which he was usually eager to receive. His fear of dust and dirt had increased. What frightened him particularly was the thought that dirt from the street, mixed with dog faeces might get into his room, where he feared it might spread uncontrollably everywhere, and he would never be able to get rid of it. He was also afraid that other materials (such as flour and butter) might stick to his fingers and he might inadvertently spread them to other objects and finally all over the place. And, he continued, he could not go to his parents' home anymore, because he was afraid, he might have a panic attack and start sweating – he was afraid he might get up at night, go to his parents' room and stab his mother unknowingly. Paul added that he was afraid he might be perceived as homosexual because he sometimes blushed in front of a man. Then he might also start to sweat, and this was awful: He was afraid he would never be able to get rid of this sweat, just like of the dust.

Regulation of Psychic Reality Through Sensory Perception

Paul started the second session by telling me that when he was small, he chased his mother's hens with a stick until she stopped him. He also used to put a stick up their cows' anus while they were defecating, and he masturbated. Moreover, he had a ritual in which he watched himself in the mirror while he was defecating, which aroused him sexually. When I commented that he seemed to be reprimanding himself by confessing to all his "sins", he interrupted me and said he was unsure whether I was strict and strong enough to work with him – he had the impression I was too mild-mannered and quiet, just like his mother, who had been unable to make him leave the parental bed until he was seven years old. And he continued, that in the previous session the light in the room had become so dim that he had nearly fallen asleep. Paul felt that I understood him, but he was afraid he might become dependent on me. He wished I was stricter and stronger, just like the psychoanalyst at the outpatient-clinic who had referred him to me. Having said that, he continued by telling me that he knew a lot about psychoanalysis, especially about free association. He talked incessantly for the rest of the second session.

His first relationship with a girlfriend lasted for one and a half years and ended a few weeks before he came to the clinic. It was with her that he had sexual intercourse for the first time. It was on the girl's initiative – he had always thought he would never be able to have sexual relations with a girl.

Paul was the family's fifth child. His mother was 43 when he was born. His two brothers and two sisters were all many years older (the brother closest in age was 10 years older, the eldest 20 years older than him). He saw his mother as small, thin, quiet and patient, but also anxious and always appeared to suffer in silence. He described his father as a big, strong and hard-working farmer. Being the youngest child, it was virtually impossible to gain access to the father.

Several months into analysis, Paul described for the first time a perceptual disturbance or hallucination, which raised the question as to whether this was a neurotic or psychotic symptom as well as the question regarding what type of reality loss he was struggling with. He missed a session due to a "misunderstanding": He came to the session at 1 p.m. and I wasn't there, because about 2 weeks before he asked me to reschedule this session to 7 p.m. In the session the following day, he said, "In the afternoon, I started crying and then my sense of smell was ruined." He explained that this was quite familiar to him: a very specific olfactory sensation occurring when he was sad and distressed. He could no longer perceive any (external) smells because this specific smell overpowered everything else. Even though he had known this state for a long time,

Paul was almost unable to describe it. His sense of smell and taste, very pronounced, like all his sensory perceptions, was suddenly lost. He then noticed a specific smell or taste that drowned out everything else: the smell of burnt hair. He associated it with a scene in his childhood home: He was lying on his parents' bed on a Sunday morning, his mother was in the kitchen, and he could see her blow-drying her hair before she went to church together with his father. This smell tended to appear when the patient was in a certain emotional state where he felt he had "ruined his sense of smell", which was usually linked with the feeling of being excluded and ignored. Later on, he described this experience as a manifestation of a very specific psychological condition that separated him from the world. It usually lasted for varying periods of time, sometimes hours or even days, without him being able to do anything about it. But he knew that while it was a nuisance, it was also rather important to him, as it allowed him to withdraw from reality and from others, and also to assure himself of this withdrawal.

It can be assumed that the withdrawal from reality the patient described was an attempt to make the concrete situation easier for him. At the same time, it blocked his sense of smell, which prevented him from experiencing new perceptions and imprisoned him in a painful memory that was evoked by the specific smell.

The patient's increased interest in sensory perception came up quite early in analysis: Already in our first conversation, Paul proudly told me that he could accurately recall and reproduce the external world with the help of his sight, hearing, smell, taste and touch. He claimed he could draw very well, even perfectly, because he was able to perceive every visual detail in a very precise manner and put it on paper. All his other senses – especially smell and taste and hearing – worked very well, too.

But in the course of the analysis, it soon became clear that the patient's sensory perceptions, visual and especially olfactory, turned into an effective tool to avoid contact with his objects and distort his relationship with reality. Over a certain period, it was extremely important for Paul to prove to me and to himself that he could actively trigger this specific olfactory illusion, described above. This "ability" allowed him to feel in control of situations, as he could switch off all the smells from outside.

Around the same time, he also mentioned that sometimes, his perception of reality changed altogether: "Everything becomes so narrow, and then I see everything only two-dimensional, and my sense of smell is ruined, it's weird but it seems to be the only way for me to have control."

At this point, a detail from the patient's history seems important: He reported that he had slept between his parents on their bed until he was seven years old. It was only when Paul's school teacher gave a comment to his mother – in the boy's presence – saying that this was a rather peculiar arrangement, that he himself decided, out of shame, to sleep in his own bed from that point on. He remembered this scene with a lot of shame and with resentment as well. He recalled that from then on, he had had a strong wish to ensure his performance at school was perfect, which he succeeded in doing during his school years.

Loss of reality and sense organs

Freud's remarks on loss of reality and my clinical experience with this patient rises a number of questions: What happens in this moment of olfactory disturbance? Is it a perception, a sensual memory, an hallucination? And in whose service is the distorted sense of smell – is it part of a neurotic or a psychotic defence? Does it allow Paul to change his inner world or does it help him recreate the old outer world a new one, in order to spare himself the disappointment of losing the old one forever?

Interestingly, the way Paul characterised the olfactory sensation indicates that it emerged for the first time in the context of a disappointment – the patient was left behind while his father and mother went to church together. However, the possibility remains that the so called "ruined smell" eliciting the memory of seeing, hearing and smelling his mother handling a blow-dryer, served as a screen-memory[1] covering up[2] all the frightening perceptions he had during the nights, staying in his parents' bed. I will come back to that later.

Important in this context seems the observation that, while reporting this symptom, the patient maintained the ability for reality-testing. Paul clearly identified the hallucinated perception as belonging to his inner reality and never expressed the suspicion that it might be an odour originating in external reality.

On the contrary, Paul emphasised on several different occasions that it was an "olfactory image" emerging within him that separated him from the external world, isolated him, blocked his access to the world. In the atmosphere of the analytic sessions, it became clear, especially through the countertransference experience, that the patient used this perceived smell as a means of depressive withdrawal which interrupted contact, by positioning an "internal stench" between himself and the analyst.

Freud recognises the complex connection between the perception of an unpleasant inner reality and the emergence of hallucinations or memory images in the 7th chapter of "The Interpretation of Dreams", where he wrote the impressive description of "hallucinatory wish fulfilment." In an attempt to keep the external, failing reality bearable for as long as possible, the infant hallucinates a satisfying experience, but in order to achieve actual real bodily satisfaction, he or she has to stop the regressive path from memory image to hallucination and instead seek the path via external reality in order to arrive at the longed-for perceptual identity (Freud 1900). But even before that, in one of his case histories, Miss Lucy R., (Freud, 1893) Freud recognises that sense organs can be venues of psychic conflict and serve as "organs of conversion" that allow for the discharge of tension.

Freud describes the olfactory sensations of his patient, Mrs. Lucy R., as a loss of the sense of smell and recurrent subjective olfactory sensations, at times a constant smell of burnt pudding. Freud suspected that the smell occurs because a forbidden idea has been repressed and excluded from associative processing, while the affect associated with this idea has been discharged through the olfactory organ.

In Lucy's case, it was even more complicated, the smell of burnt pastry masked another memory, that was closely associated with a traumatic scene in which her hopes had been dashed: The smell was actually cigar smoke, and the traumatic scene was one where Lucy was being rejected by her boss, with whom she was in love and whom she had hoped to marry. Analysis was able to reveal the traumatic scene, and the patient recovered. Freud makes a more general point about hysteria in this case history:

> The hysterical method of defence [...] lies in the conversion of the excitation into a somatic innervation; and the advantage of this is that the incompatible idea is forced out of the ego's consciousness. In exchange, that consciousness now contains the physical reminiscence which has arisen through conversion (in our case, the patient's subjective sensations of smell) and suffers from the affect, which is more or less clearly attached to precisely that reminiscence.
>
> (Freud, 1893, 121)

When Freud states that the sense organs can also be used for hysterical defence, i.e. for the conversion of excitement, as in Lucy's case, he implies that the sense organs are involved in the process of a neurotic loss of reality. Freud elaborates on this in his essay "The Psycho-Analytic View of Psychogenic Disturbance of Vision" (1910), stating that spontaneous psychogenic visual disturbances occur as a result of dissociation between unconscious and conscious processes in the act of seeing; the phenomenon of loss of vision is an expression of a psychic fact, not its cause.

For the disturbance of vision, he outlines the following process for the sensory organ being taken into the service of defence:

> The ego will have lost its dominance over the organ, which will now be wholly at the disposal of the repressed sexual instinct.
> (Freud 1910, 216)

After clarifying the origin of the symptom of a "visual disturbance", Freud returns to Miss Lucy R. in the same paper (1893), and provides an explanation of the role of the sense organs in the development of neurotic symptoms:

> If an organ which serves the two sorts of instinct increases its erotogenic role, it is in general to be expected that this will not occur without the excitability and innervation of the organ undergoing changes which will manifest themselves as disturbances of its function in the service of the ego.
> (Freud, 1910, 217)

In these cases, Freud argues that in the process of repression, the cathexis is not withdrawn from the rejected idea, but from a sensual perception linked to that idea. And Freud underlines that the blind eye remains "seeing" for the unconscious.[3]

Lucy's smell disturbance and my patient's ruined sense of smell seem to simultaneously express the sensory disturbance and a painful feeling of rejection. For my patient, the ruined sense of smell established a perceptual identity with a previous situation, it satisfied and at the same time covered up a desire: the desire to remain connected to the mother in spite of the real separation. The unconscious desire to smell the mother and be enveloped in her smell is masked by the perception or hallucination of mother's unpleasant smell, the smell of an absent, disappointing, stinky, repulsive mother.

Both Lucy and my patient seem to have preserved the ability to test reality, since they expressed awareness of the change in perception. In contrast to psychotic patients, they were not immersed fully in a world created as a substitute for reality – they only were immersed in a substitute reality at this special instance.

Visual and olfactory images as fetishes

Surprisingly, a little later in analysis, the patient seemed to use the distorted sense of smell and taste in a different way. In the course of his associations, Paul suddenly interrupted and mentioned that he perceived a visual image or the specific olfactory image of the specific odour, which stopped his associations and thoughts. Here are sections of a session that illustrates this:

Monday:

The patient asked me if it was possible to change the time of his regular sessions. It took some time to work out a solution, but I was going to respond to his wish within a period of two days.

(On the couch)

P: Now I'm about **to ruin my sense of taste.** I felt so good playing around with you and the sessions…I felt really well on Friday. On Thursday, after the session, I was angry because I felt I hadn't worked seriously – so the session hadn't gotten me anywhere.

Here with you, I'm always going through a rollercoaster of emotions.

It is hard to talk about certain things – it is so humiliating – and it is shameful to get an erection in here. And I get nothing from you… During the weekend, I had to copy the receipts from last year's analysis, my parents need them for tax purposes.

A: During the weekend you were busy thinking about me, copying receipts.

P: (interrupting me) A whole year!

A: And then you come here, full of positive feelings and enthusiastic, and when you're here, you get into a state of mixed and confusing emotions.

P: Yes, exactly.

Now I see **big buttocks** – I'd rather see you as a defecating **asshole.**

Andrea didn't come to the cinema with us on Saturday, I invited her when we were at the party – she didn't come, didn't even call – I called her four times, couldn't reach her… maybe something had come up.

My mother has a voice like a hen – first she is in bed with me and then she leaves me in the middle of the night.

She called today – she calls more often now, and she also sends parcels… I am happy about that… she said, "but you are coming home on Christmas Eve" – but I would like to postpone it again, I want her to know how it feels to have to wait, to be so disappointed.

A: You came here today to fulfil a wish of mine – as you put it – and now you are disappointed.

P: When I asked my question, I thought, an analyst would not answer such a question right away. I was disappointed because I thought you would have to ask someone else first. I thought that the change might not be possible this week, that perhaps you'd be able to accommodate my request in November. I thought you'd have to talk to your husband about it – yes, I thought of your husband first and then of your other patients. Thank God I haven't seen any men in here... but maybe I've been unconsciously overlooking them – there used to be one here.

It's so hard to give something up, to not cling desperately to someone, I'm afraid I wouldn't be able to get away – I'd give up everything else, my studies, my diploma... Why is it so hard to be independent (and stand on my own two feet)?

These sudden images of the "big buttocks" and "defecating ass" or a "triangle of pubic hair" which came up in very early sessions, later only "pubic triangle" as I will present in the next vignette, frightened him when they first appeared in the sessions. But very soon after, these images tended to turn his mood into one of excitement and triumph. He interpreted them as stop signs for himself and for others, indicating that one should not go any further.

In this session, Paul seemed to be fighting against his close attachment and sexualised and incestuous connection to me. He felt drawn in, which frightened him, and he desperately tried to free himself from this entanglement.

The patient remembered experiencing intense experiences in his parents' bed, where he slept until he was seven years old. He described being exposed to smelling, tasting, hearing, seeing, he felt that he should – "not thinking at all" – because this might get him expelled from the bedroom. Thinking would have meant linking his sensual perceptions to the reality of the situation, in which he witnessed his parents as a couple or even having intercourse. Paul's overinvestment of his sensual perceptions allowed him to avoid emotions that were "too powerful to be contained by the immature psyche," as Bion (1959) put it in his paper "Attacks on linking".

Once, in a darkened lecture hall, Paul noticed that his sensory perceptions intensified considerably all of a sudden, and he fell into a trance-like state, losing almost completely his ability to concentrate and think. This seemed to be another indication that the patient could get into states in which his perceptions intensified, but he was not allowed to give them any meaning or to allow any connection to his inner ideas in order to avoid overflowing anxiety and sexual excitement.

In the first instances when these images came up in sessions, the patient seem to be flooded by visual perceptions, images of body regions or body parts, and he realised that they stopped his flow of thoughts. Later on he seemed to call up these images and use them to prevent and stop his train of thoughts and certain memories or emerging emotions. With this, Paul withdrew from the analytic situation and from contact. Soon the sadomasochistic quality of his actions became clear, both in the atmosphere in the room and in my countertransference. On the one hand, these images appeared to autoerotically satisfy the patient's voyeuristic and renifleuristic[4] desires, and on the other hand, they helped him push me away. He enjoyed that he could no longer been reached either by me or by the reality of the session or his inner reality. Paul took a sadistic pleasure in keeping me away from him and torturing me by projecting the desire of closeness into me.

The images were used to mask a separation, a feeling of being excluded and the reality of the analyst's unavailability. At the same time, the images were used to represent, and hold on to, the incestuous and exciting connection to his object. The threat of separation as a consequence of his incestuous desires was held in check and simultaneously represented by the images. In this respect, the hallucinated images fulfilled the conditions and characteristics Freud used to describe the fetish: it obscures the perception of external reality while confirming an internal reality. In this case it seemed to be a (narcissistic) fetish maintaining a narcissistic equilibrium, by warding off the threat of separation/castration as a result of his incestuous desire and simultaneously representing the desires through the images.

This enactment in the session is similar to his acting out after he stopped sleeping in his parents' bed. He had already conveyed in the first interview that he had had a highly charged interest in genitals and incestuous wishes around this time, and he described that he had closely watched the cows in the neighbour's barn and was especially interested in their defecation. He then tried, in secret, to drill into the cow's anus with a stick while she was defecating. The image of a defecating asshole seems to refer to his own puberty, when he developed a masturbatory practice in which he watched himself defecate with a mirror without inserting anything – he called it shit-masturbating. The act of defecations seemed to be highly charged, at the one hand it was important for him to know that he can get rid of the "shit" on the other hand he has to control what comes out of him, what he loses, what he is separating from. The possibility of controlling the act of separation by observing it seems to be sexualised and eventually transformed into images that serve as a narcissistic fetish that covers up the separation and castration, as mentioned above. I think it is important to point out, with Nicolas Abraham and Maria Torok (1984), that these images are not real symbols, but an attempt to symbolise what cannot be symbolised. The real symbol, the verbal expression of the patient's emotional state, i.e. the incestuous desire and fear of castration, is simultaneously concealed and revealed by the image.

Considering that the patient slept in his parents' bed for so long, we may assume that he had to switch off intense sensual perceptions and resort to the perverse defence of introducing fetishistic images in order to avoid being overwhelmed by anxiety and excitement. In the sessions, these visual and olfactory images, which depicted and obscured reality at the same time, seemed to act as a seal (Morgenthaler, 1984) preventing psychotic breakdown.

At the same time, the states of producing images blocking perception, or even the specific state of not perceiving, were accompanied by excitement of being in control of reality that later turned into sadomasochistic enactments during the sessions.

Monday:

Paul arrives on time; when I enter the room I realise I have forgotten to close the curtains – I close them.

P: And now that, too – you forgot to close the curtains, I am feeling extremely stubborn now, nothing works, everything goes wrong.

Now I see a pubic triangle.

I ruined my sense of smell after the session here, and I didn't get it back for quite a long time.

I had the feeling you didn't give me your blessing for going to the party.

I'll never get closer to her.

Today on the underground, I wouldn't let anybody get close to me – I saw several girls but couldn't get closer. I ruined my sense of smell and nothing worked anymore

(jerks his arms and legs impatiently and with growing anger).

P: (little pause) Now I'm starting to sweat – what was it? Now I think about blank metal – like an axe – my father had one... rabbit... an axe in a sheath.

A: Sheath?

P: Father and mother argued a lot... Mother scolded father on many occasions, for instance for not taking his shoes off when he came home from work, and father said, "okay, okay okay." At that moment I think about castration – I think it is psychoanalytic jargon – it's useless...

A: (feeling anger) And you're trying to provoke people into stopping you – you're trying to force them into doing something, for instance kicking you out of the students' residence – and maybe even force me to kick you out from here?

P: I'm afraid I've made you furious with me. I can't start anything, I am so discontented with myself, my penis is so small, my hips are so broad, my head is so flat and small, I'll never get together with a woman, I can't imagine that a woman would ever want to be with me – now I'm losing my grip on reality, I can't see clearly anymore – I thought about undergoing surgery of my hips, just to change something.

In this small excerpt from a session in which I had to close the curtain after he had already entered the room, Paul seemed to see it as my mistake, my weakness, but at the same time he perceived it as an attempted seduction. Me deviating from the routine opened up the possibility that there might be no more limits, that I might be unable to withstand his onslaught. This scared him and he tried to stop it with the image of a pubic triangle. At the same time, he got into a more and more excited and anxious state, which resulted in a sadomasochistic enactment in the session. It was only through my harsh, perhaps even sadistic remark about his desire to be kicked out, which freed him from his claustrophobic condition created by the entrance scene. In his eyes it re-established a boundary between him and me that reduced his fear but triggered a masochistic self-punishment fantasy. In the last part of the session described above, when he seemed to be overwhelmed by anger and fear, Paul himself was able to describe that his senses became prominent, his vision blurred, and he was in danger of losing his sense of reality.

The patient used this alternation between functional states using sensory impressions (altering the perception of the external world and interrupting the connection to inner-psychic perceptions) as his main defence. But as described above, in parallel to this, he also resorted to a fetishistic use of visual and olfactory images for his denial of reality.

Ferenczi describes similar observations in the sessions with a patient who also used hallucinations/illusions as a defence, as "the last means of escaping the conscious recognition of certain pieces of insight" and observes how regression to the sense area brought excitement. (Ferenczi, 206).

Psychotic experiences

As the analysis progressed, it became increasingly clear that there were a number of other changes in sensory and reality perception that accompanied the smell distortion with which Paul was trying to maintain his equilibrium. Already in the first description of the condition, when he felt rejected, disappointed and left alone by me, he described a perception he called a reality change: The whole world suddenly appeared two-dimensional and flat to him, it lost its depth, and the sense of space was missing. The world thus also lost its immediate tangible meaning, it appeared empty and only theoretically accessible. (cf. Bion 1964) This paranoid withdrawal and distancing from the outside world was always accompanied and supported by an "olfactory corruption" that also blocked the inner world and brought it to a standstill.

It was only with the help of supervision and regular discussion of my patient that my confusing countertransference reactions became clearer to me, as did the switch between the phases of sorrow, anxiety and meaningful contact to a sudden interruption of contact and an aggressive yet anxious distance, like mocking and spitting at me with his words when he reported that he had ruined his sense of smell. These sudden changes seemed to indicate that there were different levels of functioning intertwined. A non-psychotic, more neurotic part that helped him go on functioning, despite his distinctive obsessional symptoms, was often interrupted by a "mad" state, where he seemed to be completely overwhelmed by unconscious material and had to resort to psychotic functioning. Especially in a period in analysis when he started dating women, Paul often felt overwhelmed and retreated into a paranoid "ruined smell" state, which lasted for hours, sometimes even days.

Especially in situations when he wanted to approach a woman but was afraid of being turned down, he came to the session full of anxiety and hate and with a distorted sense of smell. It became clearer that in such situations of fantasised rejection, he seemed to quickly turn to massive projective identification and block his sensual experiences as a way of protecting himself from the re-entry of projected parts, of himself and the object, like Bion (1957) describes so brilliantly for his patient who used his eyes for this process. I think in those moments, my patient split and destroyed parts of himself and his object he was in contact with, resulting in minute particles tinged with his hate. He then dispersed and projected these particles via his olfactory sense, "smelled them out" into the atmosphere around him and warded off the re-entry of these parts through a ruined sense of smell.

At the beginning of analysis, he mentioned his great fear of minute particles from dog faeces, dust, flour or butter, which could enter his apartment unnoticed and suddenly disperse everywhere and soil everything uncontrollably. Now, it is possible to understand that these particles were also minute and hated parts of himself and his objects, that he projected into the atmosphere around him (a kind of materialised smell) he had to prevent from re-entering.

In the process of Paul's analysis, this particular defence, like most of his defences, could be easily taken over by his sadistic superego, which then controlled him and his world. Identified with this superego, he tried to actively and triumphantly regulate how much of reality he was to take in through his perceptions. On the other hand, though, this state also tortured him, by robbing him of his senses and cutting off his connection to himself and others.

In periods when the "mad" state persisted, the patient presented himself as the smelly object to me. During this periods, he refused to wash his clothes and neglected personal hygiene, thus willingly invading my space and my senses. Sometimes he spoke about it rather desperately: He mentioned that he could not help it because this was the only way he could keep coming to our sessions and not feel overwhelmed. At the same time, he accused me of forcing him to resort to these "methods" to keep me under control.

Hallucinatory state versus endopsychic perception

In another clinical situation later in analysis, probably protected by the analytic setting, Paul seemed to regress even more and displayed a serious but ambiguous way of losing his grip on reality.

Thursday: (last session of the week)

P: It is unbearable to realise that you do have a life of your own, that you are married or something like that.
   I will bind you inside me and torture you... like the cow... the whole weekend – so I can avoid making anything out of my own life.
A: It hurts... it causes you pain to realise that you are separated, so you're trying to get rid of this pain – to hold on tight, to fly into a rage against me or to take revenge, getting me and the whole world under your control...
   Maybe it isn't big enough to call it pain...
P: The word can't be big enough – it is a pain and it seems unbearable... (different voice) I won't bear it...
A: Now it sounded as if someone else inside you was speaking.
P: Yes – there is a split inside me then.
   One is saying, keep quiet, relax – if I have to pee and other men are around, for instance.
   And at the same time the other voice is saying, don't give in, don't submit.
   One of my nephews said to me, "Why should I start a relationship with a woman when we will separate anyway after a while?"

Regulation of Psychic Reality Through Sensory Perception

Mira isn't the superwoman I want – two women didn't call back even though they promised to do so... maybe I am too impatient, but there could be a response from somebody someday.

But I can't wait.

I'm sure I'll come on Monday and I'll have to unload a huge rage.

I expected the session today to bring me a lot of insight – but now I realise that I only know some things on a cognitive level. I had hoped it would go deeper.

A: You came here with the intention to be careful, to not trust.

P: Yes, you know me, the worst thing is being disappointed unexpectedly.

That is like being full of something, like atoms in their structure or the whole body is full of small, soft red particles – now I'm afraid I want to impress you... now I've ruined my sense of taste... and then suddenly everything is sucked out of me – vanishing through my feet... there is a film called "Body Snatchers", and the whole body is filled up with rage and hate and control and a special picture of you to which I hold on tight.

Towards the end of the last session of the week, Paul's visual perception got an increasingly hallucinatory character and his psychic state seemed to disintegrate for moments, which he expressed in a visual image of the "whole body full of small soft red particles". In the moment when he described that his inner world dispersed into fragments, he seemed to be clearly psychotic, which could be understood as the hallucinatory experience of psychic dissolution and disintegration. But this process seemed to be complete only with the patient's report of desperately clinging, and "holding on tightly", to a certain image of me. In those moments Paul seemed to experience a struggle between positive, "soft red" feelings towards me and a fear of being pushed back and abandoned, while holding on to me, which led to an inner surge of destructive, "red" rage.

But at a closer look, this hallucinatory state was preceded by a brief moment of depressive pain, which was unbearable and to which he responded with fragmentation and disintegration of perception. This is a dynamic Betty Joseph describes in her paper on pain (1976).

> [...] a particular type of psychic pain that I believe belongs to the emergence from schizoid states of mind in which projective identification is strongly used. I have attempted to discuss it as a borderline phenomenon, on the border between mental and physical, between shut-in-ness and emergence, between

anxieties felt in terms of fragmentation and persecution and the beginnings of suffering, integration, and concern.

(Joseph, 1976, 99)

When the "red particles" appeared in the analysis for the first time, they did so in conjunction with images not only of rage and hatred, but also of pain and shy tenderness. The hallucinatory experience of the red particles escaping through his feet may be understood as a pictorial description of his inner situation dissolving and being expelled.

Paul described a visual transformation of his inner reality, and these images resembled what Freud describes as "endopsychic perceptions", which he relates to Silberer's "functional phenomena". As Silberer (1909) and, with him, Freud pointed out, a person may have endopsychic perceptions that capture aspects of his or her inner world and transform them into visual images. These phenomena are described to occur mainly in hypnagogic states, as they exist before falling asleep, but I think it is justified to postulate that these phenomena can also be found in regressed states that occur within a session. Fausto Petrella's description of these phenomena following Freud and Silberer: that a psychic fact, the content of a thought or the form of a thought can be represented by visual images. He classifies them as "material[5] or "functional autosymbolic phenomena" when either the content or the form of the thought is visualised. (Petrella, 122)

Paul seemed to be able to transform his inner psychic reality into a visual perception as a functional autosymbolic phenomenon, which he used as a defence against the psychic experience. This allowed him to "see" and observe his inner reality but at the same time keep it at bay.

Summary

The clinical data obtained in a 4-times-a-week analysis with one patient ("Paul") over a period of 7 years illustrate that he used sensory perceptions to ward off his inner reality in the neurotic sense; especially his olfactory perceptions were put in the service of repression – he lost his sense of smell.

At the same time, Paul seemed to use a mechanism that Freud describes for psychosis when the patient establishes a temporary psychotic world through a (negative) hallucination, to extinct all smells coming from the real word. An even more explicit process in this respect was a threatening form of visual hallucination in a situation where the collapse of the patient's internal world was imminent – in this case, the hallucination seemed to be a manifestation of a dispersed and unbearable mental condition and allow him to project this condition onto visual images. His defensive use of his senses was in the service of moderating his perception of internal and external realities and their temporary loss and substitution. In these sessions, the patient's behaviour seems to fit Freud's description:

> Probably in a psychosis the rejected piece of reality constantly forces itself upon the mind, just as the repressed instinct does in a neurosis, and that is why in both cases the consequences too are the same.
> (Freud, 1924, 185)

A third form of defence emerged in the patient's sessions: Paul used fixed visual or olfactory images as a fetish against a frightening external and internal reality, in order to deny it and at the same time triumph over it.

The "ruined sense of smell" seemed to be a hinge between neurosis and psychosis, between the loss of internal or external reality; for a moment, the patient lost them both until the excitement or anxiety has subsided. At times Paul turned this loss into perversion: a denial of and triumph over both realities at the same time.

Especially in (close) relationships with women and eventually later with his partner, it took several years before he was able to refrain completely from the defensive use of sensory organs. He reported that the use of fetishized images only happened in analysis.

Notes

1 Freud writes; "a 'screen memory' as one which owes its value as a memory not to its own content but to the relation existing between that content and some other, that has been suppressed."(Freud, 1899, 320)
2 Like in the Freud's case "Miss Lucy R." (1893) see later
3 As regards the eye, we are in the habit of translating the obscure psychical concerned in the repression of sexual scopophilia and in the development of the psychogenic disturbance of «**vision**» as though a punishing voice was speaking from within the subject, and saying, "Because you sought to misuse your organ of sight for evil sensual pleasures, it is fitting that you should not see anything at all any more", and as though it was in this way approving the outcome of the process. (Freud, 1910, 217)
4 Freud used the term Renifleur, defined as a person who is sexually aroused or gratified by odors, in his case history of the "Ratman": "It turned out that our patient, besides all his other characteristics, was a renifleur. By his own account, when he was a child he had recognized every one by their smell, like a dog; and even when he was grown up he was more susceptible to sensations of smell than most people." (Freud, 1909, 247)

While voyeuristic desire originates in a sexualisation of the sense of sight, renifleuristic desire is a sexualisation of the sense of smell.

5 A "material" autosymbolic phenomenon was illustrated by an oral communication of Eva Kohut (Vienna): One patient suddenly had the image of being carried in a sedan chair initiating an unwanted nap during the day: "I let myself go" was the visualized content of the thought.

References

Abraham, N. & Torok, M. (1984). "The Lost Object – Me": Notes on Identification within the Crypt. *Psychoanalytic Inquiry* 4: 221–242.

Bion, W.R. (1956). Development of Schizophrenic Thought. *Int. J. Psycho-Anal.* 37: 344–346.

Bion, W.R. (1957). Differentiation of the Psychotic from the Non-Psychotic Personalities. *Int. J. Psycho-Anal.* 38: 266–275.

Bion, W. R. (1959) Attacks on Linking. *International Journal of Psychoanalysis* 40: 308–315.

Bion, W. R. (1962). Learning from Experience. *International Journal of Psychoanalysis* 3: 55–58.

Breuer, J., Freud, S. (1893). *On The Psychical Mechanism of Hysterical Phenomena: Preliminary Communication from Studies on Hysteria.SE II*, 1–17.

Ferenczi, S. (1952). First Contributions to Psycho-Analysis. *The International Psycho-Analytical Library*, 45: 1–331. London: The Hogarth Press and the Institute of Psycho-Analysis.

Freud, S. (1893). *Miss Lucy R, Case Histories from Studies on Hysteria*. Vol. II106–124.

Freud, S. (1909) Notes Upon a Case of Obsessional Neurosis. *The Standard Edition of the Complete Psychological Works of Sigmund Freud* 10:151–318.

Freud, S. (1938). *Die Ichspaltung im Abwehrvorgang*. GW: XVII, 59–62.

Freud, S. (1899) Screen Memories. *The Standard Edition of the Complete Psychological Works of Sigmund Freud* 3:299–322.

Freud, S. (1900). The Interpretation of Dreams. *VII The Psychology of the Dream-Processes. SE Vol.IV* 509–627.

Freud, S. (1910). The Psycho-Analytic View of Psychogenic Disturbance of Vision. *SE. Vol. XI* (1910): 209–218.

Freud, S. (1911). Formulations on the Two Principles of Mental Functioning. *SE, Vol. XII*:213–222.

Freud, S. (1925). Negation. *SE Vol. XIX*:233–240.

Meltzer, D. (1973) *Sexual States of Mind*. Sexual States of Mind. 139:1–185.

Morgenthaler, F. (1984): *Homosexualität Heterosexualität Perversion*. Qumran. Frankfurt/M. Paris.

Petrella, F. (1993). Endopsychic Perception / Functional Phenomenon. *Rivista Psicoanal.* 39(1):115–134.

Index

Note: Page numbers followed by 'n' refer to notes.

Abraham, K. 31
Abraham, Nicolas 148
Abramovic, Marina 124
"affective hebetude" 37
Andrade Jr, A.M. 19
anticipatory anxieties 97
"anticipatory terror" 97
Arendt, H. 130, 131, 132
Arieti, S. 95
Aulagnier, P. 9, 73, 76, 77, 85n1, 114, 128, 129

Bell, D. 9, 10, 11, 12
Benedetti, G. 95
Bentall, Richard 89
Bion, W.R. 4, 7, 8, 9, 11, 12n1, 17, 18, 19, 20, 21, 42, 43, 44, 45, 52, 56–57, 66, 67, 68n2, 68n5, 73, 75, 79, 80, 92, 95, 98, 99, 121, 123, 129, 130, 147, 151; *Second Thoughts* 18; *Taming Wild Thoughts* 18
Blos, P.: *On Adolescence* 128
Borges, J. L. 95, 122
Boyer, Bryce 31
Britton, R. 43, 53, 54
Brunet, Marie-France 9

Caper, R. 53
childhood sexuality 2
clinic of psychosis 15–31
"community care" 88
contemporary psychiatric treatment 88
continuist model 97

degree of psychopathology 43
delusional beliefs 68n3

delusional systems 104
delusional thinking 3, 97
delusion formation 57–58, 91, 94
De Masi, F. 21, 31, 91, 95; *Vulnerabilitá alla Psicosi* 20
deobjectivization 83
discursive listening 85
Donnet, J-L. 9, 79, 84; *L'enfant de ça* 79, 80, 81

Echo 126–127
embryological remains 18
emotional system 20, 21
emotional tyranny 136
emotional unconscious 20, 21
emotional valence 136
endopsychic perceptions 152–154
"enforced homosexuality" 90
"enigmatic messages" 11
environmental deprivation 22
evidence-based medicine 87
"exceptional patients" 134
explicit insanity 130–137
external reality 2, 3, 6, 7, 11, 12, 17, 20, 36, 37, 39, 40, 45, 52–53, 54, 55, 56, 58, 60, 62, 67, 72, 79, 88, 93, 94, 95, 96, 115, 143, 144, 148, 155

Fairbairn (1994) 95
Federn, P. 31, 93
Felton, June 18
Fenichel, O. 5
Ferenczi, S. 88, 150
Fetichism 30
Freeman, T. 95
Freud, S. 1, 2, 3, 4, 5, 6, 8, 9, 10, 11, 12, 16, 17, 18, 19, 21, 26, 27, 30,

31, 34, 35, 36, 37, 38, 39, 40, 41, 42, 44, 45, 50, 52, 53, 54, 55, 56, 57, 58, 66, 67, 68n2, 70, 71, 72, 73, 74, 77, 78, 79, 80, 85n1, 87, 88, 90, 91, 92, 93, 94, 95, 97, 108, 109, 110, 111, 112, 118, 120, 121, 126, 130, 132, 134, 139, 143, 144, 145, 154, 155, 155n1, 155n2, 155n4; *A 17th century demonological neurosis* 121; differentiation of neurosis from psychosis 54–56; *The Future Prospects of Psychoanalytic Therapy* 16; *Introductory Letters* 15; *The Loss of Reality in Neurosis and Psychosis* 37, 38; Metapsychological Supplement to the Theory of Dreams 4; Negation 6, 12, 53, 55, 56, 66, 70; *The neuro-psychoses of defence* 35; *Neurosis and Psychosis* 35; *Outline of Psychoanalysis* 16; *Psychopathology of Everyday Life* 121; "The Psycho-Analytic View of Psychogenic Disturbance of Vision" 144
Freudian theory 74
Freudian thinking 95
Fromm-Reichmann, F. 94
Fundamental Anthropological Situation 11
The Future Prospects of Psychoanalytic Therapy (Freud) 16

Galeano, Eduardo 127
Giovacchini, P.L. 21
Green, A.: *L'enfant de ça* 79, 80, 81
Green, André 9, 77, 79, 80, 81, 84, 97, 127
Grotstein, James S. 104n1

hallucinatory crisis 128, 135
hallucinatory disorder 133, 136
hallucinatory state *versus* endopsychic perception 152–154
hebephrenic schizophrenia 57
Heimann, P. 27
heterogenous psychic apparatus 74
Hinshelwood, R. 92, 94, 99
Hockney, David 120

Impasse and Interpretation (Rosenfeld) 17, 19, 31
instinctual energy 90
internal psychic reality 71
interpersonal movement 94

intra-psychic model 95
Introductory Letters (Freud) 15
Isaacs, S. 45, 68n1

Jackson, M. 95, 100
Joseph, Betty 153

Katan, Moritz 98
Kernberg, O. 31
Klein, Melanie 7, 9, 11, 16, 17, 18, 19, 21, 22, 30, 45, 52, 56, 66, 68n1, 79, 93, 94; *Notes on Some Schizoid Mechanisms* 16
Kleinian group 42
Kleinian theory 9, 118
Kleinian thinking 95
Klemperer, V. 121

Lacan, J. 85n1, 117
Laing, R. 95
Laplanche, J. 11, 112
Laufer, E. 128
Laufer, M. 128
L'enfant de ça (Green & Donnet) 79, 80, 81
The Loss of Reality in Neurosis and Psychosis (Freud) 1, 37, 38, 120
Lucas, R. 98, 99

Maltsberger, J. 121, 126
material reality 53, 112–113, 116
Mc Dougall, J. 136
Meltzer, D. 118, 121, 127, 129
Memoirs (Schreber) 3
mental disorders 3
mental health 52, 59, 89
Metapsychological Supplement to the Theory of Dreams (Freud) 4
Moguillansky, C. 12
Money-Kyrle, R.E. 18
mute insanity 131, 136

narcissism 3, 5, 15, 77, 90, 91, 126
narcissistic equilibrium 148
narcissistic modality 136
narcissistic neuroses 30, 38, 91, 108, 109
Narcissus 126–127
Negation (Freud) 6, 12, 53, 55, 56, 66, 70
The neuro-psychoses of defence (Freud) 1, 35
neurosis: from psychosis 54–56; psychosis, and organization of personalities 41–46; transference 15, 37

Neurosis and Psychosis (Freud) 30, 35, 120
"Neurosis Psychosis" 70–71
neurotics 116; functioning 34, 39; organisation 43; pathologies 108; symptomatology 139
non-psychotic personalities 56, 96–98, 99
non-psychotic thinking 92, 97, 98, 104
Notes on Some Schizoid Mechanisms (Klein) 16
Notes on Symbol Formation (Segal) 19

objective reality 52, 112
Oedipal conflict 8, 135
Oedipal rule 135
Oedipus 70
Oedipus Complex 70, 90, 98, 118, 119, 121
"olfactory corruption" 151
On Adolescence (Blos) 128
operational efficacy 136
"organs of conversion" 144
Orwell, G. 60
Outline of Psychoanalysis (Freud) 16
"An Outline Of Psycho-Analysis" (Freud) 6

Pankow, G. 95
Pao, P. N. 95
paranoid schizophrenia 100–104
pathological narcissism 42
"pathological organisations" 42
Pérez-Sánchez, A. 9, 10
"perfection neurosis" 140
persecutory anxieties 94
personalities 56, 96, 99; neurosis, psychosis, and organization of 41–46; non-psychotic 56, 96–98, 99; psychotic 42, 46–50, 57, 96–98
Petrella, Fausto 154
Pichon-Riviere, E. 95
"plaques tournantes" 97
possessive insanities 130–135
possessive loyalty 134
possessiveness 112, 118, 119, 120, 123, 124, 125, 126, 131, 133, 134
Post-Freudian contributions 9
Post Freudian psychoanalysis 74
Prado, Almeida 31
primal violence 116
"Project for a Scientific Psychology" 26, 54
psychical reality 112–113
psychic catastrophe 57, 61

psychic functioning 70
psychic reality 2, 3, 10, 52–53, 62, 67, 123
psychoanalysis 1, 3, 9, 15, 27, 30, 42, 50, 87, 88, 89, 93, 118, 127, 141
psychoanalytical approach 15, 17, 18
psychoanalytical listening 80
psychoanalytic dialogue 10, 22
psychoanalytic movement 7
psychoanalytic "observation" 93
psychoanalytic theories 3, 56, 80, 118, 126
psychoanalytic thinking 3, 9
"The Psycho-Analytic View of Psychogenic Disturbance of Vision" (Freud) 144
"psychoneurosis" 2
psychopathology 10, 35, 41, 42, 43
Psychopathology of Everyday Life (Freud) 121
psychosis 3, 41–46, 70–73, 78–81, 87; clinical case 81–85; clinical implications 98–99; clinic of 15–31; Freudian and post-Freudian objects in 90–91; paranoid schizophrenia 100–104; psychotic and non-psychotic personalities in 96–98; psychotic anxieties 89–90; pursuit and destruction of object 93–95; theories of origins and the object's role 74–78; treatment 9–11
psychosomatic disorders 136
psychotic anxieties 56, 89–90
psychotic disorders 3, 73
psychotic elements 42
psychotic experiences 150–152
psychotic functioning 16, 34, 39
psychotic manifestations 4
"psychotic neighbourhood-organisation" 49
psychotic organisations 43, 49, 96
psychotic personalities 42, 57, 98; in psychosis 96–98
psychotic reality 99
Psychotic States (Rosenfeld) 19, 31
psychotic symptoms 12
psychotic thinking 18, 92, 98
psychotic transference 17, 19, 27, 93

Racker, H. 27
Rashomon effect 127
reality, question of 11–12
relational reality 112, 115
Rey, H. 95

Robbins, M. 95
Rosenfeld, D. 94, 95
Rosenfeld, H. 17, 19, 21, 31, 60, 104n2; *Impasse and Interpretation* 17; *Psychotic States* 19, 31

Sandler, J. 2
Scarfone, D. 10, 11
Schaeffer R. 21
Schatzman, Morton 115
schizoid disturbances 20
schizophrenia: Bion's work 56–57; clinical example of delusion formation 57–58; clinical features of 57; clinical material from schizophrenic patient 58–62; Freud's differentiation of neurosis from psychosis 54–56; psychic reality and external reality 52–53; session 62–66; thesis 53–54
schizophrenic patient psychic reality 53
schizophrenic psychoses 37
schizophrenic thinking 20
Schreber, D. 54, 57, 67, 70, 90, 91, 112, 115; *Memoirs* 3
Searles, H. 9, 31, 73, 75, 84, 94
Sechehaye, M. 95
secondary violence 76, 117
Second Thoughts (Bion) 18
Segal, H. 17, 19, 20, 21, 46, 94; *Notes on Symbol Formation* 19
Sémelin, J. 121
A 17th century demonological neurosis (Freud) 121
sexual delinquency 128

Silberer H. 154
Skale, E. 10
Splitting of the Ego in the Defensive Process 30
"The Splitting of the Ego in the Process of Defense" 72
Steiner, J. 42
Stern, A. 31
Strachey, J. 1, 3
stress vulnerability models 87
Sullivan, H. 94
symbolic equation 19

Taming Wild Thoughts (Bion) 18
theory of psychopathology 95
theory of representation 73
"topography" 2
Torok, Maria 148
traditional psychoanalytical treatment 133
transference-countertransference relationship 104
transference neurosis 15, 37
Two Principles of Mental Functioning 2, 3, 7
The Two Principles of Psychic Functioning 35

unconscious fantasy 46
unconscious mental processes 45

Valon, P. 88
Vulnerabilitá alla Psicosi (De Masi) 20

white psychosis 9, 79, 80
Williams, P. 10
Winnicott, D.W. 22, 31, 93, 95, 96, 113

For Product Safety Concerns and Information please contact our EU representative GPSR@taylorandfrancis.com Taylor & Francis Verlag GmbH, Kaufingerstraße 24, 80331 München, Germany

Batch number: 08319008

Printed by Printforce, the Netherlands